Start-Up Guide for the Technopreneur

Start-Up Guide for the Technopreneur

Financial Planning, Decision Making, and Negotiating from Incubation to Exit

DAVID SHELTERS

WILEY

John Wiley & Sons Singapore Pte. Ltd.

Copyright © 2013 by John Wiley & Sons Singapore Pte. Ltd.

Published by John Wiley & Sons Singapore Pte. Ltd.
1 Fusionopolis Walk, #07-01, Solaris South Tower, Singapore 138628.

Other Wiley Editorial Offices
John Wiley & Sons, 111 River Street, Hoboken, NJ 07030, USA
John Wiley & Sons, The Atrium, Southern Gate, Chichester, West Sussex, PO19 8SQ, United Kingdom
John Wiley & Sons (Canada) Ltd., 5353 Dundas Street West, Suite 400, Toronto, Ontario, M9B 6HB, Canada
John Wiley & Sons Australia Ltd., 42 McDougall Street, Milton, Queensland 4064, Australia
Wiley-VCH, Boschstrasse 12, D-69469 Weinheim, Germany

Library of Congress Cataloging-in-Publication Data

ISBN 978-1-118-51847-2 (Hardcover)
ISBN 978-1-118-51849-6 (ePDF)
ISBN 978-1-118-51848-9 (Mobi)
ISBN 978-1-118-51850-2 (ePub)

Typeset in 10/12pt Garamond-Light by MPS Limited, Chennai, India.
Printed in Singapore by Ho Printing Pte. Ltd.

10 9 8 7 6 5 4 3 2 1

To the world's best parents:
Dennis and Donna Shelters

Contents

Preface

In this book, I share insights and experiences accumulated during my many years as an investment banker, business broker, and financial advisor to numerous entrepreneurial ventures. My aim is to assist entrepreneurs in strategic planning, fundraising, negotiations, organization, and financial decision making with the hope that those aspiring entrepreneurs may sufficiently and efficiently fund their enterprises through progressive stages of development and ultimately achieve optimum financial success with a highly profitable exit. My intention is to prompt entrepreneurs to think finance and strategy in a holistic manner and within the appropriate context by discussing the various stages typical entrepreneurs face from incubation to exit.

The inspiration behind this book is my personal interest in empowering entrepreneurs to realize their full creative potential and achieve maximum profit from their hard work, sacrifices, and intellect. My goal is to provide effective mentoring to entrepreneurs so they may avoid the dangers inherent in business start-ups in general and dealing in the realm of venture capital in particular. Too many times I have witnessed start-ups with very promising and innovative products fall victim to financial starvation. I have also witnessed many instances in which venture capitalists (VCs) take advantage of entrepreneurs' vulnerable financial position and financial inexperience and impose terms that ensure that the VCs, not the founders, reap a disproportionate share of the profits. Other times VCs impose such suffocating control as to impede the innovative energies and development efforts of the founding partners, resulting in either underachievement or eventual failure of the venture.

I currently conduct a "Finance for Geeks" presentation series at tech conferences throughout Southeast Asia. This has given me the opportunity to meet numerous bright entrepreneurs from varied backgrounds who are extremely interested in the financial dimensions of starting and operating a start-up. I am constantly impressed with the passion and innovative ideas that are shared with me. The entrepreneurs' lack of experience or knowledge in financial matters also is striking. I always leave these conferences feeling that so many promising entrepreneurs would benefit enormously from engagement with an experienced mentor. Several attendees urged me to publish a book based on my presentations. I am grateful for such encouragement and the opportunity to serve as a mentor to a larger audience.

This book is unique in several ways. No other books examine the issues specific to entrepreneurs in a comprehensive manner. Indeed, entrepreneurs would be wise to consider this book a primer before reading books that examine more specific areas, such as venture capital, writing a business plan, and negotiating term sheets. Reading this book first should enable entrepreneurs to more effectively comprehend, synthesize, and place in proper perspective the information in these follow-up books. The purpose of the book is not to provide all the answers or a blueprint for success. Rather its aim is to stimulate readers to think in strategic terms. Another unique feature of this book is it is based almost exclusively on practical experience. I am not an expert on the academic discipline of entrepreneurialism and am not qualified to compose a treatise on that topic. Indeed, the material in this book may run counter to academic dictates in some areas. However, I strongly believe that experience trumps theory in illuminating a path of success for entrepreneurial ventures.

This book is not an instruction manual but a thought-provoking and enlightening mentoring/coaching instrument. It poses more questions than it answers. However, the right questions must be asked before answers are to be sought.

The standard definition of mentor is an experienced advisor offering personal guidance and support. A mentor serves as a coach, helping others to learn, rather than teaching them, to maximize their own performance. My definition of mentoring is very simple: Mentoring helps people discover how to think and what to think about. The ideal mentor is someone who can accomplish this by imparting personal experiences of both success and failure.

Often aspiring entrepreneurs express a desire to hear success stories. Although it is important to read about and try to emulate successful entrepreneurial venturers, successful entrepreneurs faced critical situations where they had to improvise, endure, and triumph. Every entrepreneurial venture that I have been involved in faced failure at some point. Failed entrepreneurial ventures offer just as valuable, if not more valuable, lessons.

Being a successful entrepreneur requires being a jack-of-all-trades. Many start-ups have founders with a passion for and expert knowledge in their particular innovative product or service but are inexperienced in and possibly intimidated by the financial aspects of starting, growing, and profitably exiting a business.

The challenge for many entrepreneurs is that they are not familiar enough with issues of finance to recognize what questions they need to ask and answer in order to learn. Once they pose such questions to themselves, they are in a position to take full advantage of their keen logic and intellect and direct some of their passionate energies to the business aspects of their venture. Therefore, my mission is not to provide answers; it is to impart wisdom. Entrepreneurs are far smarter and more familiar with their innovations than I; and much more aware of their goals thus, they can answer the important questions much better themselves—once they know what they are.

Overview of the Contents

This book has been organized to reflect the natural sequence of events experienced by entrepreneurial ventures, from conception to successful exit.

Chapter 1 presents finance terms and concepts to serve as a basis of understanding the themes of the next chapters.

Chapter 2 presents the central tenets of the book related to knowing your investor." In *The Art of War*, written more than 2,500 years ago, the Chinese military advisor Sun Tzu stated that most battles are won before they are fought. Although presenting and negotiating with investors is not a life-or-death struggle and offers more opportunity for mutual benefit, the founding partners of an entrepreneurial venture should approach and prepare their dealings with prospective investors as diligently as a military general does before engaging in battle. Sun Tzu advised that, in war, good intelligence is vital, one should always keep the initiative, obedience is more important than skill, one should avoid unnecessary destruction and take no wasted (blind) actions, and one should avoid enemies' strong points and attack enemies' weaknesses. I am not calling for an armed insurrection against venture capitalists; however, my views regarding diligent planning and preparation, issues of control, the insufficiency of merely possessing a superior product, the need for efficient fundraising, and knowing what prospective investors are looking for are all aligned with Sun Tzu's teachings. It is no surprise that to this day successful businesspeople continue to read the ancient military doctrines postulated by Sun Tzu, the ultimate mentor.

Chapters 3 and 4 consider the importance, considerations, and objectives in constructing an effective business plan and financial plan. Both documents should be composed from a strategic perspective and synchronized.

In Chapter 5, the dialogue turns to the preparation and execution of various types of funding presentations and prospectus materials consistent with the principal tenets and observations of the previous chapters.

Negotiations are the important topic of discussion in Chapter 6. The intent of the first five chapters is to place you in the most favorable negotiating position in terms of both positioning and preparation. In Chapter 6, we examine how to formulate an effective negotiating plan utilizing strategic thinking.

In Chapter 7, we examine how an entrepreneurial venture organizes itself for optimal corporate governance and to manage relations with new investment partners and other internal and external stakeholders.

Chapter 8, the final chapter, explores the various critical elements related to establishing and managing effective decision-making processes and structures before discussing how to optimize financial decision making in practice. Samples of the various funding and prospectus documents mentioned in the book can be found at the author's blog at www.financeforgeeks.com.

I hope this book helps to inspire entrepreneurs to think in strategic terms and improve as planners, fundraisers, strategists, negotiators, and business partners.

Acknowledgments

A special debt of gratitude to several family members needs to be acknowledged. My parents have always given me their full, unconditional support to pursue whatever I believed was right and encouraged me to think independently. My grandfather, Dr. Donald Dashnaw, has been a great source of inspiration as well. His tireless efforts in serving people, acting on his convictions, and writing several books on his fascinating life certainly have been sources of encouragement for me to become a mentor and write my first book. I also would like to express my gratitude to my cousin Stephanie Torta for her valuable advice on the publication process.

I particularly would like to express my gratitude to Benjamin Scherrey and his talented young staff at Proteus Technologies, a successful software development firm based in Thailand. Serving as his chief financial officer, and jointly mentoring local start-ups have permitted me to gain valuable insights into the inner workings of tech firms and improve my sparse knowledge of software development and project management.

Thank you to all my friends and associates who graciously agreed to review my draft manuscripts. A special thanks to Ian Korman, who has been a trusted associate and tireless advocate of strengthening the Thai start-up scene. His valuable insights and advice regarding publication has been a great source of encouragement and enlightenment.

Last, but not least, a collective thank you needs to go to the entire publishing team at John Wiley & Sons who have exhibited great patience in working with me as a first-time author. At times the publication process has been daunting but their amenable support has helped me endure and is a source of encouragement to continue as an author if I have the good fortunate of such opportunities in the future.

CHAPTER 1

Finance for Start-Ups 101

An appropriate starting point for this book is a review of some basic financial terms and concepts that will be useful in understanding the principal themes to be found in the ensuing chapters. This chapter consists of seven sections: fundraising stages, risk/return, types of funding, capital structure, intellectual property, valuation, and exit strategy.

Fundraising Stages

According to standard definitions, a company's fundraising stage is determined by a number of factors, including the number of employees, amount of revenues, capitalization, profit, and the status of product development. For purposes of this book, it is more accurate and useful to define a fundraising stage as a period during which the cost of funds, whether in terms of equity dilution or rate of borrowing interest, is comparable throughout such period. Reaching the next fundraising stage requires progression to the next stage of business development and/or attainment of the necessary financial objectives permitting the solicitation of additional capital at more favorable terms vis-à-vis a higher valuation or a lower interest rate that can be secured from prospective lenders. The significant implication is the derived value of raising funds efficiently via raising only the necessary funds in each funding round at the lowest cost of capital currently available to reach the next fundraising stage. Determining the "necessary" amount of funds and identifying the sources of funding currently offering the lowest costs of capital requires a financial plan.

This section consists of four subsections, beginning with the necessary preparation required during a prefunding period followed by the three successive fundraising stages: seed, series A, and series B.

Prefunding Period

The prefunding period is the time between the conception of business idea and the organization of this idea into a business plan. A series of important questions must be answered during this stage:

- Is your idea a possible solution to an identifiable problem?
- Are you uniquely qualified to execute such an idea?
- Who would benefit from effective execution of your idea?

Without an affirmative answer to these questions, the idea, although possibly worthy and interesting, may not present a business opportunity for you and prospective investors. If you can answer yes to these questions, the next issues must to be considered:

- *How much development time is required for your product or service?* This consideration is particularly important in the fast-changing world of technology. If you expect it will take five years to develop something that would almost certainly be obsolete at the end of those five years, perhaps your business idea is not meant to be.
- *Do like-minded individuals/competitors exist?* If you and a partner want to attempt to do something a big company like Yahoo! has already decided to spend millions of dollars on for research and development (R&D), perhaps you are contemplating an overly ambitious endeavor.
- *How willing are you to pursue this business opportunity and accept all the inherent sacrifices and risk?* Are you willing to have a Ramen noodle lifestyle, living a meager existence in which all of your earnings or savings is allocated to funding the venture at the expense of other personal spending options?
- *Do you have considerable family obligations,* such as kids demanding your time, a spouse preferring a sufficient and stable income?
- *What if this business venture does not succeed?* How much have you risked? Is there a contingency plan for you?
- *What if it does succeed and requires heavy and extended duty?* Are you capable of making such a commitment?
- *Can you reasonably envision investors assuming the risks and potential employees sharing your passion?* Will others be willing to patiently share in your pain and suffering?

The main objective of this stage is to write a business plan that can provide answers to the first set of questions and offer a framework on how the idea can be executed.

Seed Funding Stage

The seed funding stage is the first true fundraising stage occurring between the composition of a business plan and the completed development of a working prototype. The primary objectives of this stage are proof of concept through the development of a working prototype and protection of intellectual property (IP).

The development of a prototype has to progress to at least the point at which it can be offered on a trial basis to test users with the expectation that useful and actionable feedback can be collected. The prototype must be sufficiently presentable to prospective investors, who are primarily interested in determining its commercial viability.

Proof of concept is defined as being able to actually show a product or service to be useful to someone other than yourself and there is a waiting and prepared market for it. There are several ways to demonstrate proof of concept. The most common and effective proof of concept techniques include alpha/beta user testing, various customer feasibility surveys, and surveys based on Kano analysis. The latter effectively measures customer responses utilizing a practical and actionable customer preference classification system.

During this stage, it is strongly recommended that you protect your intellectual property either by filing patents or by writing hard-to-replicate software.

The amount of seed funding to be secured is determined by the amount of funds necessary to develop a prototype to present to both prospective investors and test users, costs associated with conducting proof-of-concept exercises, and filing and other costs associated with protection of any intellectual property. Common seed stage funding sources include individual friends and family, angel investors, early-stage venture capitalists, public funding agencies, and private incubators/accelerators.

Series A Funding Stage

The series A funding stage is when you evolve from being an R&D enterprise to being a business. The primary objectives of this stage are to begin generating revenue and validate the existence of your business through the execution of a successful commercial launch. Now is the time to implement your marketing plans, establish acceptable payment methods for your customers or users, formulate an optimal pricing policy, select the best channels of distribution, secure favorable arrangements with key vendors, and commence working relationships with any comarketing partners to demonstrate commercial viability to your investors, activities that go well beyond proof of

Fundraising Stages	Stage of Development	Primary Stage Objective	Primary Use of Funds	Typical Funding Sources
Seed	Business planning Research and Development	Proof of concept Protection of IP	Developing and producing a prototype	Angel investors early-stage VCs Public funding Incubators Friends/Family
Series A	Commercial launch	Prove commercial viability Commence revenue	Execute commerical launch	Venture capitalists High-net-worth angels
Series B	High growth stage	Profitability Scalability	Building scalable infrastructure Hiring operational personnel Market expansion	Private equity firms Strategic partners

FIGURE 1.1 Fundraising Stages

concept. Prospective investors will ask you to "show me the money." The best way to accomplish this is to point to paying and satisfied customers as well as mutually beneficial relationships with strategic partners.

From a fundraising perspective, the series A funding stage is the most crucial and tricky of all the funding stages. Up to this point, only a modest level of funds, if any, has been raised, and the investors, if any, are people who most likely provided funding to you based on personal trust. It is hoped that you have succeeded in accomplishing your seed stage objectives because now your fundraising efforts will likely be directed toward securing greater funding amounts from individuals and investment groups with a set of defined investment criteria and with whom you have no prior personal experience. The series A funding stage is the primary domain of venture capitalists.

Series B Funding Stage

The series B funding stage is when your company needs to become profitable. The primary objective of this stage is to fund increasing growth in a sustainable manner and demonstrate exponential financial returns. For a technology company, this usually means having the funds necessary to staff support teams, achieve maximum scalability, and expand into new markets. The primary series B funding sources are private equity firms and strategic partners that find your product promising after your successful commercial launch.

The number one challenge entrepreneurs face during this stage is managing growth, which is one of the top reasons why most businesses fail. Failure to meet the explosive growth frequently experienced by successful tech start-ups has often proven to be the death kiss for so many promising entrepreneurial ventures. Securing sufficient series B funding to fund scalability of infrastructure and hire operational and support staff is critical to ensuring that this welcomed growth is supportable. (See Figure 1.1.)

In Chapter 4 we examine using strategic financial planning as a road map to navigate the successive funding stages.

Risk/Return

An important concept to understand is the relationship between risk and return. The greater the perceived risk, the greater the expected return.

Factors considered by prospective investors that may increase or decrease their perceived risks of investing in your venture include the time to realize returns, the amount of funds to be invested, growth prospects in the market targeted, probability that the product will be commercially successful, and level of confidence in the capability of management in executing its plans. A primary objective of your fundraising efforts is to credibly reduce the perceived risk of investing in your venture to improve your chances of attracting an investor and secure the most favorable terms possible. The better you are in achieving this objective, the higher the perceived valuation of your company will be, thereby commanding a higher equity share price or lowering your venture's cost of capital at any given point.

At the earlier fundraising stages, the longer time to realize returns (higher risk) is somewhat mitigated by the comparatively modest amount of investment funds required. However, you may unnecessarily forfeit such risk mitigation if you solicit for more funds than needed to achieve your objectives in a given fundraising stage. Therefore an understanding of the risk/return relationship is vital in increasing the probability of success and efficiency of your fundraising efforts to ultimately maximize your returns.

Another aspect of risk/return to be considered is the relative risk/ return for the founding partners. As mentioned, the earlier people invest, the greater their return in relation to their assumed risks compared to later investors. The founding partners, original investors who must put forth extraordinary efforts for a successful exit, earn the highest returns in proportion to the amount they actually invested. The founding partners assume four primary risk categories, which can be divided into quantifiable or nonquantifiable.

The quantifiable risks include:

- *Actual monetary investment.* This includes the actual amount of money or other tangible resources committed to the venture.
- *Financial opportunity cost.* This refers to the financial sacrifice assumed by founding partners to pursue the entrepreneurial venture. If a founding partner had to turn down a $100,000-per-year job offer, the opportunity cost equals the annual salary being forfeited multiplied by the years required to be dedicated to the venture. Opportunity costs are often the most significant but overlooked costs borne by a founding partner and should never be discounted.

The nonquantifiable opportunity costs (risks) include:

- *Blood and sweat.* The personal efforts, added stress, and other nonfinancial sacrifices or hardships need to be counted. If an outside investor invested the same amount of money at the same time as a founding partner, the founding partner's greater efforts than those of a more passive investor should be accounted for at time of exit.

- *Political capital expended.* The risks, added strains, and obligations placed on personal relationships and the professional reputations of the founding partners entitle them to a greater proportion of returns.

A successful exit strategy requires extraordinary efforts on the part of the founding partners that go well beyond their financial contributions. They should be awarded accordingly.

A proper understanding of risk and return is necessary to attract funding on terms of mutual benefit to founding, current, and prospective shareholders. In Chapter 2 we discuss the various risk mitigation factors that can be employed to reduce the perceived risk of your venture.

Types of Funding

Equity and debt are the two primary types of funding from external sources, each with pros and cons and each with specific characteristics and ideal conditions in which they are to be sought. Internal (self-) funding is the best option if and when possible. Whether it is initial funding capital (founding capital) drawn from you and your founding partners' personal resources or capital funding allocated from generated revenue, internal funding will avoid incurring any obligations to external parties and establish your skin in the game—a demonstration of a personal financial sacrifice to be incurred if your business venture fails. Sacrifices include such things as opportunity costs, actual financial investment, placing at-risk personal relationships and professional reputations, assumption of stress, and time away from family. A value needs to be placed on such sacrifices when determining an appropriate share of potential financial returns. We illustrate the importance of establishing such perceived value in future fundraising efforts and negotiations with prospective investors.

The reality is that at some stage, you will very likely need to solicit funding from external sources either because you can't fund an immediate or planned specific need or you have insufficient funds to support projected or current growth. The types of funding to be secured from external sources include private equity, debt, alternative variations of both, several different public funding options, and incubator or accelerator programs that are either publicly or privately funded and managed.

Private Equity

The most common way for your start-up company to raise capital funds is through the sale of shares in your company. In this way you are adding outside investors as additional business partners. This is the ideal, if not the only, way for early-stage companies to secure sufficient funds in a timely manner. This type of funding has its pros and cons. An immediate injection of such capital can be used to fund rapid growth. Equity investors who receive common shares do not have legal claim to your tangible and nontangible assets if something goes wrong. To a large extent, their interests are closely aligned to yours: the ultimate success of the business. They are willing to share your risk so they may share your return. However, as voting share-holders, they will also want to share in company decision making. Passive investors, who do not want much direct involvement in the affairs of the business, are rare but ideal regarding the issue of control. The greater the percentage share of equity outside investors hold in your company, the less your potential control of the company. Control assumes many forms. It can be exerted through voting rights as shareholders, board membership, lever-age that exists due to company's financial dependence, and numerous other sources. Issues of control are discussed further in later chapters. Another disadvantage of accepting more equity investors is the reduction of the founders' equity percentage in the company, which reduces the return they can expect upon the future sale or acquisition of the company.

Debt Funding

Debt financing typically is made available by retail banks or specialized investment banks. During early fundraising stages, this type of financing may be difficult to acquire as the lending party requires minimum levels of cash flows to ensure that the borrower has the ability to make the debt payments (i.e., service the debt). Unlike the situation with equity investors, lenders will have claims on your tangible and nontangible assets (i.e., perhaps your core intellectual property [IP]) upon default. It is much more difficult to raise funds through sale of equity if you have considerable debt on your balance sheet because prospective equity investors prefer their funds be used for value-added activities, not paying off or servicing an existing debt. Prospective investors will also be cautious about investing in a company whose assets, especially core IP, has been secured by debt holders with more senior claims upon liquidation. A major concern for prospective equity investors is the risk of default on debt payments that can result in the loss of company control of to debt holders; it should be for the founders and other shareholders as well. A debt holder's interests may not be aligned with the interests of the com-pany. Debt holders naturally are more conservative in decision making, as they are primarily interested in getting their principal returned and collect their interest earned in a timely manner. Therefore, they are more interested in cash flows (ability of your company to service the debt) during the term of the note than in making capital expenditures for the long-term success of the company. At the very least, it is annoying and distractive to have a debt holder opposing decisions that are being made in the best long-term interests of your shareholders. Another con with debt financing is the possibility of losing control of company to the debtors in the event of debt payment default. Debt financing does have two distinct advantages: Debt holders do not have a controlling interest (i.e., shareholder votes) in your company, and the assumption of debt does not dilute the equity share of the founding partners or other shareholders.

Given the characteristics of both equity and debt financing, it is understandable why equity raises are more prevalent at the early stages. Once the company achieves the means to service debt (i.e., revenues), the risk of liquidation has been significantly reduced, and a future equity raise is neither foreseen nor necessary, it is preferred to end the dilution of equity and assume debt.

Alternative Types of Funding

There are four specific types of funding that an entrepreneurial venture may encounter that offer a variation of debt and equity characteristics. They are convertible debt, equity warrants, factoring, and licensing/revenue sharing agreements.

Convertible Debt

Convertible debt is a hybrid of both private equity and debt in which a debt note is executed and there are conversion terms. The investor usually is permitted to convert the remaining principal and possibly accrued interest balance into equity either at any time during the note term or only at the end of term.

Convertible debt is very favorable to the investor but may not be so good for the entrepreneur. Basically a convertible note is a dilutive debt instrument. It represents the best of both worlds for the investor and the worst of both worlds for the entrepreneur. In the event of liquidation, the investor enjoys all the protection afforded by debtor rights; if the company succeeds, the investor enjoys the returns of the higher-risk-taking equity investors. Until the note is converted, it remains debt on the company books, making it much more difficult to raise any type of debt or equity funding. Unfortunately, convertible debt has become a preferred way to raise early-stage funds. The primary reason cited to structure early-stage funding this way is the ease of raising such funds from a legal and pricing point of view. It may be true that in many countries, such as the United States, the legal fees and paperwork associated with a convertible note may be notably less compared to an equity placement. Also, by eliminating the need to value an early-stage company, as is necessary with an equity placement, funding negotiations can be conducted much more easily. However, as we discuss in great detail in Chapter 2, we are not seeking "easy" money; we are seeking "good" money. Making it easier to secure "bad" money in which you become insolvent from day 1 makes it difficult to secure future funding and has initial investors see your future actions more through the lens of debt holders than shareholders who are sharing the same risks as the other founders. In my opinion, this is not a good trade-off. Until a funding round is reached whereby sufficient operational and financial objectives have been achieved to serve as a basis for a valuation, investors should be treated as founding partners; the percentage equity interest they are to be granted should be based on the factors presented in the risk/return section. During my extensive experience with entrepreneurial ventures, I have seldom witnessed an occasion where early investors felt slighted after a successfully concluded funding round. I have too often seen painfully protracted and costly funding negotiations for later-stage funding, if they do not doom the negotiations altogether, by a preceding debt placement. This can be particularly true for tech entrepreneurial ventures with valuable IP; the convertible debt holders typically and reasonably hold the IP as collateral, and later-stage investors who are considering investing a far greater amount cannot justify such a large investment if they have no claims to the IP from which future cash flows depend.

Entrepreneurs should not propose this type of funding structure to prospective investors. If a prospective investor, especially at an early fundraising stage, offers convertible debt, it should be approached cautiously. When we discuss financial planning and efficient fundraising in Chapter 4, we demonstrate why any type of debt funding should be delayed, if possible, for later fundraising stages and how to properly space funding rounds by determining the appropriate time to execute them. Doing this will help avoid slighting earlier stakeholders.

Equity Warrants

A second alternative funding type is equity warrants, a substructure of private equity. Equity warrants grant the holder the right to purchase a specified number of shares at a specified exercise price. They may or may not specify a term. They share all the characteristics of equity with one important exception. A warrant holder does not have shareholder rights, particularly controlling voting rights, until such warrants are exercised. Once warrants are exercised, the warrant holder becomes a shareholder. Additional funding is generated (exercise price multiplied by the number of shares purchased) as well. Consequently, the higher the exercise price, the more favorable for the entrepreneurial venture and the less desirable for a prospective warrant holder. Equity warrants, when offered, usually are granted to comarketing partners and/or employees as incentives or to advisor/contractors for services rendered. They can be offered to attract prospective passive investors as well. The offering price of warrants is at a discount to the current market share price or at a mutually agreed-on price per share based on current valuation.

Factoring

Factoring is a form of bank debt financing that is relatively unknown. Under certain conditions, however, it may be an attractive alternative funding option, particularly for entrepreneurial ventures. Factoring is basically a short- to intermediate-term bank loan that accepts an account payable as collateral as opposed to the tangible assets usually required as collateral for a traditional bank loan or both tangible and nontangible assets that must be pledged as security for a debt note from a private investor. To secure factoring credit, you will need to have an account payable or executed contract with either a client with a strong credit rating or a government agency and typically at least a 6- to 12-month clean payment history with them. The lender offering the factoring credit will provide funds to you up front based on a percentage of the total account payable or contract amount. The lender will collect the account payable or contract payment(s) directly and, in determining whether to award such factoring credit, considers the creditworthiness of your client more heavily than the creditworthiness of your company. The beauty of factoring is that you are effectively leveraging the strong credit of your client to secure an otherwise unattainable bank loan at very attractive terms without providing your core assets as security. Therefore, it offers all the advantages of debt but without many of its drawbacks. It is not uncommon to see an entrepreneurial venture secure a nice contract or expand an existing one with a large client but needing up-front funds to execute its contractual obligations. This type of scenario may create an attractive opportunity to pursue a factoring deal.

Licensing and Revenue Sharing Agreements

A licensing agreement will grant the investing entity some form of right to utilize one or more of your IP assets in exchange for either an up-front or recurring licensing fee. If a party is identified that would be interested in entering a licensing deal with you, the two most important considerations are: Who is this party and to what extent are they granted such rights? Obviously you do not want to grant licensing rights to a direct competitor or anyone that can damage your strategic positioning in any way. You do not want to establish a potential competitor by granting too much right of use either. However, licensing fees are nondilutive and enhance your balance sheet via increasing the value of the IP nontangible asset as it is now considered a revenue-generating asset. Having an executed licensing agreement with a prominent firm will lend enormous validation and credibility that will only help you in future fundraising activities as well.

A revenue sharing agreement has similar advantages. The investing entity will provide up-front funds in exchange for a percentage of a current or future revenue stream of your business. It is nondilutive and doesn't carry the risk that misuse can lead to a strategic disadvantage, as with a licensing agreement. However, a revenue share will consume some of your future operating cash flow. A revenue sharing agreement represents a source of confidence from an outside party that can be favorably exhibited to future prospective investors as well.

Public Funding

Public funding offers attractive funding types as an alternative to traditional private equity or debt placement. Public funding may be made available by government agencies with mandates to achieve certain business development objectives for their particular municipality. The three most common types of public funding are matching equity, loan guarantees, and grants.

Matching Equity

Matching equity is the most common public funding program. The funding public agency matches the equity investment of private equity investors. Securing a matching equity commitment from a public funding agency will help you tremendously in securing a matching equity investment from a private investor.

Bank Loan Guarantee

A public agency will guarantee a portion or all of a loan that a bank provides to you. This method significantly reduces or eliminates the risks the bank assumes in lending you funds, which provides a bank with a large incentive to lend such funds to your business. Unfortunately, because tech start-ups have insufficient operating history, erratic cash flows, and/or lack of tangible assets to serve as collateral, such firms rarely can secure loan guarantees.

Grants

Securing grants from a public agency can be a little more difficult to accomplish than other types of public funding but offer several advantages. Grants are nondilutive and, if they are granted unconditionally, they basically are free money—the best form of funding. However, unconditional grants are rare. They require a lot of precious time and effort (i.e., opportunity cost) to both initially secure and maintain (i.e., preparing periodic reporting requirements). Conditional grants are more common; here you have to pay back the grant money once certain preagreed conditions are met. The grant money may come only in the form of a reimbursement for an already incurred expense, which is not useful if you need immediate funding. However, a reimbursement grant with no repayable conditions is free money; whenever possible, seek such grants out.

   A great common benefit of all public funding is the added credibility associated with securing any form of government support. When soliciting investors in the private sector, the value of such support cannot be overstated.

Incubator/Accelerator Programs

Recently the number of both public and private incubator and accelerator programs has increased significantly. This is a very positive development. Both types of programs provide the use of facilities, promotion, mentoring, exposure to prospective investors, and occasionally seed funds for start-up companies. An incubator or accelerator may demand in return a nominal equity share of your venture. The primary differences between the two are duration and intensity. Typically a start-up enters an incubator program for six months to a year and is usually free to proceed at its own pace. A typical accelerator program grants selected participants between 60 and 100 days to achieve a very ambitious list of criteria in preparation for an opportunity to pitch in front of prospective investors at the end of the program. Both program types offer a great way to avoid having to initially raise funds for non-value-added expenses, such as rent, computers, and information technology infrastructure. Sharing space, ideas, and mutual support with other start-ups and formerly successful entrepreneurs can be of enormous benefit to your development efforts as well.

The qualifications and cost for a start-up to be accepted into an incubator or accelerator program are minimal. However, acceptance into many accelerator programs is on a competitive basis. Given the enormous benefits at such minimal costs and risk, it is difficult to imagine why a start-up would not take advantage of an opportunity to participate in an available incubator or accelerator program. The search for and application to such programs should be one of the first considerations for aspiring entrepreneurs contemplating starting an entrepreneurial venture. (See Figure 1.2.)

Capital Structure

A firm's capital structure is the composition of its liabilities used to finance (acquire) its assets. It is basically a summary of all a company's executed fund raises. For our purposes, stakeholders are narrowly defined as including both shareholders and debt holders. Their positions will be represented in your capital structure.

The capital structure of your company is of significant importance to your fundraising efforts. It serves as a point of reference in observing and managing the rate at which your company's equity is diluted, managing relations with current stakeholders, foreseeing any control issues, and as a basis for determining your price per share, given the company's calculated valuation.

During your fundraising efforts, you will discover that every serious prospective investor will demand to see an accurate and up-to-date capital

Funding Type	Availability	Control Effect	Equity Dilution	Alignment with Shareholder Interest	Event of Liquidation	Effect on Founder/ROI upon Exit
Internal Funding (via founder's financial contribution or generated revenues)	Sufficient personal savings of founders, retained earnings or revenues	Optimal effect: No forfeiture of control to external parties	None	Fully	Optimal effect: No obligations established to external parties	Optimal effect: No obligations established to external parties
Private Equity	Existence of interested investors	Granting of shareholder voting rights and possibly a board seat	Yes. Amount based on percentage equity share purchased	Very high as fellow shareholders	Common: No preference Preferred: Liquidation Preference over common	Dilution based on proportional equity percentage amount issued to nonfounder shareholders
Debt Instrument	Sufficient cash flows or tangible assets for collateral	Constraining effects of reduced cash to service debt payments	None	Potential inherent unalignment between debt holder and shareholder interests	Senior to all equity classes	Reduced by amount of principal and accrued interest remaining due upon exit
Convertible Debt	Either tangible or intangible assets (i.e., IP) as collateral	Combination of debt and equity control effects	Yes. Upon conversion	Potential inherent unalignment between debt holder and shareholder interests until conversion	Senior to all equity classes	Dilution based on proportional equity percentage amount issued upon conversion

Factor Financing	Qualified accounts receivable as collateral	Constraining effects on cash flow and managing accounts receivable of key clients	None	Neutral	Bank factoring lender has already assumed accounts receivable as collateral	Slight effect on ROI upon exit based on exclusion of accounts receivable as an asset
Public Grant	Product/service matches investment criteria/KPIs of public funding agency	Constraining effects from compliance with eligibility and use of funds requirements	None	Dependent on degree stated company objectives and KPIs match	Claim to any payback terms	Only reduced by payback terms reaining due
Incubators and Accelerators	Meeting minimal admissions qualifications or competitive selection	Dependence on provided facilities. Accelerator participants need to follow strict work criteria and possibly grant some equity	Maybe a nominal percentage equity amount as a fee for participation	High alignment. Both program types designed to prepare participants for both immediate equity funding and eventual exit	Dependent on percentage amount and classification of equity granted	Dependent on equity percentage amount granted; usually a nominal percentage

FIGURE 1.2 Types of Funding

structure of your company. Expect investors to examine it with keen interest as it reveals much about the financial management of your company and will determine the funding structure type and amount they may be prepared to offer.

Throughout the various fundraising stages, you will need to refer to your company's capital structure to track the rate by which the company's equity is diluted by each additional equity sale. I call this rate the rating of equity dilution (RED); it is illustrated in Chapter 4 on financial planning. An awareness of RED will allow you to efficiently determine the timing, size, and offering price of your equity sales.

Current stakeholders will follow the changes in the capital structure closely as well. They do not want to see a new investor—who as a later investor is theoretically assuming less risk—granted proportionally better terms. In Chapters 4, 7, and 8 we discuss the various means to maintain the integrity of a capital structure.

It is important for entrepreneurs to monitor the equity positions of each stakeholder to avoid fundraising activities that may grant a particular stakeholder or a group of stakeholders more control and potential influence than desired. It is also necessary to account for proxies. A proxy is a stakeholder that permits another stakeholder to wield its voting rights or other means of influence. Maintaining effective control of your company is critical, particularly in the earlier stages of development. Throughout all stages of development, it is important to avoid too much financial dependence on any one funding source.

For these reasons, maintaining a clean and healthy capital structure is critical. A clean capital structure is one that is not complicated by numerous funding types and convertible instruments that can be sources of confusion for prospective investors. For example, a convertible note can "dirty" a capital structure by injecting a level of uncertainty. If and when the convertible debt holders decide to convert, the company's capital structure may be substantially altered with the consequent reduction in debt and the occurring dilution of equity. A clean capital structure also demonstrates a fair progression of fundraising in which the earliest investors, who are theoretically assuming the most risk, enjoy proportionally higher returns upon the acquisition or sale of your company. A healthy capital structure is defined as one that does not impede the company's future fundraising efforts. For example, a large debt note secured too early may cause difficulty in offering a subsequent equity placement for reasons presented earlier in this chapter.

Most important, your capital structure will serve as a determining factor in deriving your price per share. Your company's capital structure, which represents the sum of your outstanding equity securities, is a direct factor in formulating the price at which to sell equity shares.

Intellectual Property

Consider this truism: Ideas are cheap.

An idea in itself has no tangible value. If a commercial application for its use is identified, it has potential value as it can attract potential licensees. However, such nominal value is likely to be insufficient to attract high-risk investors. The value of any business is not the idea or product from which the business is built; rather the value is in the formulation and successful execution of a business plan associated with such an idea or product that generates exceptional returns for all its stakeholders. The greatest misperception by far I witness entrepreneurs have toward venture capital is the notion that a good idea or product is sufficient to attract investors. A venture capitalist will tell you it is all in the execution. If you have an amazing product but have a poor management team, implement a terrible pricing policy, or proceed without a financial plan, your venture will fail. If you have a not-so-spectacular product but have impeccable timing and make all the right decisions, you can make a fortune. I know people who have made an incredible amount of money selling outhouses to construction companies and others selling T-shirts. Not exactly flashy or innovative products, but the businesses were effectively planned, timed, and executed. I offer these examples to prove my point that ideas are cheap. However, the ideas or product originating from an innovative entrepreneurial venture have much more potential value than outhouses and T-shirts as they might change the lives and workplaces of many more people; thus, they have the potential to attract investment funds. With that said, there are numerous examples in the past 20 years of truly innovative ventures based on brilliant ideas that have failed to monetize their product or service.

For many entrepreneurial ventures, the most valuable asset they most likely possess is nontangible. It is their IP. IP can be defined as any innovation created through one's own original thinking and experimentation that may offer the possibility of securing legal property rights for the inventor. It is a nontangible asset because it is neither a physical object nor quantitatively valuated due to its original nature. Nevertheless, potentially significant value may be derived from the opportunity to utilize such IP to develop and produce a product or service that is revenue generating. The greater the number of commercially viable applications of a set of IP, the more valuable it potentially is as well. An entrepreneurial venture's IP often consists of several related innovative creations referred to as a suite of IP. Much of the initial fundraising activities of an entrepreneurial venture and the basis for its capital structure are funding the development and protection of its IP suite.

A primary objective of any entrepreneurial venture is to protect and maintain control of its suite of IP for as long as possible. The extent and means by which IP rights are defined and protected vary from one legal jurisdiction to another. Entrepreneurs can legally protect their IP in five formal ways:

1. *Patent.* A patent is a set of exclusive rights granted for a specified period of time by a legal authority to the owner of IP, as defined by the legal authority, in exchange for the public disclosure and commercial availability of the IP. Typically, the patent applicant must demonstrate the originality, utility, and commercial application of its innovation. A patent holder may license to another party the right to conditionally utilize its protected IP. The purpose of granting patents is to encourage innovation by providing a financial incentive to inventors to publicly introduce their innovations for the public's benefit.
2. *Copyright.* A copyright is a set of exclusive rights granted for a specified period of time by a legal authority to an author or creator of an original work with the potential and possibly intention to be copied or mass distributed. A copyright gives the grantee the right to copy, distribute, and adapt the protected work. As with patents, a copyright holder may conditionally confer such copyrights to another party.
3. *Trademarks.* A trademark is a distinguishing attribute (i.e., sign, logo, etc.) that is readily identifiable with a unique source (i.e., your company, product, or service). Successfully filing for trademark protection confers exclusive rights to the trademark holder to use its protected trademark to maintain public recognition of the connection between a company and its products and services. Such property rights may prove valuable when it is time to market and build brand recognition of your innovative products or services.
4. *Industrial design right.* An industrial design right is an IP right intended to protect an original and innovative visual design having aesthetic value. Typically an industrial design is used to produce a product.
5. *Trade secrets.* Trade secrets (i.e., classified or confidential information) are not formally protected other than via a confidentiality or nondisclosure agreement (NDA). A trade secret is generally not readily understandable, offers an economic benefit to its owner, and is worthy of maintaining its confidentiality. Trade secrets may include any processes, formulas, designs, practices, or instructions that meet the aforementioned characteristics. Basically your trade secrets represent the sum of all your mental efforts and experimentation to develop your product or service and from which your assets derive value.

Regardless of whether you formally protect your IP through a patent or through an executed agreement, such as an NDA, the best protection is the originality of your creation. The strongest protection is having the unique capability of profitably utilizing your innovation. Before filing for expensive formal IP right protections and selecting the prospective investors you will be sharing your IP with, you must consider three issues:

1. *The level of necessity and value in pursuing IP protection.* Often it is not necessary to protect an innovation no matter how innovative it is. Ask this important question: *Is there sufficient value to justify protection in terms of the potential revenue generation to be derived and the strategic value it represents?*

   Obviously, if an innovation is the basis for the potential financial success of a product or service, it warrants serious consideration for legal protection. An innovation also may need protection based solely on its strategic value. If a certain IP is critical to differentiate and give you a competitive advantage, protecting it legally may be a good idea. A patent or any other type of IP protection is an asset that likely increases your valuation and provides a source of leverage in funding negotiations as we discuss in Chapter 6 on negotiations. Occasionally protecting an IP is advantageous as a preemptive strike to either prevent a potential competitor from acquiring exclusive use of such IP or to establish a barrier of entry into a given market. The latter serves as a risk mitigation factor that prospective investors find desirable, as we examine in Chapter 2.

   However, there are costs and risks associated with attempting to protect your IP.

2. *Cost, time, and effort required.* In most places in the world, filing for many forms of IP protection can be expensive. Filing for a patent in the United States, for example, could cost in excess of $10,000. This is not to mention the time and effort to complete and wait for an application to be approved, and there is no guarantee that an IP filing will be successful.

3. *Cost to legally defend.* Your IP rights are secure only to the extent of your ability to legally defend such rights. If you do not file for protection, your IP may become known only by those you allow to see it. Once you file for a form of IP protection, your IP becomes publicly available. No one is physically prevented from using IP that is legally protected. All the protection allows you to do is file for a lawsuit or court action for any violation. As a start-up, you may not have the means to detect and/or legally defend against such a violation.

Valuation

Valuation is what a company is worth. How much is a company worth?

Your company and every other company is worth how much a prospective buyer is willing to pay to purchase the business. Ultimately the valuation of a company is determined by negotiations between company and investors/acquirers.

The valuation of the company is the single most important thing that needs to be determined before an equity investment in your venture can be executed. The price per share at which an equity purchase will be consummated and the basis from which such investor's return on investment (ROI) will be derived will depend on the mutually agreed-on valuation of the company at the time of the equity purchase. A high valuation will make your investment opportunity less attractive to prospective investors; a valuation too low will reduce the eventual returns to be realized by founding investors and current stakeholders. The lower the valuation, the cheaper the purchase price will be for a prospective investor. Prospective investors know this and use all kinds of tactics to work the price down. In Chapter 6 on negotiations, we examine this in greater detail. For our purposes, suffice it to say that it is your responsibility and in your best interest as an entrepreneur to select the most appropriate, supportable, and advantageous valuation model.

Numerous valuation models fit into four general categories. The four general categories, listed in order from lowest to highest expected valuation calculations, are asset based, pro forma (projected financials) based, comparable based, and strategic based.

Asset-Based Valuation Models

Asset-based valuation models place value on only those tangible and non-tangible assets possessed by company. Basically these models are utilized to calculate liquidation values and do not attribute any value to the company's past efforts or future prospects except in the imperfect valuation of non-tangible assets. Valuation of assets, both tangible and nontangible, is useful in debt placements requiring such assets as collateral. However, it is not appropriate for valuations of businesses that have accomplished anything that can be considered value added. Asset-based valuation models offer the lowest calculated valuations. Entrepreneurs should neither propose that their company be valued as merely a sum of its assets nor entertain a prospective investor who may offer funding based solely on assets. If you agree to an asset-based valuation, you are basically agreeing that you and your team have not added any value to the business thus far and do not offer any future value to the venture.

Pro Forma–Based Valuation Models

Pro forma–based valuation models represent the most common type of valuation modeling for start-up businesses. The financial (pro forma) projections of a business are evaluated to determine a valuation. From these projections, a company's profits and cash flows are drawn and revealed during a three- to five-year period. A valuation is derived from either a multiple of earnings or by one of numerous methods to discount cash flows. The multiple of earnings models will multiplies earnings before interest, taxes, depreciation, and amortization (EBITDA) by a reasonable factor based on the development stage and the industry. For a deal to occur, the investor has to accept your EBITDA and the multiple you are using. In discounted cash flow (DCF) methods, the projected cash flows are discounted back to their net present value. The discount rate to be employed is correlated with either the ROI or the annual internal rate of return (IRR) expected by the prospective investor. There exists much literature describing the various pro forma valuation models in more detail. For purposes of this book, suffice it to say that the numbers you place into your financial projections have to be supportable or at least reasonable and the valuation model you select needs to be recognized and ultimately accepted by your targeted prospective investors, and it must illustrate your business in the most favorable light. It is not a bad idea to try several different valuation models to calculate your valuation, given the same set of pro forma financials and see which one is the most advantageous.

Comparable-Based Valuation Models

Comparable-based valuation methods attempt to value your company based on established valuations of companies similar to yours, often in the same industry and marketplace. Apparent differences in the businesses are used to adjust up or down the valuation of your business. Financial ratios such as price–earnings ratios may serve as a point of comparison. This method presents many challenges. Often your company is at an earlier stage of development than established businesses in your industry. Can you compare pro forma with actual financial numbers? Comparing a private company, such as your new entrepreneurial venture, to a publicly traded company with publicly available financial statements represents another potential challenge. A variation of a comparable method is a comparison of your business to the overall marketplace in which you operate. If a business in the same market was valued at $3 million when it was at the same stage of development as your business, perhaps a reasonable comparison can be made. That comparable business may also be currently trading at a price-to-earnings ratio of 10. Why not multiply your EBITDA by 10 to calculate your valuation, as opposed to the 4 multiple currently used in your pro forma–based valuation if you believe your prospective investor(s) would find such a comparison credible?

A comparable-based valuation model should be presented only to prospective investors who are very familiar with the industry or targeted market ("space") in which you operate. To be advantageous to you, the calculated valuation needs to be higher than your pro forma–based valuation calculation as well.

Strategic-Based Valuation

There are no specific models to discuss when considering a strategic-based valuation. It is more a matter of perception of a prospective investor with strategic intentions. The complementary, enabling, and enhancing characteristics of your technologies and products or business position are the considerations that will warrant the strong attention of a strategic investor. If you are fortunate or skillful enough to be in position to attract the interest of a strategic investor, you may receive the greatest possible valuation. This is the only type of valuation that considers ridiculously high valuations. In fact, financial projections and assets are often merely afterthoughts in the minds of strategic investors. Earlier we stated that the value of a company is how much someone is willing to pay for it. Was YouTube worth $1.65 billion when purchased by Google? It was to Google, but it was not to Microsoft. Google certainly did not use an asset or pro forma–based valuation method. Why did Google buy YouTube based on such a relatively high valuation? Basically YouTube provided a significant media platform through which Google could pursue its stated mission to organize global information in an easily acceptable and universal manner. This acquisition is an example of a strategic purchase based on complementary objectives and capabilities resulting in large returns for the sellers' shareholders. A recent investment banking client of mine has attracted many different strategic investors due to its enabling core proprietary technologies. Although the strategic investors operate in different markets from each other and that of my client, the client's technologies offer uniquely strategic advantages for each investor. For example, one prospective strategic investor perceives the technology as a driver for demand of its own technologies currently in its pipeline (development stages). Another prospective strategic investor sees the same technology as a means to improve the performance of a service it currently provides. A third prospective investor views the technology as a means to enhance the marketing efforts of a major product it is about to launch and to enter a new market with in a significant way. A combination of good fortune and careful positioning has benefited my client and presents several examples of how an entrepreneurial venture can possess substantial strategic value.

Determining which valuation model is most advantageous to you depends on your ability to understand your prospective investors and identify their intentions. Generally asset-based valuation models should be avoided. Pro forma–based models are the most common valuation models that provide the most supportable and recognized valuation methods. Comparable-based models should be utilized when it is advantageous for you to do so and presented to prospective investors who can be reasonably expected to accept. A strategic investor is the most prized prospective investor offering the greatest perceived valuations of your venture. The primary objective and challenge of your business is to identify and position your business to attract such investors. In Chapter 2 we discuss ways to identify and approach strategic investors.

Exit Strategy

A business's exit strategy indicates how and when shareholders receive their returns. When presenting to prospective equity investors, you must assume that they are expecting a future sale or initial public offering (IPO) of the business to award them for their risk taking and support. Proceeding with a high-risk entrepreneurial venture without an exit strategy is tantamount to going to war without clear-cut objectives to end the war. In either case you will not find much support. If your business objective is simply to generate revenues for the purpose of providing the funds necessary to pay for stable salaries or only offer services with little opportunity for explosive growth, you will have to target your fundraising efforts to prospective investors who would be satisfied to receive recurring returns, such as a dividend or revenue/profit share. In general, it is not easy to identify equity investors willing to accept only small recurring returns as numerous investment opportunities offer stable income with much less risk than a start-up venture.

Serious prospective equity investors will want to be presented with an exit strategy that states how they get their investment and profits, when, and how much. A business can propose several different plausible exit strategies as well. The "how" is usually answered in one of two ways: a future sale to an investor or company or an IPO (an initial listing of a business on a regulated public equity securities exchange). In proposing a direct sale or acquisition of your business, you will need to mention specific potential buyers either individually or as a class and why they would be interested in being a future purchaser. Including strategic investors as possible buyers in your exit strategy makes your investment opportunity much more compelling. The "when" is presented in number of years to exit. The sooner the exit strategy, the more attractive it is to investors. However, the exit date needs to be realistic and allow your business sufficient time to reach the stated objectives to place it in a position either to be an attractive acquisition or to execute a lucrative IPO. Typically, an expected exit strategy is between five and seven years. The "how much" is presented as either a projected ROI or an annualized IRR. The greater the perceived risk investors assume, the greater their expected ROI or IRR. Investors consider the assumption of risks to be greater the earlier the fundraising stage they invest in and the longer they have to wait for an exit strategy to be realized. Typically, equity investors expect an ROI of about eight to ten times. In other words, if they invested $1 million, they expect to receive $8 to $10 million upon exit. To achieve the same ROI over a five- to seven-year period would require an average annual IRR of at least 80 percent. Your exit strategy must demonstrate such an expected return if you want to attract equity investors for your high-risk entrepreneurial venture.

The exit strategy is the end game for your business. The exit strategy you choose will determine what prospective investors to target, how to present to them, how you prepare your business plan, and how you formulate your financial plan. As we illustrate in Chapter 2, an investor's primary motivation is to make money. The exit strategy illustrates how it is going to be accomplished.

Summary

This chapter presented the basic financial principles relevant to the topics discussed in this book. The financial principles examined include fundraising stages, risk/return, types of funding, capital structure, intellectual property, valuation, and exit strategy. The fundraising stages include seed, series A, and series B. They progress from funding a prototype, to a commercial launch, to expansion. The various issues and challenges faced by an entrepreneurial venture in each stage were examined. The relationship between risk and return was analyzed to provide a basis for understanding the expectations of prospective investors, managing fundraising efforts, calculating valuation, and formulating an exit strategy. We described the various types of funding to assist in determining the most favorable funding type to solicit in each fundraising stage, given both the financial and nonfinancial pros and cons of each type. The closely related concept of capital structure was then examined to demonstrate how useful it is as a point of reference for financial decision making and its effect on prospective investors' perceptions. A discussion of IP was especially relevant for high-risk entrepreneurial ventures. The multiple values of an entrepreneurial venture's IP were presented to assist in determining whether and how the IP is to be protected. The ways in which a company's IP can be a source of revenue and leverage were also discussed. Valuation was the next financial principle presented. An understanding of how an entrepreneurial venture's valuation is determined will serve as a basis for the determination of financial objectives and ultimately the construction of an effective financial plan. Only after these financial principles have been understood and considered can you determine an exit strategy to illustrate to all current and prospective stakeholders how they can profit from their financial and nonfinancial commitments.

Achieving a successful exit is the ultimate goal of every shareholder. A successful exit requires both a firm understanding of the financial principles presented and the expectations of the various prospective investors. Knowing your investor is the topic of Chapter 2.

Know Your Investors

In this chapter, we characterize the different types of investors and discuss what they are looking for and what you should be looking for. When you know your investors (KYI) you will be able to:

- Increase the probability of securing funding for your entrepreneurial venture and on the best terms possible.
- Identify and select the business partners who offer the most advantages, both financial and nonfinancial.
- Ensure that your working relationship with new business partners will be the most productive and offer the best value.

KYI #1: Their Primary Objective Is to Make Money

Investors are not supporting a hobby, funding a cause, or trying to win first prize in a science fair. Entrepreneurs, by their very nature, are passionate individuals. They truly love the work they do and are apt to be altruistic and have a driving desire to pursue perfection in their creations. All of these are admirable traits, but if you do not properly manage or express these worthy values, you may hinder your dealings with prospective investors.

Prospective investors are not looking for an opportunity to financially support someone's hobby. It is good and advisable that investors recognize that you have a passion for what you are doing. However, when interacting with prospective investors or current business partners, it is important to project your entrepreneurial venture as, first and foremost, an attractive business opportunity. Inexperienced entrepreneurs often make a variety of expressions best kept to themselves. My favorite from unassuming entrepreneurs is "No one needs to pay me to do this."

My response: "Yes they do, if you want their money!"

Unless you are soliciting funding from a research and development (R&D) institution or a philanthropic organization and are prepared to be treated as the former, do not assume that an investor would be willing to fund an enterprise benefiting a worthy cause that offered little or no returns.

In a past life, when I was a business broker, a client charged me with identifying and negotiating for the purchase of an ESL (English as a Second Language) school. It did not take me long to discover an owner of an ESL school that was on the brink of closing and who wanted to sell her school and be retained to manage for at least one year. During my first meetings with her, I found her extremely competent in the administrative and operational aspects of running an educational institution. She had over 40 years of experience in the education profession and was personally responsible for acquiring all the necessary licenses and registrations required of establishing and maintaining such a school. During the first several years, the award-winning school was a big success and grew very rapidly. This rapid growth forced her to find a new location as the original facilities allowed no room for expansion. She was able to acquire a new location of suitable size, but the location proved inaccessible for her students, who were primarily foreign students without a car. Consequently, school enrollment plummeted. She now faced eviction from her school premises and the loss of her prized teaching staff. She had identified a new location for the school. My client and I were convinced that her selected location was ideal and that she was more than capable of operating the school, attracting more students, and retaining her dedicated staff.

Unfortunately, during my first meetings with her, I realized that she considered this school her baby. Her primary motivation for starting and saving the school was to provide the finest ESL instruction to her students (small class size, funding of noninstructional activities, etc.) and highly rewarding teaching opportunities with all the perks for her beloved staff. When we discussed the future financial management of the school, her primary motivation became too apparent. She made it very clear that she intended to pass along any and all profits to the benefit of her students and staff in some manner. I failed in my attempts to persuade her that the school would need to be managed as a for-profit business in the future and that my client (and any investor) expected returns on investment. I had no choice but to advise my client of her intentions, and he decided it would not be a desirable business opportunity. I never felt more cold-hearted than when I notified her that my client would not be investing. As I consoled her regarding the loss of her baby, the realization was undeniable that the overriding motivation of investors is to make money.

Again, investors are not funding your entrepreneurial venture to win first prize in a science fair. One of my first clients successfully developed and launched an innovative and effective form of outdoor advertising signage partly as a result of recognizing this KYI and a competitor's failure to do so. My client and its competitor were both developing a high-impression mobile advertising sign to introduce into a high-margin niche advertising market. As with most technology products, the more features developed and eventually offered, the greater the cost. The competitor intended to develop this product with all the bells and whistles. Initially my client was determined to meet the challenge and develop a bigger and better sign. Fortunately, though, after considering the potential advertising revenue base of each targeted advertising market and expectations of prospective advertising clients, my client realized that a bigger and better sign may not necessarily secure bigger and better profits. At this point, my client decided to develop a sign to deliver value, not "wow!" Features offering an increase in impression levels (capturing the attention of more eyes with greater retention) were favored over features intended just to impress. As a result, my client had to raise only a third of the funds otherwise necessary. Prospective investors liked the thrifty nature of our product development and expected my client to spend their money with the same thriftiness in the future. The better-funded competitor introduced its product to the market first at six times the price and could not generate enough ad revenues to secure profits for investors. My client launched the signage and was able to secure identical ad revenues to the competitor but achieved much greater profitability. This signage proved to be much more sustainable, offering superior value, and the competitor went bankrupt shortly after. The only consolation that can be offered to the competitor is that it would have won first prize in a science fair compared to my client.

Do not succumb to the mad scientist syndrome. Symptoms include:

- Harboring the belief that a brilliant innovation is sufficient to impress investors, attract investment capital, and crush any and all competition. No matter how spectacular and intriguing your innovation is, investors are more interested in profits. This is not the 1990s. At some point, your business will need to show profitability before you can contemplate a successful exit.
- Enjoying the development aspects of the business so much that you forget you are managing a business and fail to seize opportunities to go to market and generate revenues.
- Spending a disproportionate share of new investment funds on their most enjoyable part of the venture: non-revenue-generating R&D.
- Providing a comprehensive and intricately detailed synopsis of the technological marvels associated with your inventions in the product section of your business plan or during an in-person pitch rather than just explaining how the product works and generates revenues.

KYI #2: There Are Many Types of Investors, Each with Different Expectations and Capabilities

Types of Investors

The six different investor types, ordered by expected time of encounter from earliest to later fundraising stages, include:

1. Angel investors
2. Public funding agencies
3. Venture capital companies
4. Private equity (PE) firms
5. Strategic investors
6. Banks

Institutional investors include entities that have been specifically established to provide lending or investment funding and follow stated investment criteria in making investment decisions. Venture capital firms, private equity firms, and banks are the primary institutional investors an entrepreneur is likely to encounter. Each investor type has its own expectations and capabilities that offer both advantages and disadvantages to entrepreneurs. You must consider the differences to determine the most appropriate approaches and timing to present. If you understand the investor type, you will know what you can expect from a new business partner once funding is secured.

Angel Investors

Angel investors are individuals willing to make high-risk investments in early-stage ventures. Typically these individuals have had successful entrepreneurial experience in the areas of investment they consider. They usually are motivated by their desire to stay engaged in their past area of success but are not willing to follow the tough lifestyle they experienced during their entrepreneurial days. Consequently, they are passive investors, offering helpful advice and sharing personal experiences; one hopes that they also are very understanding and patient with your decisions and actions. The amount of capital they are either capable or willing to invest is limited compared to other investor types. However, their willingness to generally assume higher risk and their superior knowledge of the particular industry or market make them ideal investors at the early fundraising stages. The value of an angel investor goes well beyond the amount and timing of funding. An experienced and well-connected angel can give valuable advice and make valuable introductions. An entrepreneurial venture that secures investment funds and support from a strong and well-positioned angel is off to a very fortunate start.

Public Funding Agencies

Public funding agencies with the mandate and authority to fund business ventures to achieve economic development, environmental, cultural, or social policy objectives formulated by policy makers at various levels of government are good sources of funding, particularly at the early stages. As with angel investors, the amount of funding may not be great; however, public funding agencies usually serve as passive investors that can make valuable introductions and provide much-needed credibility. Public agencies can also offer other various forms of nonfinancial assistance, such as marketing promotion and access to R&D facilities. Grants with no or a very few conditions from public funding source may be considered free money that do not affect your company's capital structure and management's level of control. Public funding is the one exception to KYI #1; these funds are intended to help your firm achieve a specific public policy objective, not necessarily to achieve the greatest financial returns. To measure the effectiveness of public funding programs, public agencies utilize key performance indicators (KPIs). KPIs help public agencies define and measure progress to fulfilling their mandated objectives. An objective of a local economic development agency may be to increase the number of software development employees in a municipality by 10 percent. To achieve this policy goal, the agency has been allocated funding from the government budget and authorized to invest in business ventures engaged in software development. It is less interested in your bottom line and more interested in how many software developers you intend to employ once funding is granted.

In contrast to angel investors, dealing with government officials can be truly frustrating. Many times they have little or no entrepreneurial experience and may have insufficient knowledge or industry/technological background to fully understand and appreciate your innovative product or service. Keep in mind that the personalities of government officials often are the exact opposite of those of entrepreneurs. Most times they will not share your level of passion; thus, they are not easily excited or susceptible to being wowed. Indeed, trying to impress a public funding agency official may be counterproductive, as doing so only magnifies in their eyes the significance of your venture, and consequently the risk associated with failure in terms of their career prospects. Typically they are risk adverse; they do not expect to receive much credit for assisting a successful venture but are very likely to be criticized or demoted for assisting a failed one. Entrepreneurs who deal with public officials must be patient.

VCists

Venture capital firms are specifically established to invest in high-risk ventures that offer potentially high returns. VCists (VCs) raise funds to capitalize investment funds that they manage. Their investors entrust them to identify investment opportunities matching specific criteria and expectations, which govern the fund managers' investment decisions. Unlike angels, the VC managers who make investment decisions typically do not have successful entrepreneurial experience. Often they have attained their positions by fundraising for investment funds managed by their firm and have little knowledge and technical background on your product or market. Of course, there are exceptions. Cities with vibrant start-up communities, such as Silicon Valley, Austin, Boulder, Boston, and New York in the United States, have much more sophisticated VCs. Such vibrant start-up communities serve as fertile breeding ground of venture capital firms managed and funded by successful entrepreneurs who can definitely offer many forms of nonfinancial assistance.

The series A fundraising stage is the domain of venture capital firms. Such firms are likely to be the first institutional investors an entrepreneur encounters. During prior stages, friends/family, angel investors, and public funding programs accepted the higher risks and offered the modest funding levels demanded of an early-stage entrepreneurial venture based on personal trust and/or empathy. At the series A stage, entrepreneurial ventures typically need greater funds to execute a commercial launch. Often only institutional investors have the means to provide such funding. However, other institutional investors typically are not willing to accept the risks associated with entrepreneurial ventures at this stage of development. Venture capital firms play an important role by filling this funding gap at a crucial time in the development of a venture. Because the firms are aware of this fact, engaging with them can be challenging to say the least. KYI is of utmost importance when dealing with VCs, a point that will be reinforced throughout this book.

A subspecies of mainstream VCs is the vulture capitalist, who is an opportunistic VC preying on vulnerable ventures. As in the wild, the way to ward off vultures is not to act dead.

What attracts a vulture capitalist?

Desperation. Any firm that acts like it is desperate is the primary prey of the instinctive vulture capitalist. If you send out the vibe that you are seeking funds to avert the end of your venture, you are lining yourself up to be a hot dinner for a vulture capitalist.

More astute vulture capitalists may be attracted to your venture due to a perceived large leveraging advantage. Such capitalists may have a resource or contact that would be considered valuable to your venture. These vultures are more than happy to swoop down and attempt to dig their claws into you. Their modus operandi is to tell you about the prized possession they possess and attempt to extract unreasonably generous terms for them at your expense.

Some vulture capitalists are neither instinctive nor astute and prefer to play the numbers game. Their modus operandi is to offer funding proposals, often unsolicited, to unassuming start-ups. Their complicated proposals secure them a fail-safe investment opportunity at the expense of the entrepreneurs, where all risk has been shifted.

The most dangerous vulture capitalists are the ones who steal the food from their prey. They provide just enough funding to allow their prey to struggle through the most difficult and riskiest issues before they execute a take-over. I call two methods they employ selective liquidity and Rolodex of proxies. In selective liquidity, vulture capitalists provide only enough funding to maintain your survival until it is time for them to push you aside. These vultures say they wish they could provide more funding if only they had more funds to offer. In reality, they have enough funding to permit you to achieve break-out success, but they do not want that to occur until they take over the venture themselves relatively cheaply. Once they have taken over the venture, you will soon discover how much money these ostensibly cash-poor business partners actually have. In another favorite tactic, Rolodex of proxies, vulture capitalists introduce new investors to become shareholders and be in position to serve as proxies who will exercise their shareholding voting rights for the benefit of the vulture capitalist. By securing a majority controlling interest in the entrepreneurial venture in a concealed manner the vulture capitalist is now in position to seize control of the company from the unsuspecting founders at a favorable time of their choosing. This is an example of ill-intentioned "bad money" that is better for the founders not to accept. In Chapter 7, I provide an example from personal experience of the deployment of both tactics against a client.

To trap their prey, vulture capitalists use several tactics. They structure their funding proposals to create an almost no-lose situation for themselves by assuming very little risk in a highly disproportionate manner. A common way they accomplish this is by inserting clauses that provide airtight protection of their principal or some form of payment in kind that can be triggered by the first signs of a setback. Setting unrealistic performance triggers or offering funding only to avert cash-flow crises is a typical method employed to effect this. No business enterprise should take on a partner who has very little to lose while you are risking and sacrificing everything. Another vulture capitalist attack tactic is to structure the funding proposal in a way to make it nearly impossible for you to seek future funding without their explicit or implicit consent. Look on with suspicion any clauses in a proposal that grant venture capitalists rights regarding future funding from third parties or that place implicit barriers to your future fundraising abilities. Reasonable VCs who are betting on the success of your venture are highly unlikely to place such wording in their proposals and should welcome additional investors. If vulture capitalists know that you have to go through them for any future funding, they will have a tremendous negotiating advantage over you. You do not want to put yourself in the situation of being totally dependent on a business partner either.

It must be made clear that an overwhelming majority of VCs are not vultures and have legitimate concerns to minimize their risk and maximize their gains, just as you do. These legitimate concerns are discussed in greater detail in Chapter 6 on negotiations.

Private Equity Firms

Private equity (PE) firms are specifically established to invest in relatively mature ventures that have at least a modest financial or operational track record while still offering relatively attractive terms in an intermediate time frame (i.e., one to five years). An entrepreneur may not encounter a PE firm until the series B funding round, when capital is needed to fund growth. Similar to VC firms, PE firms raise and deposit the funds available for investment in funds they manage. This is where the similarities generally end. The investment decisions of PE firms are primarily made by firm partners or associates who often have either successful entrepreneurial or executive management business backgrounds. PE firms, unlike many VCs, usually specialize in one or a few industries. If you attract their interest, your business most likely operates in their industry or market of expertise. Consequently, they are an excellent source of valuable management and strategic advice.

Strategic Investors

Strategic investors are defined by their investment intentions more than any other factors. They could be a member of any of the previous types of investors we have discussed; however, more often they are larger companies operating or investing in the same industry or a complementary one or market as your venture. Very often they are not in the business of investing in smaller ventures but may believe an investment in your business would offer them some strategic value. A strategic investor may see your venture as a way to enter a market more easily, leverage existing operations and investments, gain a competitive advantage, or simply dominate a given market or industry. Attracting the attention of a strategic investor is a worthy objective. No other investor type can offer a higher valuation for your company. Strategic investors are the ideal investor type; for that reason, much of this book is devoted to preparing your business to attract and engage them.

Banks

If you have reached a position to deal with banks, you have reached financial nirvana, as banks offer the lowest costs of capital. A famous saying goes, "A bank will only lend you money when you do not need it." When you can finally go straight to a retail bank to secure lines of credit and simple principal and interest term loans that are sufficient to provide for all your funding needs, you have reached the finish line and have graduated to a full-fledged mature business. Until you have attained this favorable position, there is no need to consider going to a bank, right?

Wrong! Banks may offer relatively unknown but very favorable funding products. As we mentioned earlier, factoring, primarily a bank product, is a funding option that can offer excellent terms for a company at any stage of development, provided it has an established client. A bank may manage a venture or small-business development fund. Sometimes, like public funding agencies, banks offer matching equity programs. As we discuss in Chapter 4, combining different types of funding, such as bank and equity financing, in a funding round can both increase the chances of securing the sought-after funding and reduce the amount of equity dilution. In addition, being able to secure bank funding lends credibility to a start-up that will assist future fund-raising efforts and may establish a valuable long-term banking relationship—just what banks are looking for when they offer such programs to start-up businesses.

Investment Criteria

Investment criteria are sets of requirements necessary to be eligible for funding consideration from a particular prospective investor. These invest-ment criteria are usually publicly stated on Web sites or other marketing materials with the intent to attract only those investment prospects that match their interest. After reading the investment criteria of prospective investors a start-up can determine whether funding is available, given its needs and stage of development. The criteria also may indicate how suitable the investor may be as a business partner. Types of investment criteria include industry pref-erence, preferred stage of development, funding range, favored funding structure, and choice exit strategy.

Industry Preference

The investor may be interested to invest only in those ventures operating in a particular industry. The preference may be due to an investor's knowledge and experience in a certain industry, current attractive prospects of investing in a specific industry, the prescribed investment criterion of an investment fund, or a government mandate to assist local enterprises operating in a priority industry, as is the case with public funding. Angel investors, PE firms, and certainly public funding agencies often have industry preferences.

Preferred Stage of Development

An investor's preferred stage of development is usually determined by its level of risk tolerance, expected returns, and the amount of control it may seek. If an investor is willing to assume greater risk to achieve higher returns, it may prefer to invest at an earlier stage of development. The greater involvement and influence investors wish, the more likely they are to seek early-stage companies in which they can secure a higher percentage equity at the least cost and influence a company's management at an earlier date. Early-stage investors very likely include angels and public agencies. VCs occupy the series A stage, and PE firms favor the series B stage.

Funding Range

The range of funding is simply the amount of funding a prospective investor is willing to invest in each selected investment. The range of funding may be determined by the need to diversify risk, costs for executing each transaction, or funding levels in the stage of development the investor prefers to invest in. If you are seeking to secure $500,000 in this investment round and a prospective investor's investment criteria specifies investments in the $2 to $5 million range, your investment opportunity may not attract much serious interest from them. Typically the range of funding is closely correlated with the amount of funds typically required by an entrepreneurial venture currently operating within the investor's preferred stage of development and industry.

Favored Funding Structure

Investors may favor an equity investment if they are ready to accept the risks of liquidation for the prospect of achieving the highest potential returns and have the requisite shareholder rights. A debt placement is preferred if a certain level of liquidation claims is required as an assurance at the expense of shareholder rights and greater potential returns. Investors may try to have it both ways by proposing a convertible debt structure. Often investors are open to alternative funding structures if it would enable them to maximize their returns and minimize their risks, given the characteristics of a particular investment opportunity. The type of funding structure also determines the amount and nature of influence they can bring to bear on management. Angels typically will seek straightforward equity purchases. Institutional investors execute either debt or equity placement. VCs are very creative and propose complicated funding structures that are in their best interests in terms of simultaneously maximizing return on investment (ROI), hedging their risk in the event of liquidation, and securing the greatest amount of control and influence over the venture at the other stakeholders' expense (i.e., the dreaded convertible debt note). PE firms, which do not need to protect against liquidation risk and do not seek much control beyond shareholder rights, possibly a board seat, and representing you upon your exit strategy, prefer either a debt placement or most probably an equity placement.

Choice Exit Strategy

The three ways to express an exit strategy are time horizon, expected ROI (or a KPI-based policy objective in the case of a public funding program), and type of exit: initial public offering (IPO) or a sale/acquisition. Time horizon is usually expressed in years: for example, "We like to invest in companies for a five- to seven-year period." A public funding program may have a condition that funds have to be reimbursed in X number of years. Expected ROI often is stated explicitly: "We expect an eight to ten times return on our investments." Literature referring to a public funding program may state the program's objective directly: "We are looking to provide funding assistance to firms planning to hire five or more software developers within the next year." Although the type of exit usually is not specifically stated, inferences sometimes can be made, as in: "We are pleased to have taken 12 of our portfolio businesses public in the last three years." This statement would likely be found in promotional material presented by a PE firm that prefers to take companies it invests in public. This PE may have strong relations with underwriters willing to underwrite vested businesses for an IPO. The statement "We have a proven track record of executing the sale of several successful social networking sites" would be made by a firm that prefers investing in social networking sites, perhaps because it has close working relationships with large strategic investors interested in purchasing such sites.

A prospective investor's choice of exit strategy generally is closely correlated with its preferred stage of development and favored funding structure, as both indicate risk tolerance. The earlier the preferred stage of development, the larger the investment time horizon can be expected to be. A preference for equity investments usually indicates a preference for a higher expected ROI as opposed to a recurring income stream or the lower expected ROI exhibited by a debt placement preference.

A prospective investor's suitability as a business partner may be determined from its stated investment criteria, which indicates the investor's tolerance for risk (preferred stage of development), area of expertise (industry preference), amount of control desired (preferred funding structure), and whether its ultimate interests and objectives are aligned with yours (exit strategy).

Now that we know the prerequisites of securing funding from various investor types, let us examine what they are really looking for.

KYI #3: Prospective Investors Are Looking for Success Traits

What are investors looking for?

To discern probability of success, investors consider several aspects of your business for innovative product/service, competence and motivation of management, effective planning, favorable conditions, and existence of promising strategic business relationships.

You must assume that prospective investors will be able to accurately determine whether the funding requirements you solicit are credible. Likely they consider their own funding requirement projections for your venture when making an investment decision. You must also recognize that you will not enjoy any favorable assumptions on their part and will have to present a very compelling and undeniable case that your venture represents the best investment opportunity for them.

Such a compelling case will need to be made in ten areas of consideration:

1. Skin in the game
2. Innovation
3. Defined target market
4. Value proposition
5. Commercial viability
6. Risk mitigation factors
7. Burn rates
8. Strength of management
9. Use of funds
10. Traction

Skin in the Game

"Skin in the game" refers to the amount of personal risk assumed by the founding partners. The more personal risk the founding partners have assumed, the greater their motivation and, consequently, the greater the likelihood of enduring and achieving success despite adversity. There are two main ways to demonstrate skin in the game: via the amount of founding capital contributed, both initially and over time, and the amount of boot-strapping conducted by the founders. Founding capital represents the personal funds invested by the founding partners. Bootstrapping is the practice of sustaining the operations of the venture without the luxury of external financing. It is conducted by finding creative ways to finance the company's operations internally by investing more personal funds, delaying payment of accounts payable, or drawing on current meager revenues to just list a few. Bootstrapping displays thrift, resourcefulness, and determination—all qualities that prospective investors like to see. Other means of showing skin in the game may include a significant recognizable opportunity cost. An opportunity cost is the cost of forgoing any other alternative choice, such as a high-paying job. Such a cost is assessed not only in monetary terms but also in terms of anything which is of value. A primary opportunity cost of a founder in a start-up venture is the lost opportunity to be gainfully employed in a salaried position. Other such costs include the extra stress and reduced personal time associated with managing a high-risk start-up venture and the risk to one's career prospects and professional reputation. The latter perceived risk is particularly prevalent for founders with such valuable contacts and personal reputations.

Innovation

"Innovation" is defined as a new idea that represents a fundamental change in a thought process that presents a value-added result. An innovation can be a technology, process, or proprietary business model. To be innovative requires more than just being new. You have to exhibit a substantial difference that displays a high level of vision. Thus, it is important that your innovative creation evince both value and differentiation. If your product does not possess these two attributes, prospective investors may not perceive an economic value for it or may believe that it is easily replicable or not sufficiently unique to offer a marketable advantage.

Because an innovation is new and substantially different, it also inherently has a certain amount of risk, as it may compel a change or pose as a challenge to whatever existed before it. Remember, the greater the perceived risk, the greater the expected return. A disruptive innovation that has the potential to dramatically alter the dynamics of a specific market or industry holds the most potential value. Such innovative technologies, processes, or business models would truly be game-changing, groundbreaking, or revolutionary.

Defined Target Market

Now that you have an innovative creation, which market or industry do you intend to effect? Prospective investors want to know the size of the market (potential revenues) and any niche market opportunities (profit margins, likelihood of securing a notable share of market).

It is commonly believed that a business needs to identify its market. I disagree. You need to *define* your market. Your aim is to clearly define a niche market that is small enough for you to establish a noticeable presence in it and most suitable to your particular competitive advantages. In addition, the market must be big enough to attract prospective investor interest. Doing both of these things requires an astute balancing act.

It is better to seek a 50 percent share of a $100 million market than a 5 percent share of a $1 billion market. Why is this so, given that each scenario equally represents a $50 million market share?

Answer: Prospective investors, particularly ideal strategic investors, want to invest in market players. Market players are market participants that warrant the serious attention of every other market participant due to their ability to affect prices, set market standards, service key major customers that influence market demand and tastes, control or influence distribution channels, and/or command disruptive technologies. Of these characteristics, only disruptive technologies may not require a large percentage share of the market to affect.

Establishing your venture as a market player is the most effective way to attract strategic investors. Strategic investors like market players for several reasons:

- To enter a lucrative or potentially high-growth market or market segment that otherwise might have been out of their reach.
- To leverage their existing product development efforts, existing market activities, and investments
- To gain a competitive advantage over existing or potential competitors
- To dominate an appealing market

Defining a market is challenging and requires credible information to support and validate your projections and plans. However, the exercise will prove to be well worth the effort.

Value Proposition

Now that you have developed an innovative creation that has demonstrated your technical vision, it is time to reveal your entrepreneurial (business) vision by identifying your creation as a solution that will hold value for someone. How do potential users or consumers benefit from your creation? Would someone be willing to pay a premium for its use? How does your innovative product or service compare with more expensive and less expensive alternatives?

In Kano analysis, a product is distinguished via the possession of threshold attributes perceived by customers. Distinguishing product feature attributes noted in Kano analysis include "must have" and "nice to have," among others. A relative value is thus derived and must be presented to prospective investors. A disruptive innovation that answers a big problem will attract the greatest attention.

If your product is truly innovative, you certainly should be able to justify charging a premium. A start-up venture usually cannot compete on pricing with larger or more established competitors. Value is also about sustainability. In most circumstances, you will be introducing your innovation into a market composed of both small niche or start-up participants like yourself and big players with economies of scale that see you as a threat. Establishing value and becoming a must-have is the best way to endure in a competitive marketplace.

Without a perceived value, you may just have a cool creation that can win first prize in a science fair. Remember KYI #1! In Chapter 3, we illustrate how to present your value proposition in your business plan.

Commercial Viability

Thus far you have defined a target market and sketched how your innovation will create value in that market. Now you have to establish the feasibility and means by which your product or service can generate high returns in the defined market. To determine commercial viability, you must examine the dynamics and competitive landscape of the given market.

It is not enough that potential purchasers or users of your innovative product or service like your product or think it is a good idea. They must also have a compelling reason to pay for the product or service as well. Once you can envision and articulate a strong commercial case to prospective investors, you must also consider and demonstrate these criteria:

- Sufficient market demand exists for a minimal number of units necessary to achieve favorable economies of scale, meet stated revenue objectives, and ensure that a large enough market exists to attract prospective investors. No matter how innovative and valuable your product or service, introducing it into a dead or saturated market may prove unsuccessful. In a dead or low-growth market, even if customers find value in your innovation, there may not be enough of them to achieve high returns.
- Favorable market demand and favorable competitive and regulatory environments allow for profitable pricing. In a saturated market, it will be more difficult to differentiate, and target customers may not be willing to pay much of a premium for your innovation. In a highly regulated environment, high regulatory costs and/or price controls, whether implicit or explicit, may dim profit prospects.
- Sustainable market demand is determined by factors such as time to obsolescence, barriers to entry, ease of replication, and strength of intellectual property (IP) protection. Introducing a product that is easily replicated or soon rendered obsolete may be unsuccessful, particularly regarding innovations currently associated with rapid technological advances. You will need to explain your competitive advantages and how you plan to sustain them in order to validate the sustainability of your commercial viability.

Likely you will need to demonstrate strong prospects for sufficient, favorable, and sustainable market demand to make a compelling case that an attractive ROI is achievable. Here you are "showing the money" to prospective investors and ourselves.

Risk Mitigation Factors

In Chapter 1, we discussed the relationship between risk and return. By reducing a prospective investor's perceived risk, you increase the probability that you will secure investment funds and at better terms. Always present risk mitigation factors (RMFs) of your business. A risk mitigation factor is any specific characteristic or feature of your business that would reduce a specific perceived risk. Every business and associated market combination presents a unique set of RMFs.

One common RMF is the existence of multiple revenue streams, which reduces risk through diversification of revenue sources. The social networking site market provides an excellent example of this. Those social networking sites that rely solely or primarily on volatile advertising revenue are more likely to fail and, consequently, are much less attractive to prospective investors than sites that have additional revenue streams, such as subscription revenues, e-commerce, and premium services.

Another common RMF is a high degree of applicability or adaptability of an innovative product or service. If your product or service can, with minimal revision, be introduced in a number of different markets and/or provide a solution to a number of problems, you have an RMF worthy of presentation. Adaptability is a great RMF because the success of your product or service is not dependent on one particular market or market segment. If the problem you originally intended to resolve is accomplished before you launch commercially, all is not lost.

A third RMF category is the establishment of a captive target market. A captive target market occurs when potential competition is limited for a number of reasons, including the execution of an exclusivity agreement, the lack of comparable competition (as can occur when you have a disruptive innovation), or when many of your current or potential clientele are existing clients of a comarketing partner.

A related RMF are barriers to entry once you have entered the marketplace. Patented intellectual property, a granted government concession, or successfully overcoming a regulatory hurdle (i.e., completion of a difficult licensing process) may help protect you from new competition.

Draft a list of your RMFs and refer to it periodically. Add newly identified RMFs to this list as a measure of progress in your operational and fundraising positioning.

I include this section on RMFs because other discussions pertaining to presenting to prospective investors are focused on the return side of the risk/return equation. It is equally important to address the risk issue; in my experience, prospective investors ask more questions related to risk than to return.

Burn Rates

The burn rate is the sum of all the minimum fixed costs of the business. Minimum fixed costs include only those costs that would have to continue to maintain the company's existence. If the company stopped all R&D, production, and marketing activities, what expenses would remain? It is critical to understand and manage your company's burn rate because all serious prospective investors ask about it. They want to know how efficiently you manage your business. No one wants to invest in a money pit in which much of their invested funds disappear into a black hole of non-value-added business activities. The higher the company's burn rate, the higher the perceived investment risk because the rate represents a minimal level of commitment to keep the business afloat. Once a business generates enough monthly revenues to cover its burn rate, the perceived risk of the company failing drops precipitously (serving as a strong RMF). You are no longer in "survivor" mode and can negotiate with confidence and patience if necessary. At this point, the founders of an entrepreneurial venture may enjoy some peace of mind for the first time.

Strength of Management

Evaluating the strength of your management team is one of the most important considerations of a prospective investor. Many aspects of the management team will be judged. The more obvious aspects include the academic qualifications and technical and management experience of each management team member. However, too often entrepreneurs overlook or underestimate less obvious but important aspects that investors will judge.

For example, investors assess the emotional and psychological state of management to measure the level of passion, motivation, and determination. Many prospective investors understand how much stress must be managed and how long the road that must be traversed to move from start-up venture to successful exit. They want to bet (invest) in prizefighters prepared to go the distance.

Teamwork and sound corporate governance are another less obvious consideration. How well does the team work together? Is there an effective division of labor and lines of authority? Does the management team possess complementary skills and experiences? A management team that works well together (has good chemistry) provides assurance that, as the company grows, efficient and effective decision making will be maintained.

Completeness of management is a frequently overlooked dimension of management strength. Technopreneurial ventures usually have no problem in designating a team member as chief executive officer and chief technical officer. However, prospective investors strongly prefer at some point to see a complete team consisting of qualified individuals responsible for essential functions such as sales and marketing, finance, and other areas. Most entrepreneurial ventures, particularly in the early stages, do not have enough people or resources to fill and compensate these executive positions. However, it is important to at least identify willing and qualified individuals for each critical position who would be hired once sufficient funds have been secured.

Prospective investors are concerned about the loss of a key member(s) of the management team. Although your team may have grown up together as friends and would trust each other with their own children, it is wise to draft and execute employment agreements for each management team member. Doing this will make your venture seem more like a professional business and assure prospective investors of each team member's commitment. Before he considered an investment, a prospective investor of one of my past clients demanded that key management had employment agreements in place.

Prospective investors need to be confident that the management team is not only qualified and experienced in the relevant areas but is prepared to maintain effective management through potentially difficult challenges and periods of high growth.

Use of Funds

The use of funds statement is an itemized statement of how you intend to allocate funds secured in a particular funding round or placement. This statement is a component of the financials section of your business plan. We discuss the use of funds statement in depth in Chapter 3.

Prospective investors want to see what their investment funds will be spent on. They strongly prefer that funds are allocated to value-added activities, which have a positive effect on your income statement whereby the associated costs of the "use" is less than the associated profits in a timely manner. Funding a commercial launch or adding a revenue-generating feature to a product or service are examples of value-added activities. If the venture is beyond the seed fundraising stage, investors will frown on the use of their funds for non-value-added purposes, such as paying down an existing debt or R&D. Entrepreneurs should be aware of this fact and not get affected with the mad scientist syndrome, which I have witnessed all too often. Affected entrepreneurs are strongly inclined to expend a disproportionate share of new investment funds on the most enjoyable part of the venture: R&D. I had one client who had to be reminded periodically that at some point he should consider actually launching his product commercially to make money as opposed to indefinitely making product enhancements. I have seen this disease so frequently that sometimes I wonder if it is contagious.

Traction

"Traction" is defined as recognized instruments of leverage at your current disposal. "Leverage" is defined as the ability to exert influence beyond what should be expected, given the amount of success or positive recognition your innovation has received in the marketplace. The greater your ability to exert such influence or power, the greater the leverage you possess. Traction is secured through a public recognition (i.e., award, public media article, etc.), established market positioning, a granted regulatory licensing/ designation, successful patent or other IP protection filing, and the existence of a working relationship with a strategic partner. By definition, all traction increases the perceived value of your business in the minds of prospective investors.

A strategic partner is a company that has a strategic reason to establish a working relationship with you. Vendors that provide a product or service to you for the sole purpose of profit are not considered strategic partners. However, vendors with additional nonfinancial intentions may be considered strategic partners.

Comarketing partners are a very common type of strategic partners. They perceive a mutual benefit in assisting you in marketing your product or joint-marketing each other's products. For example, a comarketing partner may have a hardware product that complements your software product. You both agree that a joint marketing effort (maybe your software is preinstalled in their hardware) would be of mutual benefit. The hardware partner has preinstalled software that will provide a premium feature or service to attract more potential buyers. The software partner gets tremendous exposure to a large captive audience.

A joint developer is another common type of strategic partner. Your venture and another company may be developing two different products utilizing the same or similar technologies. Both companies may perceive a mutual benefit in sharing their research notes (i.e., what each has learned during development) or decide on an effective division of labor based on strengths and weaknesses of each company's development team. Reducing R&D costs, moving forward the date of a commercial launch, and acquiring additional institutional knowledge for your team are some benefits to be attained.

A licensee of your product or service is definitely a valuable strategic partner. It is always nice when a company pays you to utilize your innovation and simultaneously exposes your innovation to a wider audience. Several RMFs are demonstrated as well, including a diversification of revenue streams, demonstration of adaptability, and proof of your value proposition.

A distributor is another type of strategic partner. Although distributors may financially benefit from agreeing to market your product, they may see additional benefits in promoting your product alongside complementary products of other companies they already distribute. A distributor also may have new distribution channels that can be validated and promoted with your product.

Earlier we stated that the adaptability of your product or service offers an RMF that is worthy of presentation to prospective investors. Possessing a versatile product also increases the possibility of attracting more strategic partners because your innovation may offer solutions to multiple problems and enhance the value proposition of a greater number of prospective strategic partners.

Why do prospective investors love to see an entrepreneurial venture with one or several strategic partners? To a prospective investor, strategic partners offer strong possibilities of reduced risks and increased returns. Such partners also validate to the prospective investor that your innovation is valued by external parties and that the management team can identify and forge future strategic relationships. Some specific attributes that prospective investors find appealing about acquiring strategic partners are listed next.

- *Validation of your innovation.* If other companies find value in your product or service, why shouldn't a prospective investor? As we noted earlier, often prospective investors do not have sufficient technical background to fully understand your innovative product, service, or process and they may seek evidence that the innovation actually works. Before they commit to an investment, they may insist that some form of technical due diligence is performed on your product, possibly by a third party, to prove that all your claims are valid. A previous client of mine had a licensing agreement with a globally recognized media company. When a prospective investor asked me if any technical due diligence has been performed on my client's suite of innovative technologies, I merely cited the licensing agreement and named the company it was executed with. I said that that company certainly did its technical due diligence before paying us a licensing fee. After hearing that, the prospective investor decided it was not necessary to spend additional time and money to secure the services of a third party to perform technical due diligence. Having strategic partners who have faith on your innovation often satisfies prospective investors.
- *Validation of commercial viability.* A prospective investor will be pleased to discover that your product or service will be distributed through established distribution channels and may be exposed to otherwise out-of-reach markets. Such distribution channels also validate the commercial viability of your innovative product or service.
- *Credibility.* If your comarketing or joint-developing partner is a prominent company, such as Microsoft or Google, a prospective investor will expect your venture to receive instant credibility.

- *Ability to leverage the brand name of strategic partner.* Better yet, if your strategic partner has a strong brand name, leveraging its brand name to generate more revenues through association is a very desirable prospect for an investor.
- *Cost reduction.* Reducing costs and accelerating the time for a commercial launch by engaging in joint development and comarketing efforts with your strategic partners certainly delights prospective investors.

It is important that a prospective investor sees you have traction at your disposal and your willingness to wield it. Knowing that you are on the radar of market participants and have working relationships with prominent strategic partner(s) who have a vested interest in your success provides tremendous assurance to prospective investors.

Now that we know what an investor is looking for, it is time to discuss what we should be looking for in potential business partners.

KYI #4: Money Is Not Enough

Besides money, we must evaluate prospective investors on their suitability as strong business partners. What should we be looking for?

There is a big difference between "good money" and "bad money." Good money is money received from an investor who will prove to be a strong business partner who fully understands your business and market, shares your objectives, offers many types of nonfinancial support, and will not impede the execution of your plans intentionally or unintentionally. Bad money may, at the very least, not be worth the effort to secure. At the worst, it may doom your entrepreneurial venture. More often than not, the primary determinant of the failure or success of a start-up is the receipt of good money or bad money.

How do we determine if a prospective investor is offering good money or bad money?

An early indication can be gained from the funding term demands they seek. A good investor mitigates its investment risk by helping you mitigate risks associated with your business. A bad investor mitigate its investment risk by proposing funding agreement terms that establish a comparatively favorable position for it vis-à-vis other stakeholders without regard to the possible additional risks these terms may impose.

To determine if prospective investors are offering good money or bad money (i.e., reducing or increasing business risk), ask yourself four questions:

1. Do they know the space?
2. Do they offer nonfinancial advantages?

3. Are their interests fully aligned with yours?
4. Are there any issues of control?

Know the Space

The "space" is the type of business model for your entrepreneurial venture, the type of technology employed, the industry it is or will be operating in, and the market you will be targeting. A prospective business partner who knows your space will be able to understand your business, appreciate your efforts and display greater patience, be able to make excellent introductions, and be in a position to offer valuable advice and other support that goes well beyond the investment funds committed.

Good business partners can offer many valuable insights to an entrepreneurial venture. Entrepreneurs usually are well versed in the technologies and processes they work with and any advances related to their innovation. However, business operating experience in their specific industry or market dynamics may be very unfamiliar. A business partner who knows the space will be able to provide critical insights on the different individual industry and market participants, potential competitors and their expected reaction when you launch your product or service commercially, market trends and the informal rules governing the functioning of the marketplace, and relations among the various players. Such insights cannot be discovered through mere research and observation.

The importance of having such insight cannot be overstated. A former client favorably revised her marketing plan to pursue a more promising distribution channel based on the advice of a new business partner experienced in her space. When several prospective investors show interest in your venture, the presence of one who knows the space offers greater assurance to prospective investors who have yet to make an investment decision. Recently an investment banking client needed to raise capital to fund an expansion of business into a new market segment. To secure a sufficient amount of funds, a syndicate consisting of several different investors had to be organized. The first two prospective members of the syndicate who decided to consider the investment opportunity were hesitant to pull the trigger (make an investment decision) because of their unfamiliarity with the specific market segment targeted for expansion. Fortunately, we identified and offered a third investor the chance to participate. This individual was familiar with the target market, and his shared insights enabled the syndicate to make their collective decision.

An investor who knows the space is more likely to be able to offer other means of nonfinancial support as well.

Nonfinancial Advantages

Whether a prospective investor knows the space or not, a good money source can offer many advantages and means of support.

For example, a business partner who is a lawyer can offer otherwise costly legal counsel. A business executive would be a valuable source of management expertise as a business partner. An advertising or account executive can assist in the formulation or review of an effective marketing strategy. In addition, as stakeholders, such partners have a vested interest in ensuring you receive their best advice and efforts in a timely manner.

A good investor may be in position to arrange valuable introductions, referrals, and references. Quite often an investor with the means to invest is also a center of influence (COI). COIs generally are highly visible individuals who serve as movers and shakers in their respective professions or industries. They enjoy status and prestige that places them in an excellent position to draw on their personal contacts to actuate valuable introductions and preferential treatment. Indeed, a good investor introduction is a common path to engaging with a strategic partner. Other types of prized referrals produced by good investors include investors and vendors who are willing to provide a service on very favorable terms.

Similar to a strategic partner, a good investor can lend precious credibility. A former client had a considerable number of high-profile stakeholders who were willing to serve as personal references in support of the client's venture. These references certainly assisted us in our fundraising efforts.

Alignment of Interests

Nonalignment of interests may fall under two broad categories: differences of expectations or, more potentially serious, conflicts of interest. Both at the very least present impediments to executing your plans and can result in the dissolution of your company in the worst-case scenario.

Differences in expectations are generally easy to detect and resolve if you conduct a proper KYI investigation on investor prospects. A frequent expectation difference between management and investors relates to exit strategy. Although your prospectus materials clearly present your expected exit strategy (type of exit, time horizon, and ROI) of management, it is very important to confirm that investors find such expectations acceptable and reasonable.

Another potential expectation difference is a conflict between short-term interests and long-term interests. A common cause of this conflict occurs when you have both shareholders and debt holders in your capital structure. As we briefly mentioned in Chapter 1, debt holders and shareholders have different risk tolerance levels. Debt holders are more concerned with short-term cash flows to service their debt and avoid any moves that may risk the value of assets they have secured from you as collateral. Shareholders are more likely to exhibit patience and be willing to make short-term sacrifices to effectuate a higher ROI upon exit. A management team that holds founder's equity has the long-term interests of the venture in mind. To illustrate this type of potential conflict, consider this hypothetical example in which the management team has to determine the most favorable timing of the commercial launch of their software as a service. An immediate commercial launch will realize a more immediate return; however, premium features that could generate higher profit margins will not be included. Once launched, there is only a remote possibility that such premium services could be offered in the future, given the technological and/or logistical challenges required to implement at a future date. Debt holders who feel that the more immediate recurring revenues are sufficient to satisfy their debt service interests will press for the commercial launch now. Shareholders foreseeing the projected ROI multiple being reduced from 10 to 6 will be adamantly opposed to a commercial launch now without those premium features. Once I was involved in assisting a client paralyzed by such an ugly situation. It was not a pleasant experience, and the solution I proposed to resolve the crises and prevent a similar one in the future involved converting the debt holders into shareholders. Managing founders should be very conscious of the various stakeholder expectations both upon accepting investment funds and throughout operations. Otherwise they may accept bad money that could have been good money.

Entrepreneurs must be vigilant to avoid being entangled in potentially damaging conflicts of interest with prospective investors. Such conflicts arise most frequently when investors provide a professional service to you or refer you to a vendor they have vested interests in. For example, a business partner who is a lawyer and serves as your legal counsel may persuade you to take actions that will increase their billable hours. Occasionally a business partner will attempt to refer you to a vendor they have a vested interest as a stakeholder or by receiving commission-based compensation or quid pro quos.

The decision to become a stakeholder in your business may be based on an ulterior motive. A group of related investors of a former American-based client had a surprising motive for investing. I could never understand why they were constantly advising my client to avoid trying to show a profit when it was time to prepare financial statements and annual corporate income tax returns. We were trying to raise additional investment funds, and showing the highest profits permissible would decrease our cost of capital and secure a higher business valuation from prospective equity investors. After some research and inquiries, I discovered that each member of this particular investment group had other investments that earned what is considered passive income according to U.S. tax codes. Because my client was registered as a limited liability company, as opposed to a corporation under U.S. business law, any profits we posted would be considered taxable passive income for them and any business losses we reported would be considered passive losses, allowing them to write off the passive income they earned on their other investments. Perhaps they foolishly thought we could post losses every year until we executed a high-ROI exit strategy.

A possible, but rare, ulterior motive is when a stakeholder invests in your venture to gain access to your IP or leverage your relationship with a strategic partner or vendor for the benefit of its own business.

An extreme case of a sinister ulterior motive is when an investor is a proxy of one of your actual or potential competitors. I was once involved in such a scenario. A much larger competitor was trying to crush my client before we could commercially launch a very disruptive product in what the established competitor considered its space. The competitor knew we were trying to raise funds to execute the commercial launch of our product. The competitor secured the services of an experienced investor to purchase sufficient initial equity to have access to our management decision making and possibly exert some influence. Fortunately, with the assistance of an existing good investor, we uncovered the plans in time.

Not all ulterior motives are necessarily bad. It is more common that investors, particularly those who know the space, invest in your venture because they foresee or actually plan to invoke a more lucrative exit strategy than actually envisioned and presented. A good investor may have good ulterior motives.

Issues of Control

Control is the ability to directly or indirectly influence management decision making. Decisions that may be influenced include business planning, finance strategy, fundraising efforts, operations, R&D, marketing, and exit strategy. Control can be exerted intentionally or unintentionally. External control is the ability of nonfounding stakeholders to apply such influence.

Why is control, particularly external control, so important to be conscious of and attentive to? Maintaining effective control of your business is critical to ensure consistent planning, financial decision-making flexibility, a clear path in front of you, maintenance of the founders' vision, and a continued focus on a single set of derived objectives throughout successive stages of development. When founding partners surrender effective control, they effectively become mere employees rather than business partners. Someone else will reap a disproportionate amount of the returns as a result of your past efforts and sacrifices. From then on, you will be effectively working for them. As founders, you have taken the most risk and have the most to lose. You should have the most to gain as well. Before an entrepreneurial venture successfully concludes a series A funding round and begins generating revenues, no one can manage a pre-revenue venture better than the founders. The seizure of effective control from the founders before commercial launch often results in a failed venture.

Strategic investors (partners), equity investors (shareholders), debt holders, and public funding agencies all possess unique control mechanisms they can intentionally or unintentionally wield to influence the decision making of your entrepreneurial venture.

Strategic Investors (Partners)

An issue of control becomes particularly critical when considering entering into some form of binding agreement with a strategic investor (partner). Strategic investors have strategic motivations that may run counter to the objectives of the other stakeholders. They can use their voting powers, board presence, or control levels on your operations to wield unwelcome influence. An influential investor in a control position can intentionally or unintentionally affect your exit strategy as well. Keep your exit options open. Do not try to make yourself particularly attractive to a single exit option by tying yourself into that one option too tightly. If you think acquisition by major media company XYZ is your primary exit strategy, do not make yourself dependent on the company by offering it a large number of voting equity shares, executing an exclusivity agreement with highly dependent terms, jointly developing core IP with it, or utilizing its hosting environment. When the time for exit arrives, you lose negotiating leverage if one particular prospective purchaser knows that it represents your only viable exit option or that it can take actions to ward off other prospective acquirers.

Equity Investors

Equity investors assume shareholding voting rights, frequently insist on board membership, and may insert controlling terms in their funding agreements. The greater the equity interest a shareholder or a group of shareholders holds in your entrepreneurial venture, the greater their effective control. A majority equity interest allows a shareholder or a group of shareholders the authority to control the board and hire new management, including replacing you. A large, but less than majority, equity stake will give them substantial influence and enable them to be very persuasive to other stakeholders and outside parties. Generally expect that an equity investor who purchases a 10 percent or more equity stake will insist on a board seat, allowing inside access and participation in the venture's strategic decision-making process. An investor who purchases a 20 percent or more equity stake almost certainly expects a board seat.

A funding agreement executed with an equity investor may contain controlling terms that you must be aware of. The equity investor may include terms permitting veto power over certain decisions and restrictions on issuing different share classes. You must consider such terms in light of your future business and financial plans. However, there is one type of clause that should raise a caution flag for you in every situation: antidilution provisions.

An antidilution provision is when a shareholder is granted the right to purchase additional shares at a discount in the event of a future equity issuance. The purpose of antidilution provisions is to allow equity investors to maintain their current level of shareholder voting rights (control). In Chapter 6 a more detailed discussion on the different types of antidilution provisions and what to look at for will be given. The antidilution provision is good from the perspective of the "protected" investor but may not be good for the entrepreneurial venture if a large future prospective equity investor shows interest and then fails to invest due to the automatic immediate dilution of the investment and limitations of control imposed. Granting antidilution to an early equity investor may be counterproductive for the investor and a future fundraising nightmare for the founders. Equity investors want antidilution protection to maintain the equity percentage interest secured upon purchase throughout all the future funding rounds up to exit. However, such a provision ultimately hurts all shareholders and makes reaching an exit much more difficult. For a recent client, I spent most of my time and effort trying to eliminate the antidilution protection previously granted to a group of stakeholders because its existence rendered futile all my fundraising efforts. Every serious prospective investor adamantly disliked the severe antidilution provisions because it progressively increased the effective price prospective investors had to pay per share. Therefore, prospective investors insisted on a lower valuation (lower price per share) to compensate. The reduction of share price due to the lower valuation occurring at a much larger funding round was far greater than any antidilution protection that could have been enjoyed by the "protected" shareholders, who insisted on antidilution protection. This is a perfect example of "bad money" as it drastically impedes your ability to secure future equity investments. The terms of any antidilution provisions should only be accepted if they provide protection sufficient to protect in the event of a down round and maintain control for the "protected" shareholders proportionate to the control demanded by future equity investors. Excessive antidilution protection can have severe constraints on the ability of the founders to raise later stage funding. Thus, if the valuation and share price increase with each successive funding round as they should (no down rounds), then antidilution protection is not necessary. The purpose of financial planning, to be discussed in Chapter 4, is to prevent an occurrence of a down round and permit founders to accept any reasonable antidilution provisions proposed.

Debt Holders

In times of trouble, there is one big difference between shareholders and debt holders. A shareholder or group of shareholders, at most, will be capable of taking control of management only. In the event of default, debt holders can take full ownership of your venture.

Debt holders also may insist on funding terms that have controlling properties. The most common control mechanism is the obligation to make periodic debt service payments. Each venture has to set spending priorities. If the potential to lose your entire business in the event of default exists, one of your highest spending priorities should be your debt service payments. This high-priority expenditure will take away the amount funds available for other more value-added activities and your decision-making options (flexibility).

Prospective lenders often insist their debt is designated as senior. In the event of liquidation, holders of senior debt have first claims to assets. For this reason having a debt note may deter prospective equity investors, particularly those seeking preferred shares. Typically an institutional investor, such as a venture capitalist firm, will demand preferred shares to have senior claim over other equity classes. This is particularly the case in a series A round where the only existing shareholders typically only hold common shares. If a debt note has been issued to an investor or investment group before a series A round than the value of preferred shares has been diminished, establishing a severe impediment to a typical series A funding round, the existence of a senior debt note may make it more difficult to execute a future debt raise as well because future lenders would have to accept the subordination of their debt.

Almost without exception, prospective lenders demand either a tangible or nontangible asset as security for their loan. The risk of defaulting on a secured loan is the potential of losing ownership of that asset pledged as security. If that asset is critical to the operation of your business (i.e., a core technology), you are in effect risking your entire business. Future prospective investors, whether interested in equity or additional debt, may be hesitant to invest if there is the possibility that the venture could lose an indispensable asset in the event of a default.

Another debt provision that has a potentially harmful control feature is the prepayment penalty. The purpose of a prepayment penalty is to compensate the lender for loss of earned interest in the event the borrower is willing and able to pay off the loan before the expiration of its term. A stiff prepayment penalty may serve as a deterrent to pay off the debt early, which would be beneficial by lowering your cost of capital. Cost of capital can be defined as the amount of interest a lender would charge you based on your venture's current financial condition. As your business grows and becomes more successful, your cost of capital will decrease, thereby creating an opportunity for you to retire existing debt with proceeds from a funding raise on more favorable terms. It is often beneficial to pay off an existing debt to improve the capital structure, favorably alter your debt-to-equity ratio, or secure another loan at a lower cost of capital. A prepayment penalty can essentially take that option away from you and cause you to lose some control of your capital structure. A no-prepayment provision is potentially much more damaging. If a senior loan with a no-prepayment option exists, it will be very difficult to secure additional debt funding until the expiration of the no-prepayment loan because future lenders may not be willing to offer unsecured debt.

To reduce their risks, lenders may insert performance triggers in their debt terms. A lender may not be willing to lend you the total loan amount up front. Instead, the lender progressively lends funds as your company successfully achieves specified performance objectives. A performance trigger may read like this: "Once 10,000 units have been sold, an additional $250,000 in lending funds will be made available to borrower on the following terms."

Performance triggers are powerful control mechanisms. Failing to meet such a trigger causes a direct and immediate reduction in your debt funding. Thus, management is compelled to take every action to achieve these short-term performance objectives, possibly at the expense of long-term objectives and other desirable short-term objectives (i.e., higher profit margins, R&D, etc.).

Public Funding

Although the control issues that may present themselves in private equity or debt placement typically do not apply with public funding, with public funding, sometimes it is difficult to fulfill the funding requirements. Before you go down the public funding road, you have to decide whether doing so is worth the time and effort. However, once you have successfully secured public funds, the same funding requirements can serve as a controlling mechanism. Use of funds limitations are the most common example of restrictive funding requirements. Unfortunately, another common problem with public funding programs is that they are very specific on what type of businesses or projects they fund. To secure the public funding, a company may have to decide to modify product development plans to fit their creative innovation to the specifications and scope required of the public agency. If an entrepreneurial venture abandons its original vision and objectives to fit public funding investment criteria, it may be pursuing bad money. Remember, the objective of a public funding agency is to fulfill a public mandate and achieve specified KPIs. Your mission is to make money for you and fellow stakeholders.

It is also possible that in meeting the requirements of a public funding agency, you may be creating impediments for yourself in future fundraising efforts. Recently I examined a public funding program that initially appeared to be very enticing. It was basically awarding "free" money (nondilutive, no payback terms) to start-up companies that could demonstrate an innovative product in certain industries the country was currently trying to promote. One targeted industry was software. However, on closer examination, I discovered that there were some serious deficiencies with the program. The first deficiency was the total lack of expertise and experience of agency's staff in the software industry. Who was going to evaluate any promising funding candidates? What other support would the agency be in the position to give? The second great deficiency, draconian limits on how the funds could be spent (use of funds), made me decide to advise any client to refuse such funding. Public funds could not be used to pay salaries but could be used to pay contractors. The aim here was to prevent management paying themselves excessive salaries with the funds and walking away. Unfortunately, for software developers, the biggest expense is salaries. Basically, if you accepted this funding, you would have to fire your entire staff and hire them as contractors. A second expenditure constraint was that public funds could not be used for capital expenses, only for leased items. The rationale here was purchased physical assets (e.g., servers) would remain in the possession of the recipient after the public objectives were satisfied or, worse, the recipient could walk away with the purchased asset. Basically, if a company accepted the funds, it would have to function without employees and not own physical assets. Yet future investors prefer to invest in businesses with both employees and capital assets.

Summary

This chapter presented a realistic picture of what can be expected from prospective investors and what characteristics indicate whether they be as valuable business partners. A thorough understanding of four primary KYIs serve to help- readers avoid fundraising pitfalls and identify those prospective investors who offer the most value.

KYI #1: Their primary objective is to make money.

KYI #2: There are many types of investors, each with different expectations and capabilities.

KYI #3: Prospective investors are looking for success traits.

KYI #4: Money is not enough. Prospective investors need to be evaluated based on their suitability as a strong business partner.

Knowing your investors is just as important as knowing your customers or knowing your product. The basic finance principles presented in Chapter 1 and the KYIs presented here serve as a basis of understanding of the ideas and views introduced in the rest of the book.

CHAPTER 3

Business Planning from a Strategic Financial Perspective

In this chapter, we demonstrate the value of a business plan. We list both internal and external purposes of composing a business plan for entrepreneurial ventures, discuss the main objectives to be accomplished for each section of the plan, examine how the plans can be customized based on the types of prospective investors sought, and present rudiments to follow in composing a business plan.

Value of a Business Plan

The act of writing the business plan serves as a valuable thought-provoking exercise. Once completed, the plan serves as an essential reference source and basis for periodic updates. Drafting your business plan is the opportunity to incorporate your knowledge of your investors (KYI) in written form to efficiently organize and plan your business and represent your business effectively to prospective investors.

What value does composing a business plan offer?

Composing a business plan is a thought-provoking exercise that provides a method for you to set goals, priorities, and strategies. The goals, priorities, and strategies you decide on should be derived from the results of your KYI research and inquiries and what I call "discoveries" made during your brainstorming process with your founding partners. A discovery is any important, actionable notion that comes to your attention as you are composing your business plan or any other planning document. A discovery is actionable in that it prompts a revision, addition, deletion, or reformulation of a goal, priority, or strategy. As such, discoveries are key to effective business planning.

A former client had an operational software as a service business when he hired me to help decide which of two different ways to focus his business. He had struggled with the choice for a long time. When I asked to see his business plan, he informed me that he never bothered to draft one because he never needed to raise funds from external sources. My response was that we needed to compose a business plan regardless of fundraising because it would help him organize his thoughts and determine where his focus should be. Not long after we began drafting the business plan, it became very evident that his current focus and strategy was flawed and that he should pursue a new strategy—one we conceived of while we examined his business in a holistic manner. He conceded that if he had not considered all aspects of his business simultaneously, he would have never of thought of this new and unique focus.

We were able to identify the proper focus and appropriate strategy by clarifying the interrelationships of various aspects of the business. Such clarification is best attained by sitting down and writing a business plan. Unfortunately, often sections of the eventual business plan are drafted separately. At the very least, this will result in rework. At the worst, it will lead to inconsistencies and consequently poor planning. The composition of your business plan reflects a progression to your planning. You must specify a problem before you can present a solution; only then can you offer a value proposition. You must define the product and market before you can formulate a marketing plan and identify competitors. Everything has to be comprehensively described and costs estimated before the business plan ends with the financials and an exit strategy. Your business venture becomes an investment opportunity ready to be presented to prospective investors only after the financials and exit strategy have been formulated and determined.

The business plan is a working document to be constantly updated and revised in accordance with changes in market conditions, strategy, finances, product additions and modifications, and the like. Although it is advisable to avoid making changes (particularly to focus and objectives) too often, it is also advisable not to treat the content of your business plan as written in stone. Being flexible and at the same time keeping everyone on the same page is best accomplished by treating your business plan as a blueprint designed for amendment and a point of reference for everyone on the management team. Similar to continual integration software testing in which newly written code is tested often to ensure it does not cause breaks in the existing code, you must test revisions to the business plan to ensure it is aligned and consistent with the rest of the plan. If not, you may need to make additional revisions. A break in the code—an inconsistency in your plan—offers a valuable opportunity to understand the interrelationships of the different aspects of your venture.

The primary external purpose of the business plan is to present it to prospective investors with the intent to secure investment funds.

It is true that many investors have explained that they do not need a business plan from a prospective funding candidate. Many entrepreneurs seeking investment funds state that they do not need to draft a plan because investors are not going to request one. Due to this prevailing wisdom often I cannot convince funding candidates of the need to compose a business plan as preparation to answer questions from a prospective investor. Invariably the following scenario plays out:

I introduce the funding candidate to an interested prospective investor who has only read an executive summary, despite my fears that I am throwing a sheep to a pack of wolves. Inevitably both parties are disappointed. The funding candidate can answer satisfactorily only a small fraction of the questions posed by the prospective investor. A line of questioning that should take 30 minutes takes more than two hours as the prospective investor demands constant clarifications because he or she cannot fully grasp the overall business model of the funding candidate. At the end, the prospective investor gives the distressed funding candidate a long list of questions. The prospective investor expresses frustration to me that the funding candidate is totally unprepared and does not understand his or her own venture. The top recurring comments I hear are: "There is no basis for their financial projections," "They are not accounting for such-and-such risks or factors," and "Who is really their target market?"

The questions prospective investors focus on usually represent areas of research that you totally missed or conducted in a deficient manner. Writing a business plan forces you to answer the predictable questions a prospective investor will ask in a way that can be easily articulated. As we see in Chapter 5, showing command of your venture and the investment opportunity it represents is a primary objective in funding presentations.

Composition of a Business Plan

The business plan demonstrates to prospective investors that their investment criteria have been met and that the success traits they seek assuredly exist. It is a partial product of your KYI efforts.

Essential sections of the business plan in their suggested order include:

- Executive summary
- Defined problem and solution
- Product/service description
- Value proposition
- Marketing plan

- Management team
- Strategic partners
- Operational and expansion plan
- Company objectives
- Current positioning/traction
- Risk factors
- Financials
- Exit strategy

The objective of each section is to display how the associated KYI concepts are fulfilled.

Executive Summary

The executive summary is the short and sweet version of your business plan and usually the initial prospectus document presented separately to prospective investors. The executive summary is like a resume. The purpose of a resume is to generate enough interest to secure an interview from a prospective employer; the purpose of the executive summary is to generate enough interest to secure a presentation or request for additional information from a prospective investor.

Although the executive summary represents the first section of a business plan, it is usually written as a separate document following the completion of the other plan sections. A simple and effective format in which to compose the executive summary is to draft a condensed one-paragraph summary of each plan section and organize the summaries in the same order as in your full business plan. In the executive summary, it is not necessary to include a summary of all the business plan sections. It is sufficient to have these sections: defined problem/solution, value proposition, the market, competitors/differentiation, go-to-market strategy, management team, strategic partners, traction, financial summary, and exit strategy. In this way you are certain that you present all the KYIs relevant to the purpose of the executive summary in a clear and concise manner.

The executive summary should be only two or three pages long. However, it must present a compelling argument that your entrepreneurial venture represents a very attractive investment opportunity that warrants serious in-depth consideration. After reviewing the executive summary, prospective investors should have a clear understanding of your business and have little doubt that potentially very high financial returns can be attained, thereby justifying a request for a business plan, a personal presentation, or continued reading of the rest of the business plan.

Defined Problem and Solution

You must introduce your venture as a solution to a defined problem. You must demonstrate great need and demand for the resolution of this defined problem. Prospective investors need a valid reason to continue reviewing of your complete business plan. Without demonstrating demand for your solution, later discussions regarding defined target markets, value proposition, traction, potential strategic partners, and exit strategy would be rendered baseless. Consequently, defining the problem and solution is an appropriate section to follow the executive summary. This section often is titled market opportunity.

In Chapter 2, we discussed value proposition in a section under KYI #3, prospective investors are looking for success traits. We posed this question there:

- Who is facing what challenging problem that we can address?

This question can be rephrased in the following manner:

- Who is facing what challenging problem that we can address?

The best way to answer such question, especially if a venture is at the seed-level stage, is to conduct customer-driven feasibility studies through market research and customer surveys. The market research should be directed toward assessing the potential level of demand for your product or service based on feedback from customers of comparable businesses and studies conducted by prominent market research companies in your space. The surveys are to be worded to discover the real challenges faced by prospective customers on both an emotional and a practical level and provide an opportunity for them to suggest possible solutions. The importance of these prospective customer surveys cannot be overstated. You present the results of such surveys in this section of the business plan, supporting what is presented not only here but in the remainder of the business plan. Just as important, it is often the case that your initial assumptions require revision, thus influencing your overall business planning and the composition of the remainder of the business plan. Identifying an assumption to be revised is an example of a valuable "discovery."

For entrepreneurs, especially founders of information technology start-ups, such measures of prospective consumer behavior may be particularly important because they are accustomed to operating in a world of logic. I often meet entrepreneurs who assume that demand for their innovative product will certainly exist because it makes complete logical sense that it should. Consumer behavior does not exist in such a world of logic. Emotions and other illogical determinants have powerful effects on consumer behavior that can be revealed only by grassroots-level research.

For entrepreneurial ventures at the series A fundraising stage, the alpha and/or beta testing that has been performed on the product or service serves as a means to answer questions related to potential demand as well. The comments from test users may be useful in confirming your claims that your product offers an effective solution to a serious problem. If the testing results are not satisfactory, either an overall reassessment of the product/ service is in order or improvements need to made and placed in front of the testers again before your product/service is ready for presentation. If positive test user feedback is available, present it to validate your product as a solution in this section of your business plan.

Prospective investors will most likely not engage in blind optimistic assumptions and must be offered some empirical evidence to substantiate what is presented in this section. Furthermore, the bigger and more challenging a problem is, the greater the perceived value of any solution and the greater the probability that such a solution will be considered a must-have, in accordance with the tenets of Kano analysis. Thus, when composing your defined problem and solution section, you must define the problem in such a way that it is perceived as large, challenging, and costly for your target prospective customers. You must define your product or service in a manner that suggests it provides a viable and most effective answer to the defined problem.

To define a problem, you can simply list a set of challenges or problems faced by specific prospective customers or users of your product. Presenting your product as a solution requires an explanation of how it successfully addresses such challenges or problems that for reasons you need to provide have not been sufficiently addressed thus far by anyone else but your venture.

Say your product is a management tool for project managers. You can make a simple problem/solution statement like this:

> Many project managers face a tremendous challenge in effectively communicating the customer's priority changes in a timely manner to all the relevant development teams. Our XYZ product accomplishes this by enabling project managers to. . . . As a result, greater productivity and transparency is achieved, leading to vastly improved customer service.

The problem/solution statements set the context for the remainder of the executive summary or complete business plan. These statements serve as a basis from which prospective investors can judge the effectiveness of your product.

Product/Service

In this section of the business plan, you describe your products and services. Beware of the mad scientist bug! A comprehensive and intricately detailed synopsis of the technological marvels associated with your inventions is not required here. Instead, keep it simple, stupid. Prospective investors only need to know how the product works, its key unique value-added features, and how disruptive it will be. An innovative product/service is value-added when you can demonstrate that it will have a positive effect on the bottom line by either reducing the costs or increasing the revenues and/or profit margins for the consumer/user. Features that are value-added enable, facilitate, clarify, and enhance the consumer/user experience. A disruptive innovation is one that significantly alters the dynamics of the marketplace into which it will be introduced. You must clearly explain the value-added and disruptive nature of your innovation here. Utilize action words in describing the features of your product or service. Here are some examples of simple yet effective wordings for this section:

> Our customized search-and-filter functions facilitate the identification of items marked by the user.
> A unique characteristic of this financial management software is it enables traders to monitor the performance of multiple portfolios and execute simultaneous trades real time from a single interface.

Perhaps better:

> For the first time. the user is able to perform online these functions . . .

This section allows prospective investors to envision how the products and services mentioned can be disruptive moneymakers. Triggering the imagination of prospective investors in this way is invariably a good thing. Sometimes prospective investors or strategic partners who know the space can identify a new application, market segment, or exit strategy for your product(s) and venture that may never have occurred to you. This usually happens after they read the product/service section of the business plan, particularly if it has been effectively written with this intent.

Value Proposition

Now that you described the value-added features of your product or service, it is time to illustrate or quantify, if possible, its benefits to the targeted consumer or user. A quantification of any value added would be very beneficial. Does it reduce costs, and, if so, by how much? Does it allow premium pricing? If so, how much is the afforded premium? Does it permit the expansion into a larger marketplace? If so, how much larger is the newly expanded marketplace? Substantiating your value proposition will require some empirical evidence, such as focused and relevant market reports, alpha/beta testing results, customer feasibility studies, and surveys. In our discussion of value proposition in Chapter 2, we asked three questions that may be alternatively phrased as:

> How will your target consumers or users benefit from your product or
> service?
> Why would someone pay a premium for your product or service?
> How does your product or service compare with more and less
> expensive alternatives?

The next two statements are examples of value propositions that are being quantified and describe the benefits to the prospective users or consumers:

> Due to an expected 18% increase in retention rates users of our
> product can expect an average annual savings of . . .
> From our extensive beta testing experience, we have discovered
> that users in every market segment enjoyed a 25% increase in cus-
> tomer conversions with use of our service, thereby realizing a
> comparable percentage increase in both revenues and profits.

Always have evidence to support your claims when you make such quantifying statements. For example, the last statement cites tester feedback.

We mentioned in Chapter 2 that you need to compete on value rather than price. Thus, you need to justify why someone would pay a premium for your product. An example of such statement may be worded in this manner:

> The increased portability offered by our software product is
> expected to command a 20% premium over competitor prices.

A comparable value proposition statement may read like this:

> The XYZ Display is designed to achieve a perfect balance between
> cost and quality to prospective buyers. There exist more impressive
> and expensive displays where the higher purchasing price is not
> justified, given the potential ad revenue base of each geographical
> market. Several less expensive displays exist; however, they are
> deficient in material quality, design, durability, physical appeal, and

ad space. The lower-cost displays will have a much shorter operating life, generate less ad revenue per unit, and have greater costs due to more frequent maintenance, repair, and replacement.

In the previous section of the business plan, we allowed prospective investors to imagine how the product or service creates value. In this section, we hit them over the head with our value proposition. Our value proposition serves as a basis for our differentiation in the next section.

Marketing Plan

The purpose of the marketing plan is to demonstrate several things:

- The market you are about to enter into is robust and attractive.
- A defined target market is eagerly awaiting your innovation.
- You can make a strong case for differentiation.
- You compare favorably and sustainably to the competition.
- You present a winning strategy to enter and grow in the market.

To accomplish our purpose, we illustrate the fulfillment of several KYI elements associated with defined target market, value proposition, commercial viability, and risk mitigation factors (RMFs) introduced in Chapter 2. The primary sections of the marketing plan are market and industry, competitive environment, and marketing strategy.

Market and Industry

The market and industry section is a general overview of the marketplace used to place the rest of your marketing plan in proper context. Essential items to include are quantified current size and growth prospects of the market, market segmentation (distribution channels, geography, demographics, etc.), market and industry dynamics (trends, interaction between participants and suppliers, etc.), the behavioral characteristics of the consumers or users (likes/dislikes, unfulfilled needs and demands, priorities in their purchase decision making, etc.). Here also is your opportunity to define the target market in accordance with the views presented in Chapter 2. Defining the target market consists of a more detailed description of target audience and market size. A hypothetical and condensed example of ideal wording for a target market definition follows:

> The XYZ market is estimated to be about $8 billion today, growing at an annual rate of 34%. This can be segmented into a primary (developer-to-distributor) market and a secondary (peer-to-peer) market that we intend to target. The total size of the peer-to-peer

market is about $3 billion. What is driving the market growth is greater accessibility due to technological advances, more secure payment methods, and faster broadband connections. With average licensing fees of 5% to 10%, the current addressable market size can be estimated to be $150 million to $300 million. Seventy percent of the peer-to-peer market is located in Asia. The demographic profile of the user base is primarily males between the ages of 25 and 35 with average annual incomes of between $50,000 and $100,000 per year. The users prefer the peer-to-peer market due to ease of connection; however, the biggest issue most often cited is the increased risk of fraud. Our product will address this issue in the following ways . . .

To fortify your claims, you must provide statistics or other forms of evidence from credible sources that demonstrate the trends and tastes you are stating and the demand you claim exists for your product/service.

Competitive Environment

Following the description and analysis of the market, the prospective investors' attention shifts to the competitive environment. The aim of this section of the marketing plan is to identify both direct and indirect competitors and emphasize the strength of your competitive advantages. The relevant KYI sections to reference include innovation, defined target market, value proposition, commercial viability, RMFs, and strategic partners.

There are several ways to identify and provide a brief comparative description of your direct and indirect competitors. One way is simply to present each identified competitor in summary form. A more effective means to compare is to create a matrix illustrating differences in such areas as features offered, target geography, level of service, operational focus, stage of development, and others. Present indirect competitors separate from direct competitors, and explain why they are considered indirect competition. Indirect competitors are typically companies that do not directly participate in your target market but may affect the dynamics of your target market in a marginal manner. The purpose of identifying such indirect competitors is to further delineate your defined target market and note the existence of potential competitors who are at a much greater competitive disadvantage than your direct competitors.

In this section, you present several competitive advantages that enable you to successfully compete and sustain such a level of competitiveness. The primary objectives of this section are to list and describe your competitive advantages and to differentiate your venture from the competition.

You must explain how you intend to win against your competition either by achieving greater profitability vis-à-vis the competition or by establishing yourself as the dominant market player. Perhaps you expect to be more profitable because you have devised a more effective payment system. Perhaps you intend to become the dominant market player by addressing challenges faced by the target market that are insufficiently addressed by your competition. Either way, you must provide prospective investors with a reason to believe that that at some point in time, your venture will ultimately be the champion in your space.

This is an ideal section of your business plan to highlight your RMFs. It is no coincidence that factors that reduce the perceived risk in investing in your business may double as sustainable competitive advantages. The possession of multiple revenue streams may give you a competitive advantage over competitors that rely on fewer revenue sources, particularly in markets that are either volatile or characterized by rapid technological advances. With multiple revenue streams, your business is in a much better position to manage any declines in sales or growth from any one source of revenue or market segment. Your business also would be in a much better position to profit from any increases in sales or growth from any one source of revenue or market segment. For example, if my business receives revenues from both one-year subscriptions and per-use fees, I am in a more favorable position to survive a sudden short-term decline in usage than competitors who have only pay-as-you-go models. Another competitive advantage may be derived from the added flexibility of possessing a very versatile or compatible product or service. If your innovative software product and that of your competitors are currently competing for desktop users and suddenly a dramatic increase in demand for your software product by mobile phone users occurs you possess a valuable competitive advantage if your product is compatible with existing mobile phone technologies and your competitors' competing product does not have such compatibility. Possessing patented intellectual property (IP) and holding captive markets offer competitive advantages as well. This section is the place to show prospective investors that you represent the eventual champion in your defined target market.

Why not? You defined it.

Marketing Strategy

Now that prospective investors are familiar with the market you have defined and targeted and its competitive environment, it is time to present a marketing strategy. The goal of this section is to explain how you are going to establish yourself as a market player as defined under KYI #3 in Chapter 2. A market player cannot be ignored because of its strength in one or more areas of marketing execution famously known as the 4Ps: product, price, placement, and promotion. You can display a strong presence in each of the four Ps in the ways discussed next.

Product   Marketing the unique features of your product or service is an effective way to differentiate and garner the attention of the marketplace. You can achieve differentiation by emphasizing the innovation and proposed value of your product or service. How can this be accomplished? In your marketing materials or sale campaigns, you must include information on how this product is unique and what benefits consumers or users will enjoy. Such benefits may be derived due to the product's must-have and/or other desirable features previously not available to the target market. Also discuss other benefits, such as increased capabilities or enhanced user experiences. If your product or service is very disruptive in nature, you must effectively communicate how a new environment for consumers or users may become reality and the beneficial implications. An example of such an illustrative notice statement may read like this:

> For the first time XYZ collectors will be able to trade online in real time, creating a liquid market and accurate pricing for their collectibles. Being first to market grants inherent advantages recognized and understood by strategic investors.

Price   Pricing strategy can be defined simply as how you answer the question: How much should I charge for my product or service? Pricing policy answers this question.

Do not underestimate the importance of formulating the most optimal pricing policy. Pricing can make or break your entire business. If you price too high, you compromise the revenues required for securing initial traction and/or your ability to secure valuable market share. If you price too low, you may make your exterior stakeholders (customers, suppliers) happy while you earn the scorn of shareholders expecting exceptional returns. High revenues and low profit margins are fine if you are a major grocery retailer. They are not so great if you are managing a high-risk entrepreneurial venture whose shareholders have loftier return on investment (ROI) expectations. One of my clients possessed a major fault: He determined pricing policy at the negotiating table with prospective clients. After closing deals, he often boasted of being successful in closing the deal, the size of the deal, and how pleased the counterparty was. When I asked him how this deal affected his company's bottom-line, he would invariably answer, "Basically we break even on the deal." I had to remind him frequently that at some point he should try to please his shareholders as well and that break-even deal after break-even deal will not achieve this. The end result of his poor pricing policies was that although the product had great commercial success, the exit was not successful for the shareholders who had funded the product. Clients and suppliers enjoyed substantial business growth and profits derived from the product at the expense of the venture shareholders who assumed all the risk.

You must consider many factors when determining a pricing policy. They include market characteristics, costs, and pricing objectives (i.e., differentiation, profit maximization, and maximizing market share). Online searches show many different types of pricing methods. However, most do not apply to high-risk entrepreneurial venture positioning to attract investment funds. For example, the simplest pricing method is the cost-plus method, where the price is the cost plus a percentage of such costs. This certainly is not a preferred pricing method to attract strategic investors expecting exponential growth, market player positioning, and a high ROI. Remember, you do not want to compete on price alone either. Thus, competition-based pricing, where you set your price competitively with the competition, is not preferred either. More differentiation is required to justify a high-risk investment in your venture.

To formulate an effective pricing strategy for an entrepreneurial venture, you should consider value-based pricing and premium pricing. Value-based pricing uses the measured perceived value of your product/service for target consumers/users to determine a price level. In value-based pricing, you compete based on innovative features, winning functionality, and a superior user interface, not price. Premium pricing is setting the price deliberately high to enhance the perception that your product/service has superior quality and reputation. This favorable perception should be justified as well; if you cannot charge a premium for your product or service, you are not demonstrating sufficient differentiation vis-à-vis the competition, and not make a compelling case to prospective investors that you can achieve exponential returns. You can illustrate your strength in this area through value comparisons or premium pricing. To illustrate a value comparison, you may want to position your product or service in the middle of a price matrix with an explanation of why your product is a better buy compared to higher-priced and lower-priced competitors. The higher-priced alternative products are not worth the extra cost because their benefits are only marginally superior to your product. The lower-priced alternative products may lack must-have features or have hidden costs. If your product is priced in the upper part of the price matrix, you must offer a strong and irrefutable explanation of why such premium pricing is justified and, more important, why consumers or users will be willing to pay such a premium. Perhaps the primary advantage of the technology or process behind your innovative product or service allows you to offer it at attractive pricing yet at comparable or superior quality to competitors. This situation can occur when you are entering a price-competitive or price-sensitive environment in which you are compelled to market at the lower part of the price range. In this situation, you must accomplish three things in composing this section:

1. Tell prospective investors that your intention of offering a relatively low price, when you can justifiably charge a higher price, is strategic in

nature: that is, you aim to secure dominant market share and/or directly attack a key competitor.

2. Demonstrate that attractive profit margins justifying a lofty expected ROI can be attained despite the comparatively low pricing.
3. Assure prospective investors that you will not be cutting corners to sell at the price indicated. (Cutting corners results in inferior quality that may put you at a competitive disadvantage immediately or in the future.)

The objective of your pricing strategy is not to be the price leader (i.e., lowest price) but to be the price setter. As the price setter, your pricing is recognized as the most accurately derived based on true value or degree of innovation. Once the price of your innovation is established as the benchmark price in the target market, you will have a direct influence on the pricing strategies of other market participants who use the benchmark price as a point of comparison. Congratulations, you are now a market player! Be prepared to draw the attention of strategic investors.

Placement Selecting the most effective distribution channel(s) for your product is critical in capturing the optimum level of exposure to your target audience. The greater the exposure, the greater your level of influence and the greater the probability of establishing yourself as a market player. In this section, you need to explain why your primary distribution channel is the best channel and why a few specific other channels may serve as additional advantageous avenues. Traditionally, selecting the most effective placement meant selecting those distribution channels that offered the highest probability of maximizing sales volumes and profit margins, given the type of product or service and targeted consumer or user. These objectives remain valid. However, there are other considerations with strategic objectives as well. The proper selection, utilization, and destruction of existing distribution channels or establishment of new distribution channels can help establish your business as a market player. How do you know when you are on the way of becoming a market player?

Scenario 1: Your innovative product or service dramatically alters how a distribution channel is utilized.
Scenario 2: Your innovative product or service presents a disruptive technology that either replaces or renders obsolete an existing distribution channel for a given target market.
Scenario 3: The act of introducing your innovative product or service establishes a new distribution channel for that given target market.

An example of the first scenario is a venture that has created a legitimate trading exchange for a certain class of virtual assets. An unintended effect is the creation of a speculative trading market for such virtual assets. iTunes is a perfect example of scenario 2. When Steve Jobs introduced iTunes, he inflicted serious damage on the traditional retail sales channels for recorded music. A past client provides a good example of Scenario 3 as they intend to supplant the accomplishment of Steve Jobs by introducing a disruptive technology that may establish a new distribution channel for music. Consequently, the client is not having difficulty attracting the interest of strategic partners and investors.

Creating any of these scenarios will attract maximum attention from prospective strategic investors. Strategic comarketing partners will be intrigued and may want to help you achieve what are possibly mutual strategic objectives.

Promotion There are traditional promotional methods and traditional promotion objectives (i.e., increase sales, project a good image) that remain valid and should be executed. However, you also should promote in support of your strategic objectives. Do not limit yourself to promoting just your product features. Promote the uniqueness and innovation of your product and the resulting beneficial implications. Using innovative forms of promotion will enhance the image of your product as unique and innovative. Live demonstrations, contests, and advertising on unconventional advertising media may be very effective if you can identify or create such promotions appropriate to your innovation and target market. What kinds of media coverage can you expect from media outlets? Free favorable publicity is certainly something worth pursuing. The target audience of your promotional efforts should include consumers/users of your innovation, potential strategic partners, and prospective investors.

The Four Ps represent your marketing plan once you have entered the market. Successfully launching your product or service commercially requires an effective go-to-market strategy.

Go-to-Market Strategy

What is a go-to-market strategy, and how should one be formulated? A go-to-market strategy is your plan to execute a commercial launch of your product or service and all the efforts associated with going to market, including hiring sales and marketing personnel, advertising, required software development or hardware purchases to enable the execution of launch, and so on. The commercial launch represents the initial offering of your product or service for public purchase through the execution of your marketing plan with the intention to commence generating revenues. Although your innovation may have been made available earlier to the public for alpha and beta testing, the product offered in the commercial launch is more refined and includes all the features required to make the product commercially viable. Pricing has been set to achieve profits either at the onset or some point in the not-so-distant future. A "soft launch" occurs when you commercially launch your product before you are either fully capable of executing your marketing plan or have all the product features planned for the launch deployed or activated. This typically occurs when it is deemed necessary to not delay the commercial launch for strategic or other reasons (i.e., being first to market, prohibitive delay costs). Another reason for a soft launch is insufficient funding or preparations with comarketing partners to fully implement marketing plans are not complete.

The key to formulating a successful go-to-market strategy from a strategic and fundraising perspective is to execute, utilize, and validate as many of your KYIs and components of your marketing plan as soon as possible, either upon or shortly after the commercial launch. The relevant KYIs to be validated include commercial viability, defined target market, value proposition, and especially the various RMFs. The effectiveness of your comarketing relationships and the use of funds (series A funds secured to execute your go-to-market strategy) may need to be validated as well. The components of your marketing plan to be validated include your pricing strategy, selection of sales distribution channels, and choice of sales promotions.

A successful commercial launch is critical to the future success, if not existence, of your entrepreneurial venture. A failure at this point may be impossible to overcome. It is highly advised that you go to market at full force. You do not want the success of your entire commercial launch to depend on only one of your several selected distribution channels or a single promotion technique. In a soft launch, you may forfeit the opportunity to compare different placements and promotions and effectively analyze your pricing.

A successful execution of your go-to-market strategy provides prospective investors for your next (series B) funding round the opportunity to observe the effectiveness of your business model and enables them to have greater confidence in your future growth strategies and implementation. Your management team will also have the opportunity to make a comprehensive postlaunch analysis to identify any necessary or desirable revisions to tactics and overall strategy.

Management Team

The purpose of this section of the business plan is to convey the strong attributes of the management team and why they represent the best personnel to execute the business plan. This section may be the most important section of the entire business plan and needs to be crafted with much more diligence than is usually the case. Over the years, I have come to realize that this is an undeniable truism in the world of venture capital: Investors do not invest in products; they invest in people.

A common mistake I see in drafts of this section is merely stating the team members, titles, and general responsibilities of each position. Prospective investors are very aware of what the duties of a chief financial or chief technology officer are.

A typical format for composing this section of the business plan is a simple listing of the personal biographical statements of each management team member. Executive biographies should include relevant comparable work experience, education, valuable business relationships, degree of access to pertinent information, history of working relations with other team members, and skin in the game, such as opportunity costs assumed. An example of an effective executive biography presented in the management team section of a business plan is presented next.

The CEO of Robots-R-US is Mr. William Bowen.

Mr. Bowen is a Founder Partner and Investor of Robots-R-US. He earned a Bachelor's Degree in Electrical Engineering and an M.B.A. from the University of Wheeler. Mr. Bowen brings 15 years of consulting and management experience in the robotics industry. For over a decade he was a partner in the successful and highly reputable engineering consulting firm of Bowen & Tiff. During his consulting days, he had the good fortune to deal with several prominent executives, high-ranking government officials, and top innovators in the robotics industry. He intends to leverage his valuable relationships and experience to establish a strong market position for Robots-R-US. Mr. Bowen's business partner was Mr. Brandon Tiff, the cofounder and CFO of Robots-R-US. During his time at Bowen & Tiff, Mr. Bowen served as a consultant to National Robotics, one of the leading robotics manufacturers. At National Robotics, he had a good working relationship with their COO, Mr. Robert Bristol. Mr. Bristol is now owner of Bristol Robotics, a current key strategic partner of Robots-R-US. Mr. Bowen declined a lucrative offer to serve as CEO for Automation Labs International to pursue this current venture.

It is not enough merely to present the qualifications, skills, and professional relationships of each management team member. You must also demonstrate that this team is complete, committed, driven, battle hardened, work well as a team, and collectively have skin in the game. You must use the proper format and wording to present these strong attributes effectively.

I submit that it is more effective to begin or end this section with a brief characterization of the management team as a whole. In this brief summary, you should note these attributes:

- *The completeness of the team.* Ensure that every core function of your business has a qualified member of the management team directly responsible to demonstrate accountability.
- *An indication of the team's skin in the game.* You can show this in part by referring to members of the team as founding investors or founding partners rather than just using the individual's management title. To evince a collective skin in the game, briefly describe situations where the team has had to endure together and the sense of obligation existing to the other team members. A battle-tested team is a team that not only has demonstrated a strong commitment to the venture but also has much to lose as a team, due to their collective sacrifices. A strong determination to work things through to success must be evident.
- *The existence of strong team chemistry among the team members.* If it is apparent to prospective investors that management team members are on the same page and function well as a team, their expectations of a successful exit will be greatly elevated.
- *Any previous shared business experiences or motivations.*
- *Evidence of commitment*, such as the existence of executed employment agreements for each management team member as advised in Chapter 2.

To augment the strength of the management team, particularly a relatively inexperienced one, assemble and include a board of advisors consisting of reputable individuals, preferably ones who are recognized as knowing the space and can be depended on to serve as at least good references. In this section, also include a biographical statement of each board advisor and the reasons why he or she is inclined to assist your venture.

Now that you have gained the confidence of prospective investors, it is a good time to introduce the strategic partners your management team will be working with to achieve mutual objectives.

Strategic Partners

This section should begin with a brief introductory statement indicating your objectives in working with the strategic partners. Then provide a description of each strategic partner. Each individual portrait should include:

- The strengths, capabilities, and positioning of the strategic partner
- Their motivation for partnering with you

- Nature of partnership, such as a codeveloper, comarketer, and so on
- What your expected benefits are in a variety of ways (e.g., financial, strategic, etc.)

A sample effective strategic partner narrative may read something like this:

XYX Corporation is a Hong Kong based multinational media company with principal operations in electronic media and print media. Their electronic media operations include pay-television, Internet, and instant-messaging subscriber platforms. Print media activities include publishing and distribution of magazines, books, and newspapers. In June 2004, XYZ acquired a 65% interest in ABC Holdings Limited, the operator of an instant messaging platform in China called XY, which subsequently developed into the leading business of its kind in China and rapidly expanded into neighboring Asian countries. In February 2005, XYZ acquired the Japanese Internet interests of CCC Corporation, which has a 90% share of the Chinese Internet services market. In May 2006, XYZ purchased a 70% interest in the Korean media group AAA, publishers of dozens of newspapers and magazine titles. XYZ's most significant operations are located in Asia, from where it generated approximately 67% of its revenues and 80% of its operating profits in 2009. The strategy of XYZ is to create media content, build brand names around it, and manage the platforms distributing the content. XYZ then delivers its content in a variety of forms and through a variety of channels, including television, Internet services, newspapers, magazines, and books. Our intention is to provide XYZ with our unique media content that can be delivered through each of their distribution channels and assist them in managing their Internet services by licensing to them our proprietary technologies. In return, we expect to establish a strong brand in multiple media markets and geographical areas, particularly our target market, the Asian Internet space where they hold a dominant position. We are excited to pursue a mutually beneficial marketing partnership with them.

If you make a compelling case of why a strategic partner would want to work with you, most likely you have just made a compelling case for why a strategic investor should invest in you.

I advise concluding this section with a summary of the cumulative benefits offered by your strategic partners. It is useful to display a planned overall strategy to identify and secure additional strategic partners. A demonstration of several large and prominent strategic partners with vested interests in the success of your business certainly provides strong assurance to prospective investors that your venture will be successful.

Operational and Expansion Plan

In this section of the business plan, you give a detailed description of how you are going to execute the plan. These areas are discussed: pricing policy and revenue streams, production, service and support, research and development, employees, vendors, logistics, and operational and expansion milestones and timelines.

Pricing Policy and Revenue Streams

An explanation of how and why your products and/or services are priced is of immense importance. Formulating a successful pricing policy whereby the optimal point on a supply and demand curve is selected is of critical importance to the success of any venture, regardless of the quality of the product or service. Pricing too low will hurt your profit margins; pricing too high will cost you market share (i.e., sales losses). Sophisticated prospective investors will be very interested in seeing the thought process behind your pricing as an indication of your business acumen. Demonstrating multiple revenue streams will serve as an advantageous risk mitigation factor as well.

Production

You must provide a depiction of the production facilities, locations, and processes. You also must explain how and why such facilities were designed and the locations were chosen, and how the production processes were derived. If different stages of production occur at different facilities, what is the basis for such division of labor? What are the production capacities of the business? At what production levels are economies of scale enjoyed? How scalable is your product or service? What are your plans to increase production to meet the demands of growth?

Service and Support

Once your product is commercially launched, what services and support are required? Are there multiple levels of service? If so, what are they? Who will perform service and support for your product, a dedicated in-house team or an outside vendor? Have standards of quality been established and are support policies in place? Will your company utilize a customer relationship management tool (CRM)? Given your growth expectations, how will you service and support requirements increase? To answer this question, it may be advisable to present a general model of how you correlate the number of customers/users and the number and composition of the necessary services and support staff. This model should also be represented in your pro forma financials. Also present your crisis management contingency plans in the service and support section. Crisis management is discussed in greater detail in Chapter 7.

Research and Development

What are your plans and necessary efforts to make continual improvements to your existing commercially offered products and services? Are you going to add to your product mix a selection of product offerings? Is the business planning to develop spin-offs or accessory products? Will new features be added? Will research and development (R&D) efforts include increasing scalability? If so, what is the level of scalability targeted, and how does this relate to projected market demand? To justify the itemized R&D, you must cite expenditure findings (market reports, Kano analysis, testing surveys, etc.) indicating whether each listed feature or other R&D outcome is a must-have or a value-added feature.

Employees

How many employees will you have? What is the breakdown of the types of employees needed and their required academic and skill levels? How will you identify and attract such employees? Describe your hiring process. What is the availability of employees satisfying your required skill sets? It is advisable to provide an organizational chart delineating lines of authority and accountability. It is also important to describe the working relationships among the various operational groups. Are there mechanisms and communication procedures in place for timely and effective communication? Mention any corporate governance policies and documents (i.e., code of conduct, employee handbooks, etc.) in this section as well.

Vendors

What are your production inputs and required services? Who will be the suppliers and service providers to support your operations? Do you have multiple suppliers and service providers for each production input or support service? What vendor qualification methods do you intend to employ and do you have any specific standards that must be met? What are the determinants in securing favorable terms with vendors? Providing a listing of order processes and delivery times for each vendor would be ideal.

Logistics

How will you deliver your product or service to consumers or users? If outside parties are primarily responsible for distribution, what are your contingency plans in the event a problem arises with one or more of these parties? If multiple production facilities are utilized, how will the unfinished product be transported from one facility to another? Will there be expected delivery delays due to uncontrollable factors, such as customs inspection or other forms of regulatory compliance? How reliant is your service on local infrastructure, such as bandwidth or quality of Internet connectivity?

Operational and Expansion Milestones and Timelines

Here is where your growth projections are revealed and aligned with the other information from this section. If you execute the operating and expansion plan of your business properly, you should expect to attain such milestones and timelines. The significance of each milestone needs to be articulated. What happens once 10,000 units are sold? Does this trigger the participation of a comarketer? Is an economy of scale achieved in production? Set reasonable milestones that can be achieved because stakeholders will follow your progress and prospective investors may use these operational milestones as a basis for performance triggers to determine the future availability of funds.

The objective in drafting and presenting your operational and expansion plan is to convey to prospective investors that you know what it takes to accomplish your company objectives and are aware of all possible challenges. This plan should state reasonable milestones and timelines that can be monitored and show the value-added activities that will be funded with their investment. It is important to set milestones that both display a sufficient level of ambition and are reasonable; as you succeed in reaching your milestones, you increase the confidence and enhance your credibility with both current stakeholders and prospective investors. Consequently, your negotiating position will be strengthened when engaging in future fundraising activities.

Company Objectives

This is the time to disclose your ambitions correlated with the success traits elaborated under KYI #3. You are a for-profit entity seeking to maximize the ROI for both current and eventual stakeholders, presenting a strategic investment for prospective investors and proving your attractiveness to potential strategic partners. Your company objectives must demonstrate that these are the primary goal of all your efforts. The company objectives you list must be comprehensive, including all facets of your business. They must also signify strategic value and potentially high ROI and be expressed in terms based on the expected criteria prospective acquirers will consider at exit to make a purchase decision. Upon exit, what will the prospective suitors primarily base their evaluation on? Profit margins, revenues, market share? If you believe market share will be of primary importance, it may be advisable to state company objectives on such terms.

The company objectives section should be presented in three parts: short-term, intermediate, and long-term objectives. The short-term objectives are what must be accomplished to qualify the venture for the next round of funding. Accomplishing the intermediate objectives will get you through the subsequent funding round; long-term objectives will enable you to reach a successful exit. In addition to a written description, present each company objective on a timeline, noting the points at which progress toward a particular company objective is or can be achieved. Primary objective categories that together represent a comprehensive listing of your strategic and financial ambitions are listed next.

- *Market player.* A primary company objective should certainly be the establishment of your business as a market player in the target market defined. This will excite and grab the serious attention of any prospective strategic investor or strategic partner. Now you will need to define market player in your particular target market. How much market share do you intend to secure? What leverage will you be able to wield once you have attained the defined market player position?
- *Exponential growth.* Prospective investors, especially if you are in an early stage of development, are expecting minimum ROIs of eight to ten or average annual internal rates of return (IRRs) of at least 80 percent. To accomplish these levels of return, most likely your entrepreneurial venture will have to grow exponentially. How much exponential growth do you intend to achieve? Demonstrate how this is feasible given the size, dynamics, and growth projections of the target market.
- *Continued innovation.* Entrepreneurial ventures often operate in very dynamic markets with constant and rapid technological advances. To sustain competitive advantages, you will have to make at least a minimum amount of enhancements to your commercially launched products and services.
- *Diversification.* Relying on the sale of one product or service will create doubts as to your competitive sustainability in terms of competitiveness and risk mitigation, not revenues. Prove your vision and creativity by setting a goal of periodically adding to your product mix through your proprietary technologies and processes. Show that you can diversify your revenue streams and mitigate market risk by establishing multiple applications for core technologies and expanding your market via customer type or geography. Such diversification serves as an RMF, as discussed in Chapter 2.
- *Target market expansion.* How do you plan on expanding your markets (i.e., growth strategy)? For example, under what circumstances do you decide to enter an additional market? What are your go-to-market strategies for each instance? Do you have favorable market positioning,

helpful contacts, or strategic partners ready to assist you with expanding into these targeted markets? If so, who and how?

- *Strengthening the management team.* An important source of value for your business is the know-how, skills, management experience, completeness, and professional relationships of each member of the management team. State goals indicating your intention to expand these valuable attributes by adding new team members, as management demands dictate, and continual improvements to proficiencies and business relationships of existing team members. Describe the important background information and contacts possessed by managers you intend to hire and why you need to recruit such managers, given your operational and company objectives.

- *Securing additional strategic partners.* Doing this demonstrates to prospective investors that you realize the enormous potential of increasing your leverage and capabilities by continuously adding strategic partners. As your business grows, you may discover that many strategic partners who either did not know of your existence before or snubbed you when you were just a tiny start-up are now interested in being your friends. This certainly occurs as you establish yourself as a market player. Prospective investors need to know that you have a strategic vision to take advantage of any progress you may achieve. It is now time to match the benefits offered by each prospective strategic partner with your operational and overall company objectives. Also explain what your pitch will be to each different prospective strategic partner and present a timeline showing when each prospect should be approached.

- *Exceptional revenues and profits.* Simply state in summary form the annual outcomes of your pro forma financials. It is essential to show strong cash flows and extraordinary profits.

Organizing company objectives in this fashion will prove useful in formulating your financial strategy, the topic of Chapter 4.

After you have worked on your company objectives, it is time to focus on the current positioning and traction of your business.

Current Positioning and Traction

To show what has been accomplished thus far and what can be expected given the current status of the business, a section of the business plan should be devoted to the current positioning of the company, the traction that exists to achieve the company's future aspirations and how you intend to leverage such traction.

Next is an example of an affirming traction statement secured through an award or recognition:

This past November our recently released ERP software won the "Best Innovative Software" award at the XYZ Technology Expo, beating over 120 other software products in a demanding competition. This prestigious recognition directly secured 15 additional clients who attended the expo. Favorable public relations since that time have resulted in many more executed and pending service contracts.

This statement attests to current market positioning:

On May 30 of this year we had a highly successful commercial launch of our software as a service. The actual unit sales numbers for the first three months exceeded our initial projections, and third-party reviews of our service have been overwhelming positive, with our product receiving high marks for usability and cost savings for our clients.

A statement indicating traction through a current working relationship with a strategic partner is provided next:

Through our comarketing partnership with ABC Corporation, we have garnered instant credibility in the CRM software marketplace as evidenced by . . .

Here is a statement testifying to traction guaranteed by the successful granting of a regulatory designation:

Our company became only the third and last company to be granted a government concession to offer the XYZ wireless service in the following municipal markets . . .

By illustrating your existing market positioning and traction, you are declaring past success, providing added assurance of sustainable competitive advantage and the potential to utilize leverage to achieve optimum returns, and provides further proof that you are on your way to becoming a market player. Everyone likes a winner!

Risk Factors

It is advisable to disclose any risk factors associated with investment in your venture. Risk factors are simply anything that potentially could go wrong with your venture, such as external effects, possible future failures to meet obligations, and other areas that you disclose to warn investors and potential investors. General areas of risk and some examples include:

- *Industry.* Government regulations, competitors
- *Operational.* Lack of operational history, dependencies on key vendors etc.
- *Technical.* Vulnerability of intellectual property, inability to fully develop technology
- *Customers.* Dependence on specific revenue sources, barriers faced by potential customers, other market risks
- *Management.* Inexperience, risk of losing key personnel
- *Financial.* History of deficient working capital, necessity for additional financing
- *Nature of investment.* Illiquid, majority control possessed by founding management

Businesses that effectively identify their risk factors can anticipate and adapt to changing conditions. Inserting a list of risk factors in your business plan sets an example of transparency and builds trust. Investors do not like surprises. In a former life, I was a currency trader licensed as a commodity trading advisor on the American futures markets. Regulations required that the most prominent prospectus document presented to prospective clients was the risk disclosure statement. This document had to be formatted and worded in accordance to stringent specifications. It was the most difficult document I have ever composed. After writing it, I could not imagine how prospective investors would ever be crazy enough to open trading accounts. The document I wrote mentioned every conceivable potential disaster trading in futures could inflict. It was clearly a document intended to scare away all but the most diehard risk takers. However, I soon realized its many great benefits:

- As a trader, I became fully aware of all the potential dangers to be attentive to and my duties and responsibilities as a trustee of other people's money.
- Clients knew they were fully informed and should not expect any surprises.
- I was certain that after reading such an intimidating document, clients who agreed to open a discretionary trading account would accept the ups and downs of the market and hang in there when times get tough.

These points are very important to recognize. Almost every business will have its ups and downs. During the down times, there is a real possibility that you may either incur the wrath of stakeholders or have to seek additional funding from existing investors. Establishing an atmosphere of full disclosure (transparency) and trust is the best assurance that you will have supportive business partners. The importance of transparency is emphasized in Chapter 7 on corporate governance. A list of risk factors also serves a valuable internal purpose. Earlier we explained the value of taking inventory of your RMFs as a way to measure progress in your fundraising positioning. The flip side holds true as well. Consider identified risk factors as potential opportunity costs worthy of your time and expense to reduce or eliminate when such opportunities present themselves. As we discussed elsewhere, mitigating downside risk allows you to assume greater upside risk to secure greater upside returns. This section illustrates a perfect example of a "discovery" and how the business plan has both internal and external purposes.

Sample Risk Factors

Company Has a Limited Operating History, a History of Working Capital Deficiencies, and May Never Become Profitable

The company was established in 2007 and has a limited operating history and a history of limited working capital. The company has generated only nominal revenues to date and may not succeed in its business model of generating revenue from subscription and advertising fees. The company does not currently have the funds necessary to repay outstanding obligations. There can be no assurance that the company's operations will achieve profitability at any time in the future or whether, if profitability is achieved, it will sustain such profitability.

Company May Not Be Successful in Obtaining Sufficient Additional Financing to Continue Its Business or Realize Its Business Plan

In addition to the $1 million that the company is seeking in this offering, it may need to secure significant additional funding to continue its business. If we are successful in raising $1 million, we will disperse approximately half of the net proceeds and immediately pay off outstanding payables of approximately $500,000. Another $500,000 will be allocated for continued developmental and operational expenses for the six-month period following commercial launch. If the company is unable to obtain adequate additional financing, it may not be able to develop its technology further, commercialize its products, or continue its operations.

Continued

Company May Be Unable to Develop Its Technology Fully

The company is planning to commercially launch its innovative subscription service from beta testing after a significant delay from the initial expected launch date. Although the company believes that it has adequately addressed the technological issues that led to the delay, there is no guarantee that all such issues have been resolved. The company may not have the necessary financial and technical resources to complete the development and testing of subsequent planned service offerings within projected time frames or at all. Regardless of the company's successful efforts, competitors may develop comparable services superior to those of the company.

Company May Not Be Successful in Generating Subscription Revenue, Which Is a Key Element of Its Business Plan

The company's business model relies heavily on its ability to generate subscription revenue from the use of its premium subscription service or any other products it develops. Given that the premium subscription service is currently available to beta testers free of charge, there is no guarantee that subscribers will be willing to pay a subscription fee for continued use. The company will not begin to charge subscription fees until the beta test is complete and a successful commercial launch is executed at least three months from now. Beta users may be discouraged from continuing their use once they are required to pay a subscription fee for the service. The company anticipates that the number of registered users could decrease significantly once subscription fees are charged. The company ultimately may fail in its strategy to generate subscription revenue from the use of any of its services. If the company receives no or little subscription revenue, its business and prospects will be materially adversely affected. In such case, the company would not realize its projections and would need to reevaluate its business model.

Financials

The financials section is your opportunity to numerically display your potential financial success. There is a good reason why the financials section is placed second to last in the business plan (only before exit strategy) and formulated second to last (only before the executive summary). Here is where the expected sales figures given in the marketing plan, the revenue and growth objectives stated in the company objectives section, and the expenses explicitly stated or implied in the operating and expansion plan are consolidated and translated into numbers. It is critical that this financial translation and consolidation be accomplished in a credible manner by ensuring that no inconsistencies exist. Obviously, it is not good for prospective investors to detect any inconsistency; however, failing to identify and implement the necessary revisions from a realized inconsistency will cause a lost golden opportunity to identify "discoveries" and improve your overall business planning, which is equally unfortunate. Earlier in this chapter, we mentioned the concept of discoveries and its importance. The formulation of your pro forma financials presents the best opportunity to identify these valuable discoveries.

In addition to ensuring consistency with the rest of the business plan, there are several other items to note during the formulation of your financials.

- *Base your financials on your entire business, not just your champion or primary product.* You are not trying to secure project financing; you are attempting to attract an ideal business partner. Diversification is important in both mitigating the perception of risk and being a worthy company objective. Although the primary software retail product may put you on the map and represent 80 percent of projected revenues and profits, it is still beneficial to note the lower-risk but much more stable software development project work the company can rely on more steadily. The multiple-revenue sources and the existence of perhaps less impressive but more dependable revenue sources will assure ideal business partners. It is important to explain why the continuance of such low-risk, low-return project work will not serve as a drag on the development and/or marketing of the higher-value innovative products you are championing. The existence of stable cash flow may also be a determinant in securing lower cost of capital or less dilutive financing. For example, recurring revenues may permit a portion of the funding to be less dilutive credit financing.
- *Be attentive to discoveries.* You have a higher change of uncovering discrepancies in your business plan when you are constructing your financials than during the composition of any other part of your business plan. A common example of a discovery during the drafting of financials is when the potential revenues from a particular revenue source cannot be justified given associated costs to implement.
- *Where possible, present the pro forma financial statements, in multiple scenarios, including worst case, expected case, and best case.* Set the parameters of possibilities for prospective investors and demonstrate that you recognize and understand the different potential outcomes of your venture.

- *Do not specify actual months in the pro forma statement but rather the number of months from commencement of the statement.* Instead of "February 2013," use "Month 1," and so on. The starting point for a pro forma statement is usually some important event, such as securing funds currently being solicited or a commercial launch. You simply do not know the exact timing of these key events often contingent on something else occurring and it is a much better point of reference for a prospective investor who may ask themselves, "Where will this company be six months after they receive my funds or 12 months after commercial launch of XYZ product?"
- *Include the direct costs of implementing any stated revenue source in the financial projections.* This typically may not occur either due to a careless oversight or an intentional attempt to inflate the profit margins by only stating revenues and not costs. Regardless of the reason, direct costs are relatively easy for prospective investors to decipher and they are an easy way to discredit your entire financials presentation if not disclosed.
- *Recognize that what you state may be used against you.* Keep in mind a prospective investor may base performance triggers on your numbers. Presenting reasonable and believable numbers is more than just an issue of credibility.
- *Do not be too conservative in your financials.* The prospective investor will do that for you. Just ensure that you have a clear model that reasonably substantiates your numbers.

In a nutshell, the financials section illustrates how your business is to make money. The section includes several different components: actual (if you have had an operating history) and/or pro forma financial statements, capital structure, valuation, use of funds, and funding requirements.

Actual/Pro Forma Financials

Actual financial statements are financial statements that have already been prepared based on actual performance. If audited financial statements of your business exist, include them in the financials section before the pro forma statements. Pro forma financial statements are prepared in advance of the time periods they cover; thus they are forecasts. They mark the first time that you inject the dimension of time into your business plan. They represent the future financial projections of your business and should extend out three to five years. The three primary pro forma financial statements to be formulated and presented are the income statement, cash flow statement, and balance sheet. Pro forma income statements provide an important benchmark or budget for operating a business throughout the year. They enable you to make operational decisions, such as changing pricing or decreasing costs. Pro forma cash flow statements illustrate cash outflows and inflows on a timeline. They help identify potential cash flow problems that may occur when a cash shortage develops due to payments and receipts operating on different time schedules. A pro forma balance sheet shows the assets and liabilities of the business. It helps to project how the business intends to manage its assets in the future.

Assume that all prospective investors will closely scrutinize and put to the test every number in every statement. Welcome and facilitate their efforts, particularly by presenting the pro forma income statement on an Excel spreadsheet, which enables them to insert their own numerical inputs. By doing so, prospective investors are testing your financial model (accepting your assumptions) rather than testing your input numbers. It is preferable that they test your model rather than your input figures because you can and must formulate a model that can withstand intense testing better than you can substantiate forecasted numbers. Additionally, there are several different scenarios of how your business progresses. A reliable and trusted model must exist so you can examine multiple future scenarios merely by changing the inputs. This ability is important for both your management team (effective planning purposes) and prospective investors. Although the numbers you input must be reasonable to appear sane, no one will believe your numbers anyway. Why? There is a very high probability that the numbers ultimately will prove inaccurate. Prospective investors need to believe in the financial model that you used to derive the various possible outcomes. Let them prove to themselves that your pro forma financial statement is believable. When I consider this truism, I recall the movie titled *My Big Fat Greek Wedding* in which the mother convinces her husband to agree to a decision he would be expected to oppose by making him believe that the decision was actually his.

Consequently, the most important thing to remember when constructing your pro forma financials is that the strength and credibility of the financial model utilized as a basis for your pro forma financial statements is far more important than the actual numbers you insert into them.

Capital Structure

You need to display the capital structure of the company, presenting the positions of all equity and debt holders. Prospective investors reviewing your business plan may become part of this capital structure someday and will be very interested in what they are getting themselves into. As mentioned in Chapter 1, the capital structure reveals how the fundraising efforts have been managed thus far. It will be a significant consideration as to whether they invest or not, and what the preferred funding terms should be for the investor such as whether the investment should be debt or equity placement and what funding terms to demand to protect against identifiable investment risks as revealed by the composition of the capital structure). (See Figure 3.1.)

Total Authorized Shares:	5,000,000
Equity Securities Outstanding:	
Total Common Shares Outstanding:	1,426,577
Total Warrants Outstanding:	405,513
Total Equity Securities:	1,832,090

Warrant Types:

Outstanding warrants include advisory warrants granted for advisory services rendered, bridge warrants issued to retire debt convertibility, and assignable warrants granted to a contractor for software development services rendered.

All warrant types grant holders the right to purchase one share of XYZ, Inc. common stock at an exercise price of $1.50.

Senior Debt Note:

We currently have a senior debt note outstanding, held by 15 individuals. The terms of the note are as follows:

Principal Amount:	$500,000
Accrued Interest:	$75,000
Interest Rate:	12% per annum
Payment Terms:	Full payment of principal and interest at maturity
Maturity Date:	March 12, 2014

FIGURE 3.1 Capital Structure Representation

Valuation Calculation

You must calculate a value of your business utilizing a valuation method appropriate to your type of business. You should select the best (most favorable and acceptable) valuation model. For example, a multiple of projected revenue will most likely not be the most appropriate or favorable valuation model to employ for a high-risk, high-return start-up. Such a valuation model is more appropriate for a retailer and would prove too low to attract prospective high-risk investors.

The numbers derived from your pro forma financial statements serve as the inputs for the valuation method selected. Clearly demonstrate the assumptions and calculations you perform to arrive at the valuation. For example, what discount rate or price–earnings multiple did you use in your calculations? Are we assuming the worst-case, expected-case, or best-case scenarios? Typically the valuation presented in a business plan is calculated based on an expected-case scenario and is a postmoney valuation. A postmoney valuation is defined as a valuation of the business after the solicited funds have been secured. (See Figure 3.2.)

Use of Funds

A use of funds (or proceeds) statement is an itemized statement illustrating how you intend to allocate the expenditure of the solicited funds. Remember, prospective investors are looking for expenditures to be primarily on value-added activities. In this section, only refer to the use of funds to be secured in current funding round. (See Figure 3.3.)

Projected Postoffering First-Year EBITDA	$5,270,346
One Year Leading "Free Cash" Multiple	$\times$ 2
Total Valuation:	$10,540,692
Outstanding Common Shares =	1,050,000
Outstanding Warrants =	275,000
Total Equity Securities =	1,325,000

Per Share Valuation = Total Valuation/Total Equity Securities

$$\frac{\text{Total Valuation:} \quad (10,540,692)}{\text{Total Equity Securities } (1,325,000)} = \$7.96/\text{share}$$

FIGURE 3.2 Valuation Calculation

The proceeds of this Offering, after offering expenses, will be used primarily to finance ongoing software development, fund the execution of our Commercial Launch including the hire of Business Development, Marketing, and Advertising Sales executives, fund Customer and Technical Support associated with the Company's online services, pay down existing payables, and general working capital for the next six months.

The following is an itemized list of planned use of Funds:

Fund Commercial Launch	$450,000
Customer & Technical Support	$150,000
Research & Development	$100,000
General Working Capital	$200,000
Total:	$900,000

FIGURE 3.3 Use of Funds Statement

Funding Requirements

Here is where you actually state how much funding you currently are trying to raise and what type of funding structure is preferred. In the likely event the preferred funding structure is an equity placement, you would list the amount of equity offered. This amount is derived from the present valuation of your business most recently calculated. A funding requirements declaration may be stated like this:

> XYZ Corporation is currently raising $500,000 USD to finance the expansion of our sales efforts into the Asian markets. Based on a postmoney valuation of $5 million USD a 10% equity interest representing 100,000 Common Shares will be offered at a per share price of $5 USD.

In the event of an equity placement, an immediate dilution clause will need to follow. This clause describes how the purchased shares will cause dilution by increasing the number of shares outstanding. An example of an immediate dilution statement follows:

> Assuming full subscription of this Offering and the exercise of all outstanding Equity Warrants, we would have outstanding 2,600,000 of Total Equity Securities. The fully subscribed 200,000 Common Shares represented a pre-offering equity interest of 8.33% in XYZ, Inc. The same 200,000 subscribed Common Shares represented an immediate post-offering equity interest of 7.69% in XYZ, Inc. Therefore an immediate dilution of .64% of equity interest has occurred upon the subscribed Common Shares as a result of a full subscription of this Private Placement.

Once the financials section has a graphical and monetary summary of your investment opportunity, it is time to present prospective investors with what they have been waiting for: the exit strategy.

Exit Strategy

The purpose of this final section of the business plan is to give the ultimate reason why prospective investors should invest in your entrepreneurial venture. This section answers the "how," "when," and "how much." As discussed in Chapter 1, the "how" is either a future sale of the company or an initial public offering (IPO). You need to specify which it is. If both exit scenarios reasonably exist, you should explain how each could occur, which scenario is the most desirable, and why. To strengthen a declared future sale exit strategy, list specific companies that would be the most likely purchase candidates and why. The "when" is simply stated in number of years to future sale or IPO. The "how much" is an annual return (i.e., IRR) or a multiple of the original investment (i.e., ROI). Regardless of what exit strategy scenario(s) you present, it must be consistent with the rest of your business plan, particularly the company objectives and financials.

Next is a sample exit declaration:

> The Company is cultivating strategic alliances with media, social networking, and telecommunications companies that benefit in a variety of ways from the utilization of our offered services. The benefits derived for our potential acquirers include operating on a global platform, creating demand for products in their pipelines, and offering competitive advantages related to the use of our proprietary processes and services. After building perceived future value, acquisition by one such company is the current planned exit. Media companies that would be potential suitors include Viacom and Time Warner. Social networking sites, such as Facebook and LinkedIn, and major telecommunications companies, such as QWest and AT&T, represent additional prospective acquirers. We expect the ROI upon projected three-year exit based on our current valuation to exceed 15x as we would project an acquisition price by one of these strategic acquirers to exceed the average P&E multiple of companies in our space of 12.

Business Plan Customization

In concluding our examination of employing strategic thinking in constructing a business plan, it is very important to note that the plan needs to be customized for the type of funding sought and the type of prospective investors targeted. To prepare an effective business plan, you must identify whether the financing you seek is primarily equity placement, debt placement, or public funding and whether the investors are strategic. Identification of the type of funding you seek and the type of prospective investors to approach will determine what sections of the business plan require more detail and/or emphasis.

Marketing Plan

When examining your marketing plan, the different prospective investor types have different interests in the Four Ps. Regarding product, creditors want to ride the existing waves; equity investors, particularly strategic investors, want to make new waves. In other words, prospective creditors want a product or service whose source of demand is easily recognizable with no or very little consumer or user education required. For creditors, demand must be more readily apparent because they want to see more immediate and certain revenues to permit more reliable debt servicing. Public funding agencies require a product to fit their strict definition. When reviewing your pricing strategy, prospective debt investors want prices to effect stable and recurring revenues. Equity investors, especially strategic investors, want to see premium pricing. The consideration of placement will be different as well. Prospective creditors prefer the utilization of tried and tested sales and distribution channels that can secure more dependable revenue streams. The equity investor wants to use sales and distribution channels that will make the biggest splash and permit the establishment of strategic positioning (i.e., increased market share, channel domination). Likewise, both investor types will review promotion differently. Prospective creditors who will be less likely to accept free-trial periods and other promotional techniques that delay or cut into expected revenues will favor tried and tested promotional methods. Less traditional promotional practices that can provide a decisive competitive edge will please equity investors.

Operational and Expansion Plan

Prospective creditors are very interested in identifying evidence of cost effectiveness (i.e., economies of scale) and keeping the monthly burn rate at a minimum. Any operational risk (i.e., unreliable suppliers, regulatory authority interference, etc.) that could disrupt stable cash flow will be of particular interest to them as well. Equity investors will be more accepting of continual R&D spending, the selection of more expensive but better-positioned vendors, and achieving milestones that represent nonfinancial but strategic benefits. Equity investors will favor increased initial spending on efforts to enhance scalability with long-term benefits as well. For public funding agencies, the operational and expansion plan is a very important section. The location and size of your production, service, and R&D facilities (i.e., employees) are most likely of utmost importance to them.

Company Objectives

A different emphasis will need to be placed when presenting the eight different previously listed categories of company objectives. Prospective creditors will be eager to learn that diversification and target market expansion are primary objectives of your company. Successfully achieving these objectives would increase the likelihood of more stable and greater revenues to service the debt. Prospective equity investors seeking competitive advantage and optimum ROI in the long term will appreciate seeing that you are a market player, have exponential growth and continuously innovate and strengthen the management team. Regarding the securing of strategic partners, prospective creditors would like to see additional comarketers that will have a direct and more immediate effect on revenues. Prospective equity investors, particularly strategic investors, would like to see additional strategic partners prominently displayed in your future plans that provide leverage you can use to gain strong market positioning or other competitive advantage. Both debt and equity investors want to see exceptional revenues and profits; however, creditors are more concerned with revenue streams than profits. Creditors know that they can still receive their principal and interest back, regardless of profitability. Public agencies simply like to see your highest-priority company objectives aligned with their KPIs.

Financials

Prospective creditors examine the pro forma cash flow statement and balance sheet most carefully as they most directly indicate your ability to service debt and can offer sufficient collateral to secure the debt. Consequently, you will need to pay more attention to these two critical statements when seeking debt funding. Exceptional profits in the pro forma income statement are most important to equity investors. Equity investors will care much more about the present valuation than would prospective creditors.

Exit Strategy

When presenting an exit strategy to a prospective creditor, it is best to illustrate recurring annual returns (IRR) to prospective creditors and a multiple of original investment (ROI) to prospective equity investors. Creditors will be more assured to see consistent and sufficient returns up to exit strategy to ensure that the company has the ability to pay debt payments. Regarding time horizon to exit equity investors, creditors and public funding agencies will have different considerations. For equity investors the greater the time to exit the more perceived risk there is and the lower the current valuation they will agree too. Time horizon to exit will be a primary determinate on the term of the debt note and consequently the rate of interest and the amount of periodic debt service payments required to be demanded from creditors. For a public agency the time to exit will be of interest if a grant requiring pay back terms is being considered. The type of exit is only a major concern for equity investors. Any equity investor wants to see the highest ROI possible and will be pleased with any exit type that holds the most promise to accomplish this. A strategic equity investor may likely prefer being acquired by a strategic buyer rather than an IPO.

Business Plan Rudiments

Next are some general rules of thumb to follow when composing a business plan:

- Note whether you have multiple types of users (beneficiaries of your product or service), and identify each one before composing your business plan.

  If you claim that your product/service offers benefits to different groups, you need to present a clear case for each group. For example, if both participating merchants and individual consumers stand to benefit from your service offering, you must explain how each will benefit. Often draft business plans demonstrate value to only one of many applicable target groups or fail to specify which group is being discussed when describing specific benefits. Both mistakes diminish the effectiveness of the business plan.
- Define any key terms you use, such as "critical mass" or "risks."

  I have read these statements in draft business plans; with no definitions provided.

  > As we gained more critical mass in number of users, word-of-mouth referrals will also add more momentum to our market penetration and market share.
  >
  > Therefore, risks must be minimized to ensure system performance, reliability, and availability.

  Prospective investors certainly will want to know what number of users you consider critical mass and what risks you perceive there to be.
- Counter any risk or challenge mentioned in your business plan with a means to address it.

  A common mistake is listing a number of challenges faced by your competitors without explaining how your venture will meet these challenges. You have missed a great opportunity to differentiate.
- There are several phrases to avoid in a business plan. Here are a few examples:
  - "We hope . . ." Investors are not investing based on hope. You must use stronger words, such as "we intend" or "we expect" and state why you feel confident about such prospects.
  - ". . . in ways that . . ." Investors are not investing in ambiguity. You must list and define the "ways." A phrase like "We intend to use capital in ways that maximize return on investment by investing in value added activities" is much too general and could conceivably be placed in every business plan if left to stand alone.

- *". . . will be chosen on a case-by-case basis."* Investors are not investing into unpreparedness. If left unexplained, this sentence will not tell an investor much.
- *"The advertising media used will be chosen on case-by-case basis."* You do not want to be perceived as just winging it in management. At least describe the determinants and contingencies that will serve as a basis for such decisions.
- *". . . whenever possible."* Investors are not investing in limited possibilities. Everything should be possible, or you should give a specific reason why it is not possible and how risks associated with such impossibilities can be mitigated. The following is such an ambiguous phrase:

> "We will provide operating instructions to our newest subscribers whenever possible."

> When is it not possible and why? If not possible, what is the solution or alternative?

When proofreading your business plan draft, pay attention to such empty and damaging phrases. Your familiar with the technologies, processes, and business you have devoted all your waking hours to for an extended period of time creates the possibility that such phrases may creep into your draft. Recognize that the audience is not as familiar with your business and/or product and may not understand what you are trying to convey with stand-alone phrases.

Summary

Crafting a business plan is a strategic exercise with both internal and external purposes. Internally, drafting a business plan permits the opportunity to view the entire business in a holistic manner, resulting in much more effective planning. The concept of "Discoveries" is first presented. A discovery is a realization during a planning process that leads to a revision that represents an improvement. Such discoveries are instrumental in effective planning.

As the primary prospectus document, the business plan serves an important external purpose. During the composition of a business plan, the objective is to address all the KYI considerations discussed in Chapter 2. Each individual section is drafted with this objective in mind and addresses particular KYI considerations. The business plan is organized into these sections, and each section addresses KYI factors as shown:

- *Executive summary.* Serves as the comprehensive and concise response to KYI #1 and KYI #3 considerations.

- *Defined problem and solution.* Provides a basis for the consideration of numerous KYI issues, particularly value proposition and defined target markets.
- *Product/service description.* Highlights the value-added features and disruptive nature of the product or service. This directly addresses KYI issues pertaining to competitiveness, sustainability, and market player prospects.
- *Value proposition.* Depicts the financial and strategic value of the product or service that will result in exceptional profits and ultimately a successful exit.
- *Marketing plan.* Validates the commercial viability of the product or service and explains how a market player presence is to be established.
- *Management team.* Discusses all of the desirable individual and collective attributes of a management team.
- *Strategic partners.* Demonstrates that establishing strategic partnerships is part of your overall business plan is an effective means of addressing the KYI issues of traction and RMFs.
- *Operational and expansion plan.* Presents an efficient use of funds and serves as a strong basis for your stated company objectives and exit strategy. By stating worthy but reasonable milestones, you create the opportunity to generate additional traction.
- *Company objectives.* Directly aligns the objectives with the establishment of the various success traits described and categorized under KYI #3.
- *Current positioning/traction.* Showcases evidence of sustainable competitive advantage, potential market player positioning, and leverage that can be applied to maximize returns.
- *Risk factors.* Demonstrates competence and transparency.
- *Financials.* Shows, via a timeline, that KYI #1 interests will be successfully fulfilled.
- *Exit strategy.* Provides the definitive answer to KYI #1.

Now that we have discussed how to craft a business plan from a strategic perspective, it is time to employ strategic thinking to formulate an overall financial strategy for your business.

CHAPTER 4

Financial Planning for Maximizing Returns

Having a financial strategy and a plan to execute it based on the fundraising stages is mandatory for every entrepreneurial venture seriously interested in achieving a successful exit. Too often I witness start-ups with elaborate, well-thought-out plans on how to develop, produce, market, and service their product through commercial launch and beyond. However, they fully intend to proceed without formulating some form of financial strategy or plan. Financial planning, at least on a preliminary level, is necessary initially to determine whether you have a potential viable business. Conducting effective business planning requires an informed understanding of what is and is not financially feasible in regard to your venture. To execute your business plans requires money. Without securing sufficient funds on acceptable terms and in a timely manner, every other focus of your business efforts is moot. A financial plan serves as a basis to calculate an acceptable return on investment (ROI) and determine a successful exit strategy. A financial plan with well-defined financial objectives is a must.

This chapter begins with a descriptive listing of the various benefits of formulating a financial strategy and plan for your business. Then we focus on thinking strategically in devising a financial plan, including an illustrative analogy. We then turn to the areas serving as a basis for establishing financial objectives. We introduce FREEs—fundraising effectiveness and efficiencies—on both macro and micro levels and the conceptual methods of FREE measurements before we proceed to examine the construction of an effective financial plan. The chapter concludes with some rules of thumb regarding financial planning.

Importance of Having a Financial Plan

A well-conceived financial plan enables the management team of an entrepreneurial venture to determine the type of financing with the lowest possible cost of capital, the most favorable funding structural terms, and the greatest strategic value at the time of each financial decision.

For example, if you need to fund the execution of your go-to-market strategy and you have determined that an equity placement is your best and only funding option, why increase the amount of equity to be placed to include the server purchase if you can purchase servers on much more favorable, nondilutive credit terms? Why include operating capital needs during a series B growth period with a long-term senior debt offering when you can secure a lower interest and subordinated bank revolving line of credit? These types of decisions are critical to maximizing your returns upon exit regardless of how special your product or service may be. Seeming small financial decisions have had major impacts on the ultimate success of businesses big and small worldwide. To illustrate this point, during the 1990s, numerous big American businesses conducting business overseas failed in their foreign enterprises because they did not manage their foreign exchange exposure with proper currency risk management. Although their sales revenues and profit margins were exceptional, all their operating margins disappeared in the wake of more exceptional foreign exchange losses. We already mentioned how securing funding on highly unfavorable structural funding terms may render any business success moot if another party is permitted to reap the profits.

Consider another example of a venture I have personal knowledge of with enormous potential that has very little chance of succeeding because no financial plan was developed and followed from the beginning. Despite Herculean fundraising efforts, great traction, experienced and prominent founders at the helm with superior connections, and a truly disruptive innovative service with numerous applications spanning several large industries, the company is facing financial suffocation. Without a guiding financial plan, the founders made a devastatingly bad decision at the beginning that has doomed their fundraising efforts. The primary reason for their fundraising challenges was their decision to accept a "dirty" convertible debt-funding deal at the seed-level stage. The convertible debt deal is laced with one-sided terms in favor of the investors as to question whether there were negotiations conducted and what the true intentions of the investors really are. The terms strongly suggest that the investors had every intention of ensuring that any future funding would have to come directly from them. The combination of participating preferred shares, antidilution provisions, generous conversion terms, draconian voting rights requiring unanimous consent from nearly a dozen individual investors, and, the icing on the cake, all current and future intellectual property (IP) required as collateral rendered any future fundraising efforts futile. In accepting this deal, the company became insolvent day 1. Creditors will not touch the firm with a ten-foot pole. Prospective equity investors do not want to provide funds for non-value-added uses (i.e., paying down the high-interest debt) that trigger a drastic automatic dilution of their own shares on purchase, or invest in a company in which they cannot secure any meaningful liquidation preference or highly coveted IP as collateral. This is extremely unfortunate because this venture has protected IP coveted by major corporations and a product that can revolutionize an entire global industry with enormous positive social implications. The absence of a financial plan denied the founders the chance to take advantage of all potential benefits.

There are eight areas in which having a financial plan is of significant benefit and importance: assistance in overall business planning, ensuring the health and integrity of capital structure, determining sufficient funding amounts, securing funding in a timely manner, securing funds on the most favorable terms, determining appropriate responses to new challenges and opportunities, instilling discipline and maintaining focus, and maximizing ROI upon execution of exit strategy.

Assistance in Overall Business Planning

Just as writing your business plan can lead to discoveries, drafting a financial plan can result in valuable discoveries as well. Many components of your business plan, especially in the marketing and operational plans, have expenses associated with them. Composing a financial plan compels you to assess the approximate costs of these different specific expenses. In doing so you may discover that the combined or accumulative cost of an associated expense is too great to execute and justifies an exploration of an alternate means to accomplish what is desired or identify means to reduce such costs. Financial constraints may be a determining factor on company objectives and priorities. Here you have an opportunity to look at different functions in relative terms. Contrasting different functions and plan components may result in these questions and revelations:

Service A will generate revenues sooner than Service B. Service B, whose primary expected expenditure is the purchase of physical equipment (i.e., servers), can be lease financed on much more favorable (nondilutive) terms than an equity raise as required for Service A. It makes more sense to proceed with an equity raise for just the funding of Service A and generate the cash flows from the commercial launch of Service A to qualify for the lease financing of Service B.

The combined research and development (R&D), "go-to-market," and ongoing marketing expense associated with Service A is too great to justify proceeding with its development, given the expected revenues to be generated.

When we raise series A funds for the commercial launch of Service A, will the terms be less favorable if we concurrently try to raise funds for R&D (less value-added) of Service B?

The logistics effort and expense to produce Product A and Product B independently are too great to warrant consideration. Is there a conceivable way to combine production of these two products?

The cost savings associated with locating our manufacturing facilities in closer proximity to our targeted geographic market is greater than the cost savings enjoyed by maintaining one central location.

Do we have the financial ability to simultaneously market product A and develop product B?

An effective way to financially evaluate company and operational objectives and set priorities is to contrast each one based on value added. As we mentioned earlier, a value-added activity has a positive effect on your income statement. The timeliness of such an effect is an important consideration as well. An R&D expense may offer an excellent value added but may take three years to reap the benefits. By comparing such effects on the income statement, you can quantitatively set priorities or make a yes or no decision.

Note that although it is helpful to make a financial quantitative comparison for the purpose of priority setting, other nonfinancial (strategic or incremental) factors may be priority determinants as well. Kano analysis is a preferred comprehensive method in setting priorities and should be considered in this situation.

As mentioned, composing a financial plan may lead to discoveries that results in favorable revisions to a business plan. It also enables you to monitor the progress of your business plans and financial plans concurrently.

A common type of discovery made during financial planning is a realization of the most favorable present allocation of capital funds. Often this leads to the decision to proceed to the next fundraising stage. In the use of funds discussion in Chapter 2, I mentioned a past client who was affected with the mad scientist bug and so thoroughly enjoyed R&D that he needed to be prodded into a commercial launch to generate revenues rather than indefinitely making product enhancements. In effect, I was attempting to persuade him that he was ready to take the leap from the seed to series A stage. The recurring theme to my advisory pleas was this: "Once you commercially launch a product and begin generating revenues, continued R&D can be financed with either internal financing (revenues) or a new fundraising round in which a higher price per share can be secured."

The financial status of your venture at different points in time will have an effect on both your business planning and financial planning priorities. Both plans are working documents with a degree of built-in flexibility that allows for periodic necessary changes in business strategy and operations. The interrelationship between the two plans is not as flexible, as each plan directly dictates the workings of the other.

Ensuring the Health and Integrity of Capital Structure

An effectively devised and executed financial plan will prevent a down-round type of scenario. In this situation, the integrity of the capital structure has been diminished, and current stakeholders perceive that a current funding round offers terms to prospective investors that are more favorable than the terms they received, given the assumed levels of risk. No current stakeholders want to believe that the company's valuation is somehow lower now than when they invested. Such implications seriously erode investor confidence in management. We discuss this further in Chapter 8. Maintaining the health of a company's capital structure is paramount to prevent impediments to future fundraising efforts. The real-life example I presented at the beginning of this section is a case in point.

Determining Sufficient Funding Amounts

A big question consistently entrepreneurs ask is: How much money should I raise?

Answer: Only what you need to attain the next fundraising stage.

The next question from entrepreneurs is: How do I know how much I need?

Answer: Only by formulating a financial plan.

Often I find people thinking or advising that entrepreneurs should determine the amount of money they should solicit for based on expectations of prospective investors or rules of thumb associated with stages of development. In my opinion, such advice is misplaced. These numbers are fictitious, and prospective investors will know this. The only financial expectation that matters for prospective investors is their expected returns. Because each entrepreneurial venture has different costs associated with the development of the innovation(s), general rules of thumb regarding amount of funding to be sought for a given stage of development will prove inaccurate as well.

It is not very useful to calculate the total sum of funding requirements for your entrepreneurial venture from inception to exit for two reasons. First, it is virtually impossible to secure such a funding amount all at once. Second, if you could do so, the terms undoubtedly would be so unfavorable as to prevent founding stakeholders from achieving a high enough ROI to justify their time and effort.

Constructing a financial plan forces you to place all the costs from the various functions and priorities represented in your business plan on a timeline, divided into the fundraising stages described in Chapter 1. Doing this enables you to determine the necessary funding levels at each fund-raising stage. Enough funding needs to be secured at the beginning of each fundraising stage to enable the achievement of every required company objective identified to attain the next fundraising stage. Again, the financial plan is a working document. Although it likely will prove inaccurate to project the correct amounts needed in later fund-raising stages, the most important objective is to accurately determine the amount necessary to fund the next fund-raising stage and be able to recognize when and why a revision to the projections for later stages in your working financial plan is necessary.

Insufficient funding is the biggest reason why start-ups fail. It is no coincidence that fundraising stages are closely aligned with stages of development.

Securing Funding in a Timely Manner

Two scenarios must be avoided: securing funds insufficient to cover the funding requirements necessary to reach the next funding round and securing funding well in excess of what is immediately required.

In the preceding section, we stated that insufficient funding is the primary reason most start-ups fail. More specifically, most start-ups fail when they do not secure enough funds to reach the next fundraising stage. Attempting a second funding round within a given development stage typically is a sign of doom for the business. Both current stakeholders and prospective investors will raise red flags if you follow one funding round with another offering with the same or more favorable terms. A perception of desperation or misman-agement will prevail. Neither will improve your negotiating position or credibility. After reviewing a draft funding PowerPoint pitch of a prospective client, I posed these questions and offered advice:

> Have you asked for enough funds in this funding round? You have stated your funding requirements are $400,000; however, according to your pro forma financials you burn much more before you break even, much less attain the ability to operate on internal financing. For prospective investors, the point at which you can internally finance your operations or have achieved the financial objectives required to reach the next stage of development, making possible a subsequent funding round at a much higher price per share, is much more important than a more or less symbolic break-even point. By end of second quarter, you claim to have burned $650,000 at the

break-even point. How do you make up for this $250,000 difference before you break even, and where will you secure the additional funds necessary to reach the next fundraising stage? Will current shareholders contribute these extra necessary funds? If so, by what means and on what terms?

A much worse scenario is trying to conduct a down round. A down round occurs when an equity sale subsequent to other equity purchases is executed at a per-share price lower than the prior purchase prices. The primary reason for a venture to conduct a down round is its failure to raise enough funding at the beginning of the current fundraising stage. Down rounds reduce the percentage equity interest of current shareholders. In many cases, such as with restrictive stock, it is illegal. If conducted legally, you are basically making a death wish for your venture as you have destroyed the integrity of your capital structure and the prospect of raising future funds will be very bleak.

Recently, debt holders who appear more interested in seizing my client's valuable IP than sharing the interests of the shareholders seeking an exceptional ROI upon exit advised my client's management to conduct a down round to secure needed funds. Indeed, the debt holders may participate in such a down round as well (acquire a higher percentage of my client's equity at a cheaper price) and introduce new investors (that may serve as their proxies) who would be attracted by the low price. I asked a representative of these debt holders why they would give advice that implied a lower valuation for a company that had patented valuable IP and executed a successful commercial launch of its first groundbreaking product since the last funding round. The reply: "Most start-ups experience a down round." This is not true. However, instead of correcting the person, I simply replied that most start-ups fail. We do not wish to be like most start-ups.

On the flip side, securing funds much greater than your immediate needs can be equally dangerous. Do not fall for the seductive trap of accepting an offer for more funds than what are immediately required. If an investor is willing to offer you more money than what you need immediately, the intent is to secure as much equity percentage interest (i.e., control) as possible before paying much higher prices in later funding rounds. Determine if you are granting too much control given the current funding stage, whether you can secure more favorable terms with less funding, and whether investor expectations associated with investing such a large amount can be reasonably attained by your venture in the allotted time period. At the very least, the more investment funds you accept during the life of the venture, the greater the size of the exit required to achieve an ROI acceptable to shareholders.

In sum, securing the maximum amount of investment funding offered in a given funding round may prove to be a costly mistake in terms of control and increased size of acceptable exit.

Raising funds in a timely manner will not only prevent doomsday scenarios for your venture but will result in progressively securing funds on the most favorable terms.

An effective financial plan will enable you to activate a just-in-time fundraising system in which you solicit the minimal required amount of funding during the higher-cost earlier stages. This method creates a potentially valuable fundraising efficiency with both short-term and long-term benefits.

Securing Funds on the Most Favorable Terms

Funding terms should become progressively more favorable. As a business progresses to the next advanced developmental stage, theoretically the cost and terms of funds should become more favorable due to the reduction of risks, accumulation of know-how and assets, and improved positioning/ traction and revenues. To progress to the next fundraising stage, you need to demonstrate evidence of such advances to establish a higher valuation. Establishing a higher valuation will result in a higher price per share, thereby causing less dilution upon an equity sale. Later in this chapter we show how to measure this rate of equity dilution.

Determining Appropriate Responses to New Challenges and Opportunities

Most start-ups are employing constantly advancing technologies and processes to develop and introduce products and services into highly dynamic market environments. A financial plan, as a working document, provides a means to assess from a financial perspective the various options under consideration in response to identified changes in technologies and market conditions and what the appropriate financial responses may be. For example, the identification of a new competitor or increased regulation in your target market may compel a reevaluation of the direction of your R&D efforts or the timing and nature of your go-to-market strategy. You will have to make financial decisions not only to fund any changes to your R&D or marketing efforts but also to reach the financial objectives required to secure shareholders' high ROI expectations. In another example, a new promising market may emerge for your innovative product. Taking advantage of such a golden opportunity may require forgoing some R&D efforts in the short term and reallocating funds to moving up a commercial launch. A working financial plan offers a way to make such assessments and execute such changes in strategy. Current shareholders or prospective investors certainly appreciate innovative advances and the working dynamics of a new or rapidly growing market. However, their financial expectations are not so fluid. Remember Know Your Investors (KYI) #1: Expectations for a successful exit will remain.

Instilling Discipline and Maintain Focus

A valuable tenet postulated by Sun Tzu is that discipline is more important than skill. A financial plan instills discipline and helps maintain focus. This proposition rings particularly true for entrepreneurial ventures with innovative products and services entering rapidly changing and competitive marketplaces. Such changes offer powerful challenges to the founders' ability to maintain focus on both short-term and long-term financial objectives. One challenge is the fact that taking reactive actions to new developments without considering the financial implications to your venture may prove a financial disaster regardless of whether you can meet the challenge presented from a developmental, operational, or marketing perspective. Consider the case I described earlier where a past client faced a competitor who was developing a product with all the bells and whistles. My client could have decided to meet such a direct challenge and compete from a purely product feature perspective. However, he decided to resist such a temptation after referring to his recently drafted financial plan. The review made apparent the potentially dangerous financial implications of such a path and served as a reminder of the shareholders' financial expectations. Under such circumstances, referring to a financial plan usually cures those afflicted with mad scientist syndrome.

Another benefit derived from the improved discipline and focus associated with having a financial plan is the ability to deal with the ups and downs inherently experienced by start-ups and take calculated risks in which the potential upside more than justifies the possible downside. When I was a currency trader, my trading partner and I often went through periods where we suffered losses on seven out of every ten trades; however, we were able to secure net profits during such periods because of our disciplined trading approach. We used support and resistance levels to determine where to place stop-loss market orders to limit our losses to the downside and reestablish stop losses just below a recently broken support or resistance level after successfully breaking through it on the upside. In effect, we were limiting our losses and locking in our profits while allowing our profitable positions to run as high as the market would allow. Consequently, the amount of gain for our profitable trades was typically three times higher than the amount of loss on our losing trades. Our disciplined trading strategy did two things for us. First, it allowed us to remain positive throughout the numerous ups and downs. Emotionally hanging on every trade would only result in ulcers. Our failure to make money on a majority of trades could have easily crushed our will to continue trading. The ups and downs experienced by entrepreneurial ventures can have similar demoralizing effects on its founders. Two, without our disciplined approach, we would never have had the courage to hold on to our initially profitable trades long enough to achieve such profits. Mitigating downside risk permitted us to assume more upside risk. An entrepreneurial venture protected by a significant barrier to entry, a favorable public concession, or a valuable patent may be in a better position to consider pursuing higher upside opportunities that earlier may have been considered too risky. For an entrepreneurial venture, the financial objectives found in the financial plan also may serve as clear demarcation points on which to base calculated risks. The financial strategy derived from a financial plan offers an informed and disciplined approach to making financial decisions. It is necessary to establish financial objectives based on the progression of fundraising stages. For an entrepreneur, determining when the next fundraising stage has been reached (i.e., certain risks have been mitigated) is similar to locking in your profits. The heightened awareness of the financial position and needs of the venture afforded by a well-designed financial plan enables users the ability to identify and assess calculated risks that offer a favorable risk/return opportunity. Being fully aware of your financial status and needs will prove valuable during funding negotiations as well. A formidable negotiator is one who is both informed and disciplined.

Maximizing ROI upon Execution of Exit Strategy

If you devise and execute an effective financial plan, the improvement in business planning and the periodic securing of funds on the most favorable terms at the optimal minimum amounts with concise timing precision will maximize the expected ROI upon execution of your exit strategy. A financial plan will help you minimize dilution of equity by providing a view of what funding is available at different points of time, what the various costs are, and the risks and effects of such different funding types. Thus, you will be able to identify opportunities to secure lower-cost nonequity financing when an opportunity exists. An effective business plan alone will not achieve such maximization of ROI.

Having a financial plan articulated in a holistic manner will enable the founders to make more informed decisions. Most important, a financial plan provides the means to formulate and make periodic advantageous amendments to a winning financial strategy.

Formulating a Financial Strategy

The primary objective of formulating a financial strategy encapsulated in a financial plan is to maximize the ROI upon execution of your exit strategy. Formulating a financial strategy requires you to plot out a financial course to achieve the optimal fundraising efficiency to ultimately maximize ROI. Establishing and incorporating financial objectives into your financial plan is a means to plot such a course. Efficient fundraising is a balancing act between minimizing equity dilution while obtaining enough funds to reach the next required funding round.

The strategic thought process helpful in plotting such a financial course can best be illustrated with an auto road trip analogy.

In preparation for a long road trip through a remote area, you need to make macro-level decisions regarding the most direct route (prioritized company objectives) to take and the fuel stops (funding rounds) to make. You know that as you travel west toward your destination (exit strategy), the price of gas (cost of capital/equity dilution) becomes increasingly cheaper (more favorable). There are two extreme options. One is to stop at every gas station on the way to minimize the risk of running out of gas. This may prove to be very inefficient and costly as more stops (dilution) are taken and greater instances of refueling at higher-price (lower valuation) pit stops occur. The opposite extreme option is to try to go as far as you can on each full tank, relying on your perfect judgment (pro forma calculations) and absence of unforeseen occurrences like detours (necessary priority changes). However, in choosing this option, you maximize the probability of running out of gas and getting stranded. As you run low on gas, you may have the unpleasant experience of watching your fuel gauge (operating capital) and pressure gauge (capital structure) enter the red zone. Once you run out of gas and become stranded, you may encounter vultures (opportunistic prospective investors) only interested in selling you gas at $50 per gallon. Pursuit of either extreme option would not be prudent. The best approach would be to perform the necessary research to identify and evaluate each fuel station, given its pricing and your preferred direction (company objectives), and utilize this information to select the series of pit stops that would enable you to make the minimum number of stops at the lowest aggregate cost for your trip. It would be wise to give yourself enough flexibility (cash reserves) in your trip plan (financial strategy) to deal with any unforeseen events.

Along the way, you will have to make micro-level decisions as well. During your assessment of each fuel station, additional considerations may include the quality of fuel (good or bad money) and the expected duration of the fuel stop (effort required to raise the funds). Can food (nonfinancial support) be obtained? If nature calls (need to mitigate risk), does this fuel station offer clean restroom facilities (competitive advantage)?

You can take micro-level actions in preparing the auto for the long trip as well. Leaving the SUV at home and taking the very fuel-efficient sedan (strong value proposition) would certainly be advantageous, although possibly less comfortable. A pretrip tune-up (effective operational plan) and cleaning the car (effective marketing plan) can both add to the fuel efficiency of the car.

Proper air pressure in the tires (effective management team) and adjusting the mirrors (bringing along a good investor for the ride) should make for a more pleasant and less eventful ride. Topping your brake fluid and power steering fluid (maintaining control) is certainly advisable before a long trip as well.

As in travel plans, there are many considerations in financial plans. Establishing financial objectives will facilitate the execution of a financial plan and keep you on the course plotted. Next we turn to the basis for such financial objectives.

Financial Objectives

There are five primary bases for establishing financial objectives:

1. *Burn rate coverage.* The first financial objective for any new business is to have the ability to internally finance the minimum expense requirements of your business as soon as possible. This leads to a priceless source of peace of mind and the best source of negotiating leverage and effective control. The concept and importance of burn rate was presented in our discussion of KYI #3 in Chapter 2.
2. *Revenues and profitability.* These are the most obvious bases of financial objectives. These numbers have already been calculated and presented in your pro forma financial statements. They directly address the primary objective of making exceptional returns on investments.

   The remaining three bases for financial objectives are associated with effective and efficient fundraising and can be quantified utilizing measurement tools to be presented in the next section.
3. *Minimizing equity dilution.* Minimizing equity dilution is a means to maximizing ROI for the founding partners.
4. *Optimal selection of funding or financing options.* Considering each individual financial decision within the context of an overall financial strategy is the essence of effective financial planning and funding negotiations.
5. *Maintaining effective control.* Minimizing limitations and maximizing flexibility in your financial decision making is essential to ensure your ability to implement a well-conceived financial plan and, consequently, operational plans.

FREE

You must make effective financial decisions at both a macro and a micro level. The macro level includes all fundraising activities. To maximize fundraising efficiencies and effectiveness at the macro level, you must make a focused effort to determine the most desirable path of succession for fundraising activities. Macro-level decisions include the timing, amount of funding solicited, funding type, funding structure, and funding terms for each funding round. In your business plan, you have already presented your short-term, intermediate-term, and long-term company objectives associated with the successful conclusion of the current and subsequent fundraising stages. With the company objectives serving as the basis, you must employ fundraising efficiency and effectiveness measurements from company founding to exit to determine the optimal fundraising path.

You must make efficient and effective finance decisions at the micro (project or individual purchase) level during each fundraising stage. The basis of these micro-level decisions is your operational milestones. The required expenditures to accomplish such objectives are specified in your operational plan and monetarily represented in the financials section of business plan.

FREE Measurement Tools

Rating of Equity Dilution

The rating of equity dilution (RED) is the percentage equity interest of a company held by the founding shareholders. The rate of equity dilution (RED is the acronym for "rating," which is different from "rate") is the percentage equity interest decrease realized by founding shareholders following each successive funding round. It is a measure of a company's fundraising efficiency. If the objective is to maximize the ROI for the founding shareholders upon exit, one way to achieve this goal is for the founding shareholders to hold the greatest percentage equity interest in the company upon exit.

Adjusted RED is the raw RED score adjusted to account for established future uncertainties in the capital structure of a business. An established capital structure uncertainty exists when there is a possibility that further equity dilution can occur without the need to execute a funding round whereby additional shares are issued to new investors. The four primary reasons for such uncertainty are when:

1. A convertible debt instrument exists
2. Equity warrants are issued
3. Additional equity is granted pursuant to tranche-based or performance trigger–based funding terms
4. Equity-based incentives for management (i.e., stock options) exist if such equity is issued outside of a structured incentive pool in which shares have already been issued or allocated pursuant to a previous funding agreement.

All four causes allow or provide contingencies for existing stakeholders to acquire more shares.

You can calculate the RED adjustment in one of two ways:

1. The preferred way is to be conservative and calculate the maximum potential amount of additional equity interest that is contingent. Include such maximum contingency in your capital structure by adding both outstanding equity and contingent equity and labeling the sum equity securities.
2. In certain situations, calculation of contingency equity is not so easy. The existence of antidilution terms in a convertible equity security funding agreement is a good example. In such an event, it may be necessary to determine an appropriate percentage amount to adjust the raw RED score. To estimate a useful adjustment amount, you may determine that your RED should decrease by 20 percent. Thus, your current RED of 75 may be adjusted downward to 60.

The next list displays a reasonable minimum acceptable rating of equity dilution for entrepreneurial ventures following the conclusion of each successive fundraising stage:

Seed funding round: 75
Series A (go-to-market) funding round: 50
Series B (growth) funding round: 25

Consider these numbers general rules of thumb; nevertheless, calculating RED is an effective way to plot a financial course to maximize ROI upon execution of exit strategy.

ACRE Chart

Construction of an ACRE chart is an effective way to determine how to secure funds on the most favorable terms. Based on our company objectives and immediate operational objectives, which finance options (i.e., funding types) are available, and how do we determine which finance option would be the most efficient, based on the funding requirements of this particular fundraising stage? How will each financial decision fit into our overall financial strategy?

The acronym ACRE stands for availability, cost, risk, and effect. The terms represent the criteria to be assessed to determine the most efficient finance option.

Availability. What is required to be eligible for this type of funding, and how much funding is available to be secured? Equity investments have a high level of availability. Usually all that is required is the existence of a viable and compelling exit strategy and meeting specific investment criteria of individual investors. Sufficient cash flow to service periodic payments and collateral assets as security typically is necessary for debt funding. Availability of public funding is limited to companies participating in select industries or markets or providing a priority product or service within a particular geographic or functional area. Bank credit lines require a strong credit rating and long operating history. In many locales and circumstances, some types of funding may not be offered at all.

Cost. What costs are assumed once such funding type is secured? For equity investments, the cost is the amount of equity dilution and the resulting decrease in the founders' ROI. The cost of capital (i.e., interest) is the cost for debt or credit funding. Cost may also include the amount of time and expense to secure such funding. Especially in the case of acquiring public funds, it includes any cost derived from altering the original developmental, operational, and marketing plans to qualify for the funding. For example, if you need to relocate your manufacturing facilities to a more expensive location or add an additional feature to secure such funding, securing this funding has derivative costs.

Risk. What can be potentially lost by accepting such type of funding? For equity investments, an offering price per share too low will diminish the founders' expected ROI of the unnecessarily. An offering price too high may result in securing insufficient funds or may make it more difficult to raise future funds as a higher offering price is required in subsequent funding rounds (i.e., remember no down rounds). The primary risk for debt funding is the asset(s) pledged as collateral and/or the consequences of liquidation. A potential risk of either funding type is the "dirtying" of the capital structure based on the funding terms. The primary risk of public funding is the potentially costly assumption of strict funding requirements or the commonly high costs in terms of both time and money associated with applying for public funding (i.e., composing a grant application).

Effect on cash flow. A cash flow squeeze will have a detrimental effect on the execution of all your business plans. An equity raise will have little or no effect on your company's cash flow unless dividends on preferred shares are paid. This is both rare and not recommended for typically cash-starved start-ups. Debt service payments do have a negative effect on cash flow that limits the amount of funding available to be expended on more value-added purposes. Securing a relatively large bank credit line works wonders for your cash management capabilities as long as draws are taken prudently and monies are allocated for immediate value-added purposes.

Effect on balance sheet. Positive effects on your balance sheet will serve to increase your company's valuation and provide more potential assets to be pledged as collateral. Negative effects naturally will have a direct opposite effect of weakening your ability to secure future debt funding or establish credit. Securing senior debt funding will prevent you from issuing subsequent debt more senior. Once an asset has been pledged as collateral, it cannot be designated as security for another funding. The designation of a debt as either short term or long term will have an impact on your ability to secure bank credit. Most nondebt funding, such as public grants, licensing fees, and revenue shares, will have little or no effect on your balance sheet.

You will have to undertake a comparison of the different funding types. Create an ACRE chart for each funding need. Include the different funding options on the vertical axis, and show the various criteria to be assessed on the horizontal axis.

In general, macro-level fundraising is more available for start-ups but entails greater costs and risks. Therefore, for each fundraising stage considered, apply the ACRE chart on the micro level to identify finance options that may be cheaper and provide the opportunity to reduce the amount of funding needed to be raised at the macro level. In following this logic, you must determine the total funding amount required for a particular stage, given company and operational objectives. Doing this will enable you to establish the amount of funding to be solicited at the macro level by subtracting the total amount satisfactorily available at the micro level from the total required for the entire stage. Two hypothetical examples of applying the ACRE chart at the micro level followed by two hypothetical examples of utilizing the ACRE chart at the macro level are presented to demonstrate the process.

Two Applications of ACRE Chart on the Micro Level
Scenario 1: You have identified a need to purchase 12 servers sometime during the next fundraising stage at a total cost of $100,000. The type of funding available for you in this stage in which the purchase of equipment would be a permissible use of funds include an already planned equity placement at beginning of the stage and a five-year $100,000 senior term loan at 12 percent offered by a willing individual creditor if the funds are used to purchase computer equipment and equipment leasing provided by the equipment distributor. Diluting your equity by including the purchase of servers in the required funding amount for the equity placement may be too costly if alternative financing options for equipment purchase are available. Accepting a long-term senior debt on your balance sheet also seems quite excessive, given this may preclude you from securing a much larger senior debt instrument at a later stage, when such debt

financing would be more advantageous than an equity sale and you have sufficient cash flows to service it. The equipment leasing option offers a three-year term at 5 percent. You choose the leasing option as it is the most favorable in terms of cost, risk, effect on cash flow, and effect on balance sheet. The cost of capital for the lease is 5 percent as opposed to 12 percent. The effect on cash flow is slightly better as the monthly lease payments on a three-year 5 percent lease are less than on a five-year 12 percent term loan. The risk of defaulting on the lease is the return of the servers. The risk of defaulting on the term loan may include other company assets as well. An equipment lease is a secured short-term debt on your balance sheet, whereas the term loan is a less-favorable senior long-term debt.

Scenario 2: The business you cofounded is in a growth stage of development and doing well. You have several long-term contracts with reliable paying clients and have already secured a $250,000 revolving credit line with a private bank, albeit at a relatively high interest rate of 10 percent. The company has plans to commence R&D on an innovative software product to launch commercially in the future at a total cost of $150,000 over the next three months. Recently you signed a new software development contract requiring $100,000 in the next two months to hire four new developers. The two immediate objectives of the company are to commence R&D development of the innovative software product and execute the recently executed contract. Due to the short-term nature of the funding requirements, the only available funding is the existing line of credit, a public grant specific to creating new software developer jobs in your geographic locale, and factor financing from a local retail bank. The existing credit line is large enough to provide sufficient funds for both high-priority objectives. However, it may be too dangerous to tap the entire amount and raise the possibility of a short-term cash flow issue or be forced to turn down a new contract. The available public funding would not be granted for the internal R&D project as existing developers have been tasked. Unfortunately, securing the no-interest public grant may take three months and will cost $10,000 to hire someone to write the complicated grant. The factor financing terms offer an interest rate of only 6 percent. Such a low rate can be offered because the bank relies more on the credit of your contract clients than on the credit of your own business and collects the accounts receivable directly from your clients. Given the size and strong payment history of your current monthly accounts receivable, enough factor financing funds can be secured for both projects. Thus, you decide to apply for

$250,000 of factor financing. Factoring is cheaper. The interest rate on the existing credit line is 10 percent. Paying $10,000 to apply for the $100,000 grant (only the new contract cost is eligible) would be at an effective rate of 10 percent as well. Default risk is associated with the credit line. In a factoring deal, the bank assumes responsibility for collecting on the accounts receivable, which limits the default risk for your company. The public grant carries no risk once secured. However, there is the $10,000 risk that the application is not successful as well as the risk that funds are not made available in a timely manner. Factoring is superior to public funding in terms of both availability and risk. Factoring reigns supreme over the existing credit line both in terms of cash flow and effect on balance sheet. In the factoring deal, banks give you money up front for the accounts receivable they will collect directly from your existing clients over the next three to six months. Drawing from the existing credit line will require monthly minimum service payments. Factoring will have no net effect on the balance sheet. Drawn funds from the credit line, however, will be shown as an increase in short-term liability.

Two Applications of ACRE Chart on the Macro Level
Scenario 3: Assuming that the preceding two scenarios were related to the same business, a subsequent macro-level utilization of an ACRE chart may occur. In the first two scenarios, you want to raise a total of $350,000 at the micro level. If the total required amount of funding for that stage is $750,000, then $400,000 is remaining to be raised at the macro level. Besides your planned equity placement, are any other funding types available? If so, is another available funding option(s) more efficient? You need the remaining $400,000 to cover burn rate expenses. Following the construction of an ACRE chart at the macro level, you see that the only available funding is equity placement, senior debt placement, factoring, or an increase in the current $250,000 revolving credit line. Factoring is based on your current accounts receivable; thus, you can always secure more factor financing for whatever use as long as you have sufficient accounts receivable to cover and clients willing to pay the accounts receivable to the bank directly. After examining your current accounts receivable, you determine that an additional $100,000 can be factored on top of the planned $250,000. Thus, $300,000 must still be raised at the macro level. You decide to negotiate for as large an increase as possible to the unsecured and nondilutive revolving credit line. You will subtract whatever increase you secure from either the private equity or the senior debt placement. Now it is time to compare the

cost, risk, and effects of the two remaining funding options. As a series B company, you have successfully executed two prior private equity placements and are hesitant to dilute the shares much further, given your profitable status. You also do not wish to add more shareholders with voting rights as the current management team and good shareholders are working together well. The senior debt placement looks attractive as the risk of company failure has been diminished considerably; however, much of your cash flow in the short term will be tied up with the equipment lease and factoring deal (i.e., the bank collecting much of your accounts receivable for the next four months). It may be difficult to assume a monthly debt service payment. A senior debt now may preclude securing a much larger senior debt placement in the next round to fund your continued growth strategy. The amount of funding required at that point would definitely eliminate a private equity placement due to the enormous dilution that would occur. The senior debt lender would want some of your valuable IP as collateral. Such a risk seems excessive, given the company's financial positioning and use of the sought funds. Given these circumstances, you have decided to raise the remaining funds on the macro level with the equity placement. Regarding cost, further dilution would occur; however, it is not as much dilution as would occur in the next fundraising stage if you are forced to opt for the potentially much larger equity placement at that point. The risk, effect on cash flow, and effect on balance sheet certainly favor the equity placement over the debt placement.

Scenario 4: An entrepreneur has decided to begin a start-up venture with a partner. It has been determined that it will take them 12 months to conduct a proof of concept, develop a prototype, and compose a business plan. Expenses include rent, utilities, computers, Internet, office furniture and equipment, and minimal salaries to sustain them on a Ramen noodle lifestyle at a total cost of $75,000 to complete the seed stage. As advised earlier in the book, they identified a local incubator that will provide them with facilities in which to conduct their R&D at no expense. This has reduced the amount of funding they need to raise by a third because all office-related expenses have been covered. Unfortunately, the incubator does not provide seed funding; however, the type of product to be developed qualifies for a public funding program offered by a local economic development agency. The program will reimburse $10,000 of business expenses applicable to the venture. Although it is a reimbursement, it will assist them in raising the $50,000 required on the macro level by demonstrating to any prospective investor that, in effect, 20 percent of their investment principal is guaranteed by a public funding program. Prospective investors will also like the fact that the current burn rate is mostly covered by the incubator. Two angel investors have expressed interest. One has $50,000 to lend as a two-year senior note; the other would like to make an equity investment in the same amount. To make the initial assessment to apply for the incubator program and choose between an equity or debt investment from an angel, the ACRE chart in Figure 4.1 has been constructed.

After reviewing the chart, the funding sources available are the incubator program, public reimbursement program, equity sale, and borrowing on a senior note. The former two sources come with little or no cost and risk while offering only positive effects on cash flow and the balance sheet. However, they provide only about one-third of the funding required. The remaining two-thirds of funding will need to come from either an equity sale or assumption of a senior note. The costs and risks associated with the equity sale are less than for the assumption of senior debt, given the current seed fundraising stage. The debt note option also carries greater detrimental effects on both cash flow and balance sheet. Therefore, it has been decided to apply to the incubator program first, then apply for public reimbursement before negotiating with the prospective equity investor. Securing the first two public funding sources will strengthen the negotiating position vis-à-vis the prospective equity investor.

The ACRE chart permits a way to select the most efficient combinations of funding in the most optimal order and timing.

Command and Control Rating

The RED measurements and ACRE chart are useful tools in evaluating financial factors in assessing FREEs. However, crafting a financial strategy based exclusively on financial factors will not be sufficient if your ability to execute your financial strategy has been severely restricted because you have accepted unfavorable funding terms that limit your future financial decision making. Such restrictions may be imposed due to the generation of a control issue or failure to ensure the health and integrity of your capital structure. Therefore, you must consider and measure nonfinancial factors affecting the pursuit of future finance options and fundraising activities. A command and control rating (CCR) evaluation helps in discerning good money from bad money.

An effective way to measure the preservation or loss of financial decision-making abilities or strategic advantage is to calculate a CCR. You must determine the nonfinancial pros and cons for each planned financing method on both macro and micro levels and their effects on command and control.

$75,000 Seed Funding Sought

Potential Funding Sources	Availability of Funds	Cost of Funds	Risk Assumed	Effect on Cash Flow	Effect on Balance Sheet
Incubator Program	Meet minimal admission qualifications: $25,000	Nominal application fee	None	Highly positive. Covers a large portion of a start-up's burn rate	No effect: Purchase of physical assets deferred
Public Funding Reimbursement Program	Only for expenses qualified as reimbursable; maximum of $10,000	No cost reimbursement. Effectively a nondilutive and interest-free grant	Serves as a nice nondilutive, noncontrolling funding	Positive effect once reimbursement received	No effect
Equity Placement	Meet investment criteria of identified prospective investor: $50,000	Dilution of founders' equity	Common equity: Some degree of control lost Preferred equity: Liquidation preference	Positive: Equity sale proceeds considered a cash inflow from financing activities	Increase of shareholder equity; addition to capital structure
Debt Note	Possess acceptable collateral and sufficient cash flow to service debt: $50,000	Negotiated interest to be paid during term of note	Assets pledged; potential loss of company upon liquidation; impediment to future fundraising	Note proceeds a cash inflow; service payments a recurring cash outflow	Negative effect: Addition of either short-term or long-term debt
Credit Line	Not available. Insufficient operating history	N/A	N/A	N/A	N/A
Factor Financing	Not available. No qualified accounts receivable	N/A	N/A	N/A	N/A

FIGURE 4.1 ACRE Chart

Then you will compare the effects to help you select the most favorable financing options.

Then you aggregate your evaluations of the command and control effects of each financing option within a particular fundraising stage to make a relative estimate of what degree of financial decision-making discretion you can expect to forfeit or gain since the last funding round. A CCR of 100 denotes a complete absence of any restrictions or impediments to future financial decision making and activities. A CCR of 0 signifies that your management team members are merely puppets enacting the directives of the controlling stakeholders and/or have a total lack of ability to pursue any desired fundraising activity due to lack of traction. If you believe that your effective command and control over financial decisions is at 85 percent at beginning of a given fundraising stage and you expect such effective control to diminish a further 15 percent upon successfully executing the selected funding options, you anticipate a CCR of 70 percent at end of the fundraising stage. Any dip in the CCR score below 50 prior to the series B fundraising stage should raise some red flags.

Examples of CCR evaluations at both the macro and micro levels are presented next.

CCR Evaluation Case the Macro Level

The current self-perceived CCR score is 90. You are preparing to raise $500,000 of series A funding through an equity placement, representing a 10 percent equity percentage share of the company, to commercially launch an innovative software product that helps organize and simplify planning for architectural projects. A private equity offering memorandum is to be distributed to select qualified prospective investors at an offering price of $10 per share. A complete subscription should be expected to decrease CCR by 10 from 90 to 80 because a 10 percent equity interest in company is being sold without other identifiable command or control issues. Two other equity placement options are available. One option is accepting a $500,000 funding proposal from a prominent architect to purchase shares at $9. Another option is to accept a $500,000 purchase offer at $11 per share from a retired factory worker who just won the lottery.

Which deal should be accepted?

From a purely financial perspective, the $11 per share offer should be accepted. However, after conducting a simple CCR evaluation, you determine that the most desirable offer is that of the prominent architect.

Why?

Regarding issues of control, it is better to have greater distribution of equity holdings. The extra $1 per share offered by the lottery winner, compared to the private equity offering, may not be worth having a relatively large percentage of shareholder voting rights concentrated in any one shareholder, particularly someone who does not provide any nonfinancial benefits. The $11 offer may decrease the CCR score to 75. Regarding strategic considerations, the lower $9 per share offer may be worth such concentration of equity in one investor, given the architect's position as a center of influence. The prominent architect is in a position to offer valuable strategic benefits, including introductions to the management of large architectural firms and associations and a powerful endorsement of your product to both construction and architectural industries at large. The architect may be able to offer great advice on the dynamics of the industry and future trends that may assist your company in selecting features included in future product offerings. Netting the negative factor of greater concentration with the more positive factor of securing assistance of an investor of strategic value, you project a CCR of 85. This is an excellent example of a benefit derived from receiving good money.

You certainly can pay a premium for good money while readily turning down bad money offered at better financial terms.

CCR Evaluation Case the Micro Level

Again the current self-perceived CCR is 90. The company needs $40,000 to purchase a commercial-grade optical scanner to test its recently developed medical imaging software before a commercial launch and subsequent improvements can be executed. You have three finance options. A medical equipment manufacturer is willing to donate such a scanner if it is granted exclusive marketing rights for one year. Another available option is to max out on an existing $100,000 credit line at 7 percent with a private bank that is secured with one of your highly versatile design patents. A third option is to commit to a short one-year equipment lease for the scanner at 9 percent.

After completing a thorough CCR evaluation, you have determined that the equipment lease is superior to the other two finance options.

Why?

You estimated a resulting CCR of 85 by executing the equipment lease. The short term and high interest rate would result in a relatively high monthly lease payment that would considerably reduce the amount of available operating capital for your business and have a somewhat constricting effect on other micro financial decisions in the short term. However, this option has a comparatively marginal effect on the CCR, reducing it by only 5.

Although drawing the $40,000 from the existing credit line offering lower interest and a longer term would lessen the impact on operating capital, increasing the amount of money required to "free" a critical IP would make it more difficult to conduct future fundraising if investors insist on such IP as security. You set a CCR of 75.

The exclusivity marketing deal, although nondilutive and requiring no security or debt service payments, is a significant strategic handicap by relying so much and for so long on the marketing abilities of one entity for one of your key products. A poor performance by that company might have a long-term detrimental effect on your brand as well. You set the resulting CCR at 65.

Determining FREEs with RED measurements, ACRE charts, and CCR evaluations provide important tools to formulate an effective financial strategy and serve as a basis for defining financial objectives. Free conceptual tools are used to effectively formulate a financial strategy and identify appropriate financial objectives. Now you must articulate your strategy in a financial plan.

Financial Plan Composition

The purpose of the financial plan is to clearly illustrate the financial strategy you have formulated using the various measurement and evaluation tools: RED, ACRE charts, and CCR. Indeed, the aggregation of such tools is an ideal way to construct a financial plan. The capital structure, company objectives, operational plan, and financials sections of the business plan are the primary sources of reference. Of course, your financial plan should be totally consistent with the information presented in your business plan.

The financial plan is composed on a time stream organized by the progression of fundraising stages. The total amount of funding and funding needs for each stage are noted. There are two tiers within each fundraising stage. The macro tier displays the fundraising components (variables) of your financial strategy. These components are based on the attainment of company objectives and likely have direct effects on the company's capital structure. You must include a description of each planned fundraising activity that directly affects the capital structure, as per the previously constructed ACRE charts. The description includes an approximate date, funding amount, funding type, and prospective funding sources to be targeted. The micro tier presents finance decisions made on the operational level. They are based on operational objectives (milestones) and most likely have only a balance sheet effect. Micro-level variables are the specific projects or items to be financed or purchased at this level. They should be organized based on the previously constructed ACRE charts as well.

To maintain an accurate chronology of financial events and assist in managing cash flow, the two tiers run along the shared timeline in tandem. To ensure that financial objectives are being accomplished, RED and CCR scores are stated in the financial plan at the beginning and end of each fundraising stage. The projected revision of the capital structure should be prepared for the end of each stage as well. Both macro and micro variables will need to run (continually updated) from funding stage to funding stage. Ideally there should only be one macro-level funding round in each fundraising stage, and it should occur at the beginning of the stage. The remaining finance activities during a fundraising stage ideally should occur at the micro level; for a sample financial plan, see Appendix A at end of the book.

Rules of Thumb

The following represent general rules of thumb to consider while devising a financial plan:

- *Financial plans are for internal use only.* Prospective investors should know that you have a financial strategy and plan to execute; however, they do not need to know the specific details. You want to maintain control of your fundraising process at all times. A financial plan is there to provide discipline and peace of mind.
- *Fundraising efforts need to be constant.* Do not wait until you absolutely need funds to conduct a funding round. The best time to have a funding round is when you do not have an immediate need of funds. This is why it is always best, if possible, to conduct a funding round upon the entrance into the next fundraising stage to secure sufficient funds for that fundraising stage and before you commit to any additional expenses associated with that stage. A successful funding round requires sufficient time to prepare; thus, preparation will need to begin well before the completion of the previous fundraising stage.
- *Be mindful what you are granting based on what stage of development you are in.* Whatever term is granted to an investor at any given stage may not be available to prospective investors offering significantly more funding at much more favorable terms at some point in the future.
- *Dedicate a qualified member of the management team member to fundraising efforts.* Fundraising activities should not be a major source of distraction for key personnel who are vital to other facets of the business. Someone at the executive level, preferably the chief financial officer if

you have one, should be overseeing, if not personally conducting, all fundraising activities. Your chief operating officer, responsible for assuring the successful execution of your commercial launch or growth strategy, should not spend most of his or her time making cold calls to solicit funds. It is essential that a high level of consistency exists in your fundraising efforts. Different management team members should not be at liberty to approach whoever and whenever they choose and offer varied funding terms without receiving the consent of a responsible officer who is accountable for fundraising activities and has the authority to ensure compliance with the agreed-on financial plan.

- *The financial plan can be a valuable source of financial discoveries.* As mentioned earlier, you can make valuable discoveries while composing the financial plan that may assist you in overall business planning. Financial-related discoveries can be made as well. For example, say you discover that your CCR score is unacceptable. You decide that it may be better to reduce the size of the planned equity placement offering at the beginning of the next stage and remove the purchase of XYZ from the use of funds found in the offering and attempt to get a credit limit increase on an existing revolving line of credit to fund such a purchase instead.
- *The components of the financial plan must be consistent with each other and with the business plan.* You do not want to cause a break in the code that will cause the utility and value of your financial plan to diminish. You must perform periodic continual integration testing to maintain the alignment of all your planning documents.

Summary

The beauty of having a financial plan is the enhanced ability to make finance decisions that take into account future conditions. Thinking in a time stream is the essence of effective planning.

Having a financial plan is important to assist in overall business planning, ensure the health and integrity of the capital structure, determine sufficient funding amounts, secure funding in a timely manner, secure funding on the most favorable terms, make informed responses to new challenges and opportunities, instill discipline in the decision-making process, and ultimately maximize returns upon exit. Formulating a financial strategy with the intent to achieve optimal fundraising efficiencies is the path to maximizing returns. A written, well-conceived financial plan is the means to articulate such a financial strategy.

Having a financial plan means having more control and maintaining the initiative vis-à-vis prospective investors. Whereas your business plan is out there for any interested party to view, your privately held financial plan will provide a firm basis for your dealings with prospective investors.

The key to optimal financial planning is to accurately identify expenses on both a business objective level (i.e., go-to-market strategy) and an individual item level (i.e., purchase of a server) over a time continuum divided by funding stage. Once such items are identified on both a macro level and a micro level, you can select the type of financing with the lowest possible cost of capital and with the most favorable funding structural terms at the time of each funding need.

Several conceptual tools can be utilized to compose a winning financial plan. The rate of equity dilution measuring the progression of equity dilution enables management to maximize ROI through the minimizing of equity dilution. The ACRE chart assists entrepreneurs in contrasting multiple financing options to secure funds at the best available terms. CCR evaluations provide a means for management to remain vigilantly aware of important nonfinancial considerations throughout their fundraising efforts and to maintain effective control of the financial decision-making process.

These various conceptual tools provide the means to compose a financial plan that progresses on a time stream throughout the successive fundraising stages. Such progression is two-tiered. At the macro level, fundraising activities are planned to successfully fulfill company objectives. Financial decisions made to reach operational milestones are done at the micro level. This two-tiered progression is necessary to illustrate the relationship between the simultaneous activities that occur on both levels.

Once you have a polished financial plan to go along with your business plan and acquired KYI knowledge, it is time to determine which prospective investors to present to and when. Once you have identified the appropriate prospective investors to approach and when to approach them it is time to prepare the different types of funding presentations which will be the topic of the Chapter 5.

CHAPTER **5**

Successful Fundraising

You must determine who, when, and how many prospective investors to approach in an informed manner. You must prepare and perform funding presentations professionally, clearly, in accordance with knowing your investor (KYI) objectives, and with a strategic perspective. A variety of prospectus documents and types of funding presentations are required and certain actions and analysis must be performed following each presentation. Your funding presentation to prospective investors makes an impression that will affect their perception of you as a future business partner. This perception is critically important not just in securing funds from them but in their expectations as a stakeholder afterward.

The chapter begins with a discussion on planning funding presentations by asking who and when to make a funding presentation too. A descriptive listing of the different types of prospectus documents and the significance of each follows. Then the different types of funding presentations are presented, with an examination of the content, customization, and performance of formal presentations before we identify postpresentation actions to be pursued.

Planning Funding Presentations

Devise a simple plan for soliciting funding to answer three questions:

1. Who are the prospective investors to be approached?
2. When should I approach them?
3. How many should I approach at once?

Answer the first question based on the fundraising stage you are currently in, the investment criteria of identifiable potential investors, and your determination of whether money from each investor prospect would be good or bad. If you are looking for seed funding, as mentioned in Chapter 1, angel investors and incubator programs may be your best shot. The management know-how and relationships with possible underwriters offered by a private equity firm would be ideal for a company preparing for a last funding round before an exit. Consider the investment criteria of prospective investors you have identified as well. If you are a social network site and the investment criteria of investor prospects state that they exclusively invest in biotech ventures, there is little reason to prepare a presentation to them. Say you have identified eight venture capitalists (VCs) that are available and possibly interested in offering series A funding. If three of them have a track record of closing lucrative exits of companies similar to yours, and references from successfully exited companies overflow with superlatives on all the nonfinancial assistance those VCs provided, those VCs are to be considered a potential good money sources and deserve a place on your short list. Constructing and utilizing an ACRE (availability, cost, risk, and effect) chart concurrent with conducting command and control rating (CCR) evaluations, as advised in Chapter 4, are excellent ways to establish a short list of prospective investors to present to.

Consider the following factors in determining when to approach prospects on your short list:

- You must secure the required funding for a given development stage before commencing work in that development stage.
- You also need sufficient traction to justify the amounts and terms you are currently soliciting for.
- Conducting a funding presentation soon after favorable industry or market news has been announced is advantageous. You must solicit for funding well before the actual need to receive the funds. Many times entrepreneurial venture management teams mistakenly believe that a prospective investor will respond to a funding presentation shortly thereafter; they also assume that after a successful presentation, the money will start to flow immediately. Both beliefs and assumptions are usually not valid. Prospective investors may take a long length of time to respond before responding. If the response is "yes," it may be some time before funds actually reach your bank accounts.

Approach as many prospective investors on your short list as possible, given these considerations:

- The amount of time you can allocate to effectively perform the necessary follow-up correspondence, which is discussed later in this chapter.

- Your ability to manage the multiple prospective investors you have presented too. Prospective investors may be hesitant in entering bidding wars with other prospective investors. If different funding terms have been offered to different prospective investors, the situation can become problematic. Offering different funding terms may be justifiable, given the nonfinancial considerations of selecting a future business partner. You may offer a source of better money more attractive terms. Just be prepared to offer a satisfactory explanation to any prospective investor who may raise objections.

Before you conduct a funding presentation to prospective investors on your short list, you must compose and distribute effective prospectus materials.

Prospectus Materials

Prospectus materials include any documents distributed to prospective investors for marketing or informational purposes. There exist several types of prospectus documents, which illustrate different aspects or functions of the business at various levels of detail. They include the executive summary, business plan, funding proposal, shareholder letter, technology brief, demonstration (demo) in some form, market trends and research report, and others. Each prospectus document is written for a specific purpose and composed and distributed with strategic intent as we will now explore.

Executive Summary

The executive summary is the initial and most distributed prospectus document. Its purpose is to solicit more interest and a request for either more information (i.e., business plan) or a presentation. Indeed, often prospective investors do not want to go through the lengthy details of a business plan in their initial review of the business. This document is aimed not only at prospective investors but at anyone needing a brief overview of your venture, such as potential strategic partners and government regulatory authorities. See Chapter 3 for the organization and content of the executive summary.

Business Plan

The business plan is the most recognized and most important of all documents that you present to prospective investors. Most prospective investors who express strong interest will request a business plan. As we examined in Chapter 3, you cover every aspect of your business in the business plan, and it should provide answers to every expected question from prospective investors.

Both the executive summary and business plan provide a holistic view of your business to answer the most basic questions and generate more specific questions. The remaining prospectus documents answer specific questions in a more detailed manner. They are distributed on request or when you determine that the seriousness of a prospective investor's interest or need to know warrants such documents.

Funding Proposal

The funding proposal is a brief (usually one or two pages) formal presentation of the actual investment deal you are offering to prospective investors. This is not to be confused with the funding proposal, which represents the formal funding offer from interested investors once negotiations have been concluded successfully. Generally you should draft funding proposals when you are soliciting multiple prospective investors of different types and levels of goodness. The content includes these items:

- The total amount of funding being solicited.
- The purpose for such funding. Basically what the funds will be used for. Is it to fund a commercial launch of a product, research and development, or something else?
- The funding terms. For a debt placement, list the term and interest rate; for an equity placement, list the price per share and any other material terms.
- Capital structure illustration.
- Postfunding valuation calculation.

See Appendix B, a sample funding proposal, at end of book.

Often many entrepreneurs insert a briefer version of a funding proposal at the end of their business plan. I prefer to have a more detailed and separate funding proposal for several reasons:

- Once an investor or group of investors has reviewed the business plan and feel ready to make an investment decision based on the funding terms, examining the shorter funding proposal it is less cumbersome. If they are prepared to consider just the funding terms, help them maintain their focus.
- You can insert and display a revision to the funding terms more easily in a two- or three-page funding proposal than in a 30-page business plan.
- The business plan may be distributed to other parties besides prospective investors. A strategic partner or potential vendor does not need to know the details of your fundraising activities. A widely distributed business plan can get in the hands of competitors as well. Therefore,

send funding proposals only to those prospective investors who are seriously considering an investment.

Private Placement Memorandum

The private placement memorandum (PPM) is a much more comprehensive funding proposal required when offering it to a select group of "qualified" private investors and specific terms need to be set forth pursuant to some form of government regulatory compliance. In the United States, private placements are often composed in accordance with Regulation D rules to permit the offering without meeting the formal registration requirements of the Securities and Exchange Commission (SEC). The PPM (or offering) is the most common formal type of funding proposal. It is composed of specific information and constructed in a format pursuant to the proper public disclosure requirements enforced by government regulatory authorities, such as the SEC in the United States. In addition to the funding proposal terms listed earlier and much of the information presented in your business plan, you will need to disclose the mechanics of dilution as well.

Whenever you sell additional equity in your company, the shares of both existing and the new investors are being diluted. Dilution is the decrease in the percentage equity interest of each shareholder upon an increase in the number of outstanding shares of the company. When investors purchase equity in your company, an immediate dilution of their percentage equity interest occurs because the number of shares they purchase immediately increases the number of outstanding shares, thereby representing a lower percentage equity interest than if they had held the same number of shares before such equity purchase. The equity interest before new equity purchase is referred to as preoffering equity interest. The period following a new equity purchase is referred to as postoffering. New investors are most interested in their postoffering equity interest. In the PPM, you must disclose the nature of such immediate dilution for any new subscriber (purchaser) of your equity placement.

Here is an example of a typical immediate dilution clause included in a PPM:

> Assuming full subscription of this Offering, the total number of outstanding shares would increase to two million (2,000,000). The fully subscribed 200,000 Common Shares represented a preoffering equity interest of 11.1% in XYZ, Inc. The same 200,000 subscribed Common Shares represented an immediate postoffering equity interest of 10.00% in XYZ, Inc. Thereby an immediate dilution of 1.1% of equity interest has occurred upon the subscribed Common Shares as a result of a full subscription of this Private Placement.

Two types of documents typically are distributed with the PPM to remain compliant with governmental regulations: a subscriber questionnaire and a subscription agreement. Prospective investors complete the subscriber questionnaire to demonstrate their qualification to make such a risky investment in terms of their risk tolerance, financial ability, and satisfactorily meeting the disclosure requirements of the relevant regulatory authorities. Prospective investors must sign and return the subscription agreement to acknowledge that they have fully reviewed the offering terms and are willing to accept the risks in partaking of such an investment. These formal documents are considered confidential and should be distributed only to qualified investors who have expressed a serious interest in investing.

When you distribute a PPM, you may not have to distribute a business plan with it, as the PPM incorporates information found in the business plan. The additional information included in the PPM is material that would need to be disclosed later in the due diligence stage of negotiations; thus, it serves to shorten and lessen the time and amount of work required at the beginning of negotiations.

Shareholder Letter

A shareholder letter typically is distributed to current shareholders of the business. It shares recent developments and the future vision and goals of the management team. It is an excellent way to briefly showcase recent positive developments (i.e., increased traction, favorable market trends, etc.).

If it is to be distributed to current shareholders, how can it be considered a prospectus document? Although it is not originally intended to serve as a prospectus document, it may be a good idea to use it as such.

Why? Shareholder letters are:

- *A convenient way to demonstrate positive developments for your business both internally and externally.* Hiring a valuable new member to the management team, discussing how a new market trend is a source of optimism, entering into strategic partnership, permitting a glimmer of your effective decision-making process and rationale are all things associated with the success traits discussed in Chapter 2 that prospective investors look for. Remember your KYI objectives!
- *Current.* Prospective investors like to believe they are receiving the most updated information.
- *Good advertising.* The letters demonstrate how people can expect to be treated once they become shareholders. You are displaying a professional level of transparency that will be perceived favorably.

The shareholder letter is most effective when it is distributed to prospective investors who already have analyzed your business and are waiting for your next planned funding round. It is an excellent way to maintain a positive vibe and forward momentum among prospective investors who, for whatever reason, are awaiting a later funding round to invest. A private equity firm with strict investment criteria to only invest in a later series B funding round is an excellent example of a prospective investor that wishes to "stay in the loop" despite the fact that your venture is in a stage too early for them to invest.

Technology Brief

A technology brief is a document that provides a more detailed explanation of how your innovative products or services work. You do not want to give away any trade secrets or other proprietary information, but you do want to give sufficient information to validate that your innovation(s) actually work and demonstrate the use of your advanced technologies and processes. Prospective good investors who know your space will more likely ask for such information. They would be familiar enough with the relevant innovations to enjoy reading such a brief. Give them the light reading they want.

The technology brief, however, is not composed with enjoyment in mind. It is written to comply with the requirements of technical due diligence that are anticipated with an innovative use of technologies and processes and the interest of serious investors.

Demonstrations

Some prospective investors may want to be shown how your technology works but would not consider your technology brief light reading. For these disadvantaged souls, you can offer a demonstration of how the product or service works. This can be an in-person physical demonstration or take the form of a video, DVD/CD, or online presentation. A demo represents the most effective and welcoming prospectus tool vis-à-vis prospective investors and clients. Seeing is believing!

Market Trends and Research Report

The market trends and research report is a comprehensive and in-depth analysis of the dynamics of the defined target market, including its size, the different market segments, demographics, metrics, market participants, distribution channels, competitive analysis, and regulatory environments. In the marketing plan section of your business plan, you presented a more basic market analysis highlighting just the main points and not fully conveying the exhaustive efforts your team devoted to market research. This is why you may have to answer a number of questions after distributing the business plan:

Have you done the necessary market research?
What are your marketing options?
Do you have contingency plans for the occurrence of XYZ?
Why do you think you can successfully compete in this market, given certain circumstances?

Your market trends and research report will answer these questions and exhibit your thorough understanding of the target market. After reading it, prospective investors should have confidence that you fully understand and appreciate what you are getting into. This report is an opportunity to convey your current or prospective market positioning in a favorable light, given documented market conditions and trends. The report serves as further evidence that your innovations have commercial viability and the chances of becoming a market player are very real. This report should also showcase the value of the traction you have and the strategic partners you work with.

Other Miscellaneous Prospectus Materials

To demonstrate traction and answer the inevitable questions regarding expected or actual customer feedback and market response to your innovative product or service, compile these prospectus materials for distribution:

- Alpha and beta testing results
- Customer survey results and testimonials
- Favorable public announcements, news articles, blog commentaries, and recognitions

Distribution of Prospectus Documents

You must manage the distribution of prospectus materials with strategic considerations as well. Depending on what the prospective investor demands or is expected to demand, you may present prospectus documents individually or in packages. In my experience, prospective investors seldom ask to see everything (too much to digest) and they seldom ask to see the same things. There are many good reasons why prospectus documents are composed with the expectation that they will be presented individually. Some of these reasons are listed next.

- From your initial impressions, initial feedback, and KYI research, you can determine what prospective documents to deliver. It is important to gauge the level and type of interest upon your first encounters with investor prospects. Obviously, a prospective investor with intimate knowledge of your space may enjoy your technology brief while someone like me may not be able to decipher it. A little KYI intelligence collection through research and inquiries may indicate prospects' primary interests as well.

- The situation may dictate what to deliver. You may send only an executive summary if a prospective investor is a referral that you have not spoken with or met. Perhaps you do not send a funding proposal until you are confident that serious interest exists. Perhaps a prospective investor received the full suite of prospectus materials a long time ago and just wants to be updated. In this situation, send only updated prospectus materials, such as a shareholder letter. You can ask if the prospect would like any other updates as well, saying, "If you wish, we would like to share some positive developments since you last took a look at our investment opportunity."
- In the event the prospective investor intends to redistribute, a prospective investor may request that some information on just the technology behind your innovation be forwarded to his information technology team for review or to a third party for technical due diligence. In the latter case, sending only a technology brief is sufficient.
- If prospective investors have a specific line of questions or only requests specific documents, send only the relevant or requested prospectus document. Assuming you know more than they do about what they need is risky. Do not inundate prospective investors with too much information, much of which may already have been received or would be deemed irrelevant. By having already prepared individual prospectus documents tailored to answer specific and expected questions on your business or product, you look very organized and competent by delivering a well-prepared response to specific inquiries in a timely manner.

Different Types of Presentations

We hope that the distribution of your prospectus materials has proved effective and you now have presentation opportunities. Presenting in person is the long-awaited opportunity to differentiate your venture from others and to place a face and personality to your business. Different situations call for different presentations. Therefore, you must prepare three different types of presentations of varied scope and duration: the elevator pitch, the lobby or PowerPoint pitch, and the more formal conference room pitch.

Elevator Pitch

The elevator pitch is the shortest of the three types of presentations. It is labeled so named because it is used in situations in which you have no more than 30 seconds to conduct your pitch. Thirty seconds is the approximate duration of an elevator ride and also how long you may have the attention of a prospective investor in a chance encounter, such as a spontaneous meeting at a conference. In this short time span, you only have time to present your business card, act professionally, exhibit a controlled passion for your business, and appeal to the KYI #1 senses of the prospective investor. To secure a second encounter, the prospective investor needs to recognize your venture as a unique moneymaking business opportunity. Do not waste your time and theirs by focusing on the coolness, complexity, or world-saving features of your innovative product. We cautioned about such talk in Chapter 2. Instead, focus on the problem/solution dynamic, value proposition, and how you and all the shareholders (i.e., possibly this investor) will become market players. Establish a brand recognition whereby your venture is associated with a valuable service or role. Justify why the prospect had to listen while stuck on the proverbial elevator with you.

An example of an effective elevator pitch follows:

We have developed groundbreaking technologies that will empower medical professionals and international health officials by bringing real-time collaboration and enhanced imaging and diagnostics to a targeted base of medical facilities and by leveraging that base will expand into comparable markets. Until now, medical doctors have not been able to perform surgical procedures or offer classroom instruction and interact remotely in front of their peers or students in real time. We are the first to resolve the set of technological issues previously preventing such a possibility. Global demand for such real-time interactive medical video conferencing is trending up. Predicting this trend, we have developed a XYZ prototype that allows live interactions among medical professionals, public health officials, and their peers. XYZ is envisioned as a high-end global videoconferencing system that will disrupt traditional ways of conducting medical procedures and instruction. We will become synonymous with online medical video conferencing.

You must practice the elevator pitch over and over to commit it to memory. There is usually no time to rehearse an elevator pitch just prior to the chance encounter.

Lobby (PowerPoint) Pitch

The lobby or PowerPoint pitch is the audio-visual version of your executive summary. It typically lasts five to ten minutes and is utilized in numerous circumstances when you have the attention of a prospective investor for about that length of time. Unlike the spontaneous elevator pitch, often PowerPoint pitches are scheduled to fit into a prospective investor's tight schedule or a situation when you attract the interest of a prospective investor while conversing in a public space waiting area, such as a hotel lobby or airport terminal. Another likely scenario in which to use a PowerPoint pitch is when you are presenting to a panel of judges at a conference sponsoring a pitch event or competition. Typically you are allotted only five to six minutes to make your pitch.

The content of a PowerPoint pitch is basically the same content presented in your executive summary. There is not enough time to go into elaborate detail regarding the different facets of the business. However, you must present comprehensive coverage of your business. The primary objective and challenge in this type of presentation is to demonstrate the strength of your planning and convince the audience that you know what is required and have the ability to execute it effectively. The most common and lethal questions from pitch judges are these:

So how are you going to reach and attract customers?
What is your go-to-market strategy?
Why would a customer purchase your product when there are so many alternatives?
What are the barriers to entry that you or a potential competitor has to overcome?

Just as an effective elevator pitch successfully presents your venture as potentially a moneymaking business opportunity, an effective PowerPoint pitch illustrates how your venture will be a moneymaking business opportunity. Proving your value proposition and commercial viability are key considerations when constructing a PowerPoint presentation.

Arm your laptop with such a PowerPoint presentation and be prepared to draw at all times. Frequent practice of your PowerPoint pitch is definitely advisable both to make the best impression and to master the timing.

Conference Room Pitch (Formal Presentation)

The conference room pitch is the audio-visual version of your business plan. The duration of this formal presentation is usually 20 to 30 minutes.

The typical audience is a group of angel investors or a committee of an institutional investor where at least one participant has served as the point of contact. This contact person likely has already received your elevator and/or PowerPoint pitch, distributed and made his or her own personal pitch internally on your behalf, and has arranged this formal presentation for a more comprehensive and serious consideration of your business opportunity by the whole investment group or decision-making team. Unlike the previous two presentation types, you usually have ample time to prepare a customized conference room pitch and the audience has had the opportunity to review some or all of your prospectus documents. Consequently, you should expect more informed questions following the presentation. The primary challenge in this type of presentation is to demonstrate the efficient organization and smooth functioning of the business in a comprehensive and compelling manner while offering sufficient detail to answer specific questions. More advanced questions regarding operations, competitiveness, and strategy that may arise during or after a conference room pitch include these:

How are you going to scale your product?
Why do you think you can compete against XYZ company?
Will partnering with ABC company limit your exit opportunity options?

Next we discuss in greater detail how to effectively craft, conduct, and conclude a formal presentation in the next three sections: content, customization, and performance. The chapter concludes with a section dedicated to postpresentation activities.

Formal Presentation Content

The content included in the conference room pitch is basically the same content and level of detail presented in the business plan. The key to crafting a successful conference room pitch is to present your business opportunity in a holistic manner, including every material facet of your venture and tying them all together. Failing to address an important aspect of your business or the targeted market may be deemed as incompetent, unimaginative, shortsighted, or unnecessary risk taking on your part. The questions you field at the end of the presentation should clarify or explain in more detail some item mentioned in your presentation, not ask about relevant items or issues that your team did not address previously. Because many of the components of your business have a price tag attached to it, it is important to demonstrate how each component is interrelated and justified as well.

Place special emphasis on your KYI strong points. If your innovation is truly groundbreaking and disruptive, illustrate how this is so in no uncertain terms. If you consider the superiority of your marketing plan as giving you a decisive competitive edge, do not hesitate to fully depict how this will prove true. If the value proposition is your strongest card, place it on the table. If you believe prospective investors will be heartened by the strategic partners you work with, highlight the wonderful and productive working relationship(s) you have with them. Do not sell yourself short!

Prospective investors want to believe they are being presented with the most updated information. Include in your formal presentation a recent positive development associated with your business, technology, or target market. An example is a brief description of a recently reported growth number related to your target market, a new and prominent strategic partner, successful completion of a developmental goal, or a new application for your innovative product or service that has been publicly revealed.

Concluding the presentation with a summary is an effective means to provide clarity, denote interrelationships (i.e., tying everything together), and leave an enduring impression.

Customization of Formal Presentation

Customize the presentation to appeal to the identified needs and desires of the audience.

Knowing the exact investor type you are to present to offers an excellent opportunity to customize. If you are presenting to a panel of officers at a public funding agency, highlight in your presentation a positive correlation between the promotion and use of your innovation and the fulfillment of their particular KPIs. If you are presenting to a panel of officers representing an institutional investor, at a minimum you must demonstrate that your business venture meets their stated investment criteria. Professional investors have numerous other investments competing for their attention. It is critical that you not only demonstrate that you fulfill their investment criteria but that your business is in their space, offers comparatively higher returns, and has low relative risk. Remember your KYIs. Emphasize any comparative advantages you may have over other investment opportunities that prospective investors may be considering. Most investors, especially institutional investment houses, prefer to invest in companies that may need the nonfinancial value-added services they offer. Another reason to show how you fit in their space is the added assurance they may feel in investing in a business that is or will be operating in a familiar market in which they have in-house expertise in, follow, and have extensive contacts.

Also craft this presentation to answer any questions you may anticipate from the audience, who may already have familiarized themselves with your venture either through direct communications with you (i.e., prospectus document review) or some form of prepresentation research they elected to conduct themselves. For example, include any items you wish you could have had more time to address or elaborate on in your PowerPoint pitch.

Be sure to answer any questions or concerns that your contact person might have shared with you.

Formal Presentation Performance

Presenting your investment opportunity to prospective investors in person offers certain advantages, and you can follow several practices to improve the effectiveness of your presentation.

The primary objective of conducting the presentation is to utilize the audio and visual features of this more personal presentation to convey the same information included in your business plan in a clearer, unforgettable, and illustrative manner. A text-based business plan is often inadequate to convey interrelationships among the various facets of a business. An oral presentation supported with visual illustrations is much more effective in conveying these interrelationships clearly and concisely. For example, a chart comparing the features of your product to the features of competitive products may be an impressive way to show your value proposition. An illustration depicting the financial transaction flows among your business, customers, and strategic partners is much easier for a prospective investor to decipher than a description in mere text. Live demonstrations are the best way to convey how your innovation works and why everyone will want to purchase, subscribe, or otherwise utilize it. The saying "A picture is worth a thousand words" is very true.

There are many ways to improve the probability of a winning presentation. Employ these practices:

- *Speak in layman's terms.* In a formal presentation, it is more important to achieve clarity and understanding over wowing them and technological validation. You no longer need to wow them or give an in-depth symposium on the technological feats associated with your innovation. If they were not already wowed, you would not have the opportunity to give them a formal presentation to begin with. Anyway, technical due diligence may be performed at a later time. Additionally, many finance types may not fully comprehend geek speak (enthusiastically talking in highly technical terms at hyper speed). A good way to practice delivering your presentation in layman's terms is to test with someone nontechnical and solicit feedback. This feedback will help you make the necessary revisions.
- *Project confidence and passion.* "We are excited to present this great investment opportunity to you." Place your passion on the business opportunity, not merely the innovation you created. I like to share this saying with my clients: "Have passion for your innovation at work and show passion for your business outside of work." Which of the next expressions would a prospective investor want to hear?

- The users of our new product will find its innovative features cool and interesting.

or

- We expect users of our new product to be more than willing to pay a premium for the new and enabling features because . . .

A further way to project passion and keep energy levels high enough to maintain the attention of the audience during a longer formal presentation is to be animated in, of course, a dignified manner.

Projecting confidence is extremely important as well. Showing any kind of weakness or desperation will likely doom your presentation.

- *Project trustworthiness and transparency.* Maintain eye contact with your audience. This will send a message that you are speaking truthfully and have nothing to hide. Demonstrate how you intend to share your progress with stakeholders both currently and in the future. Including comments on a recent shareholder letter and sharing some of your thought processes and instances of effective decision-making deliberations among management in making some past tactical or strategic decisions are a few effective ways to do this.
- *Note audience reactions.* Whether you take mental note or have an associate take written notes, it is important to pay careful attention to such things as posture, eye movements, and facial expressions to determine physical reactions to the various topics presented. Such telling reactions may reveal presentation discoveries that will prove valuable when preparing your postpresentation follow-ups and potential future negotiations.
- *Be prepared to answer some tough questions on the spot.* At the end of your presentation, allot time for a question and answer session. Earlier audience members had the opportunity to review your prospectus documents; may have heard one of your shorter pitches; may have conducted their own pre-presentation research; and now have just heard your comprehensive formal presentation. Expect and be thoroughly prepared for some very informed questioning. This is a good thing. The more informed their questions, the more effective was your presentation. Now is the time to provide definitive answers to their questions. You may also want to provide unsolicited answers to any blatantly obvious presentation discoveries you may have identified via your note taking on audience reactions.

In sum, the way to grab prospective investors is not to impress but to hit their sweet spots and demonstrate command of both your venture and your market.

Postpresentation Actions

After conducting a formal presentation, you must take some necessary actions, such as follow-up correspondence. If a contact person arranged the presentation it is proper etiquette to direct such correspondence exclusively to that contact person in the event the formal presentation was arranged by one.

Thanking them for their time and consideration and offering to answer any further questions, address any issues, or provide additional information is the minimum follow-up with each decision-making individual or group in attendance. Receiving a postpresentation response is very positive. Answer any questions from attendees concisely and in a timely manner. Indifference is usually a bad sign.

You may need to deliver more in-depth responses to any perceived presentation discoveries. However, answering a presentation discovery unsolicited does not show that you have much confidence in the presentation you just performed. You will need to determine a way to compel potential investors to request such information or simply provide such information in an unassuming manner. If other additional information is requested, you may have the opportunity to answer a presentation discovery by subtly commingling such information with the requested information. If no additional information is requested, you may have to include it in a nonrevealing fashion in a prospectus document or in a prepared summary of the Q&A session that followed the presentation with the stated intention of sharing with all attendees more detailed answers to the questions raised.

Another beneficial postpresentation action is to make your presentation materials readily available for future reference. An efficient way to do this is to post your presentation materials, such as your PowerPoint presentation, on Slide Share and refer members of your presentation audience to the link.

Summary

Before approaching prospective investors, an entrepreneurial venture will need to identify which prospective investors to make their pitch to, when to make such pitches, and how to manage solicitation of funds to multiple prospective investors. Investment criteria, current fundraising stage, and a good money/bad money assessment utilizing ACRE charts and CCR evaluations will be determining factors in answering the first question of whom. The answer to the second question of when is based on timing of favorable market news and your current point on your financial plan time stream. Time constraints that you impose on yourself and your ability to manage multiple prospective investors are considerations in answering the last question.

You must prepare and perform funding presentations with strategic intentions in mind. Typically the distribution of prospectus documents precedes an opportunity to perform an in-person funding presentation. There are two reasons to distribute prospectus materials:

1. *To entice a prospective investor to request further information or a presentation.* The executive summary and business plan/PPM are the two prospectus documents that commonly perform this function.
2. *To provide more detailed answers to specific questions posed.* The market trends and research report and technology brief are excellent examples of prospectus documents that fulfill this need.

There are three different types of funding presentations. Time constraints, degree of detail demanded, and the level of familiarity with the prospective investor are all factors in determining which type of funding presentation to conduct. The elevator pitch is utilized in spontaneous situations to solicit interest in your investment opportunity. Presenting your venture as a unique, potentially high-return investment opportunity is the objective. The lobby or PowerPoint pitch is performed in those brief but planned situations in which prospective investors are expected to be present. The objective is to present more evidence that your venture represents an attractive investment opportunity that warrants further attention and encourages inquiries. The formal conference room pitch allows for sufficient time to make a detailed decisive case for your venture as an investment opportunity that cannot be passed up. The objective is to answer previously generated questions and to generate inquiries associated with making an investment decision.

Once you can convince a prospective investor to commence contemplating an investment decision, you are ready to proceed to the next stage: negotiations.

CHAPTER 6

Becoming a Formidable Negotiator

You have been successful in securing sufficient interest from a prospective investor to engage in negotiations to determine possible terms of funding. A combination of effective prospectus documents and funding presentations and the independent research and inquiries of the prospective investor, now to be the counterparty in negotiations with you, has resulted in the intended outcome. However, the fun has just started. Counterparties are buyers with the intent to purchase your equity at the lowest price for them or lend you funds at the highest cost of capital to you. Simultaneously they will attempt to inject terms that will give them greater control and reduce their perceived risks, often at the expense of the founding partners and other current stakeholders. They are certainly justified to pursue their intentions. You have a strong fiduciary responsibility to negotiate in the best interests of the current shareholders while securing the acceptance of terms from your possibly soon-to-be newest stakeholder and business partner. Negotiating funding terms is both the most challenging and the most critical endeavor for the management team of an entrepreneurial venture. Strict adherence to your well-conceived financial plan will serve as a valuable guide. Accumulation of know your investor (KYI) knowledge discussed in Chapter 2 provides additional support. What remain are your skills as a negotiator. This chapter helps you sharpen those negotiating skills by effectively employing the strategic thinking concepts and utilizing results from the various planning/ analysis tools introduced in previous chapters. Sharing what is to be expected in the negotiating process is another important component of this chapter.

This chapter is organized in four major sections correlated with the four stages of negotiation: prenegotiations, due diligence, actual negotiations, and concluding negotiations. In the prenegotiation phase, we discuss leverage and such things as additional KYI research and negotiating leverage. Next we discuss the sometimes challenging and lengthy due diligence process. Favorable negotiating practices, points of negotiation, and crafting a negotiating plan are the primary subjects of the actual negotiations section. The chapter ends with an examination of when and how to conclude both successful and unsuccessful negotiations.

Prenegotiations

Once prospective investors have expressed their willingness to enter negotiations of funding terms with you, you must commence KYI research and inquiries. You also must identify sources of leverage to establish a position of strength before entering the due diligence stage and subsequently engaging in actual negotiations.

Letter of Intent

Prospective investors will express their willingness to negotiate by submitting a letter of intent (LOI). An LOI is a signed and affirming acknowledgment by the counterparty of its willingness to enter negotiations in good faith to accomplish specified objectives. Common additional components of an LOI are the parameters of such negotiations, clarification of key points, and safeguards in the event negotiations collapse. The LOI typically is nonbinding. However, it may include nondisclosure and act-in-good-faith clauses that usually are deemed binding. The LOI describes any conditions necessary for negotiations to commence and continue. A "no-shop" or "standstill" covenant establishing exclusivity in negotiations is a very common prerequisite condition demanded. Agree to such no-shop provisions only for a limited duration. A long or indefinite no-shop term effectively locks you into having to execute a deal with this particular counterparty, dramatically weakening your negotiating position. Prospective investors may insist on exclusivity because they do not want to participate in a bidding war. However, if they are competing with other prospective investors, they will need to be aware of this and you will not be able to agree to exclusivity. As we discuss shortly, having competing investors is a source of leverage for you. However, you must wield such leverage prudently so as to not ward off prospective investors.

Nondisclosure Agreement

If necessary, a nondisclosure agreement (NDA) is consummated shortly after the LOI. An NDA or confidentiality agreement is a legal contract between two parties specifying what information is considered confidential and not to be shared with third parties. It may also be more detailed, outlining permitted use of such confidential knowledge. Your entrepreneurial venture should have a standard NDA drafted to distribute to prospective investors before you disclose any information to be kept in confidence. Institutional investors may not be willing to execute an NDA because it could preclude them from conducting business with current or future funding candidates in their specialized industry or market space. However, as a professional investment firm with a public image to uphold, generally they can be relied on to maintain confidentiality. You may wish to include a confidentiality clause in any other legal instrument you sign with them, such as an LOI. Testing for integrity and reliability should be part of your prenegotiation KYI research, to which we turn now.

KYI Research and Inquiries

You must conduct serious independent research and inquiries on the backgrounds, interests, motivations, past investments, and relationships of each prospective investor you wish to engage in negotiations with. Do they know the space? Are they more concerned with mitigating risk, securing higher returns, or are strategic interests foremost on their minds? Do they have a successful investing track record? Have the companies they invested in exited successfully? How is it to work with them as a business partner, and what other benefits can they offer (i.e., industry contacts, management expertise, etc.)? Will they be able to participate in future funding rounds? What is their reputation in the financial community, particularly if they are to serve as a lead investor? These questions and any other questions derived from the KYI #4 precepts introduced in Chapter 2 must be answered.

How do you direct such research and inquiries?

Most institutional investors have Websites that provide useful information, such as their investment criteria and past clients. As we discussed earlier, the stated investment criteria of prospective investors not only state their minimum requirements but also give a glimpse into the type of business partner they may be by revealing their expectations and motivations. Question their past clients. You can directly contact them or their current business partners and ask how the investors are as business partners and what was involved in the process to secure their funds. Do this for all types of investors, regardless of whether they have a Website for you to review. Institutional investors that are publicly traded will have additional information, such as financial statements, available for public review that can indicate their financial health. Often such public companies have investor or public relations offices that you can contact for further information. Frequently they list contact information for prospective investors of their investment funds. Contact them and discover what they advertise or promise to their prospective investors. This information can reveal their commitments to investors, which indicates what they can or cannot offer you. Other sources of reference include investment bankers, accountants, lawyers, and any other entities having professional relationships with the counterparty.

Demonstrating in-depth knowledge of their business will instill a heightened sense of confidence in the competence of your management team and establish reasonable expectations in what is and is not negotiable before entering negotiations. Most important, it is a vital means to collect points of leverage that you can use throughout the negotiating process to secure the best terms.

Leverage

Ensure you have leverage in some form. Your prenegotiation research and inquiries along with your earlier KYI focus should assist you in identifying sources of leverage and how to wield them effectively.

Earlier we defined leverage as the ability to exert influence beyond what should be expected, given the amount of financial investment made. Leverage increases the perceived value of your business, which is what you want to impress on the counterparty before and during negotiations. In this chapter, we need to expand this definition to include the various sources of leverage.

Sources of Leverage

Next are examples of leverage sources that can be utilized to strengthen your negotiating position:

- *Traction.* As we discussed in Chapter 2, traction is any public recognition, established market positioning, regulatory licensing/designation, or protected intellectual property (IP) indicating strong prospects for success. Consider all forms of traction as ammunition to be dispensed at every appropriate opportunity. Each negotiating stage for investment funding provides ideal opportunities to portray your traction. Negotiations represent a give-and-take process. Traction permits you to justify the higher-multiple-based valuation being presented. It enables you to field strong counterarguments against counterparty attempts to lower your valuation by identifying weaknesses in your product/service, business model, management, and/or planning.
- *Track record.* If you can show that you have been consistently successful in meeting past milestones and expectations, the extra credibility to be garnered will increase your negotiating leverage.

- *Possession of risk mitigation factors (RMFs)*. Having RMFs will assist you in demonstrating a lower assumption of risk for counterparty, thereby increasing your leverage. The scenario we used as a basis for our sample ACRE (availability, cost, risk, and effect) chart in Chapter 4 is a case in point. Admission into an incubator program covers much of the burn rate so important to a prospective investor. The ability to guarantee a percentage of the negotiated funding also provides negotiating leverage.

You can identify leverage sources by collecting superior intelligence during effective prenegotiation research and inquiries on the target market and counterparty.

- *Ability to fulfill a prize objective of the counterparty*. If you are lucky, you may be sitting across the negotiating table from a strategic investor with strategic intentions. You may be the vehicle through which the investor enters a desired marketplace, secures a competitive advantage, or leverages your technology. It is safe to say that you will command more leverage on a strategic investor than you would on an investor primarily interested in exceptional financial returns. The greater leverage attained vis-à-vis a strategic investor is why a higher valuation (higher multiple on your earnings) can be secured. Your venture is much more valuable to a strategic investor because strategic value is much more valuable than just financial returns. Consequently a strategic investor is willing to pay more for your company than other investors although all investors are presented with the same financial projections.
- *Relative leverage of counterparty*. Leverage is two way. Does the counterparty have any benefits for you other than investment funds? If not, the advantage goes to you. If they have significant nonfinancial benefits to offer and the counterparty realizes this, it may possess a relative leverage advantage that can be brought to bear in negotiations to your detriment. Another source of leverage that counterparties possess is any legally or operationally dependent relationship you may have previously consummated with those counterparties. In Chapter 2, we cautioned against entering legal agreements that tie you in too tightly with a strategic investor (partner). There is an interesting dilemma regarding relative leverage: The more attractive a counterparty is as a business partner, the greater its relative leverage vis-à-vis with you in negotiations.
- *Existence of competitive investment groups*. Although prospective investors may avoid entering a bidding war, you can follow a prudent approach to ensure that you can apply leverage in a nonthreatening manner. Do this by making the counterparty aware that there are competing prospective investors however, wield the leverage to direct

attention on terms other than price, leading counterparties to believe that they hold a distinct advantage vis-à-vis other investment groups due to their more advanced stage in the negotiating process or in other nonfinancial matters (i.e.,"better money"). This may alleviate their fears of entering into a bidding war. Furthermore, if you have multiple investor suitors, the ones offering fewer nonfinancial benefits should expect less favorable terms from you. Some investment groups may be interested in forming a syndicate of investors if they are unwilling to invest the total amount of necessary funding themselves. Maybe they are looking for a co-investor(s) that offer complementary nonfinancial benefits and/or are willing-to share in the investment risk as well. Discovering such desires among prospective investors will certainly permit greater leverage opportunities for you. However, this could prove to be a double-edged sword if multiple investment groups effectively establish a negotiating front that, due to its size and strong co-operation can wield greater negotiating leverage vis-a-vis your negotiating team.

- *Relative sense of urgency.* You can control the pace of negotiations and secure more favorable terms any time the counterparty feels pressure to conclude negotiations. When counterparties are aware that other prospective investor counterparties are involved, injecting a sense of urgency may accelerate negotiations to your advantage. The opposite also holds true. If you have a greater sense of urgency to conclude negotiations, counterparties may use it to your disadvantage. A common tactic for prospective investors is to slow down the negotiating process if they sense that you are desperate. The aim of such negotiation brinksmanship is to compel the other party to accept highly unfavorable terms or face far worse consequences if negotiations are delayed. This is a reason why the best time to secure investment funds is when you do not have a desperate need for them and why you must secure sufficient funds for the upcoming development stage *before* the stage begins. Should you really desperately need the funds, you must exert considerable self-control to conceal such desperation.

- *Ability to dictate the pace of negotiations.* I cannot stress the importance of this factor. The side that holds the time advantage possesses the initiative in the negotiating process. Just as a warring army with the initiative is able to select the most favorable battlefield conditions, a negotiating party with a time advantage can select the most favorable negotiating conditions.

Our primary mission in the prenegotiation stage is to amass as much leverage as possible. The greater your leverage vis-à-vis the counterparty, the greater the amount of negotiating capital you will be able to expend throughout the entire negotiating process.

Negotiating Capital

Negotiating capital is defined as the perceived relative strength of the negotiating parties that dictates how strong each counterparty believes it can be during the negotiations, with the understanding that negotiating capital wielded is negotiating capital expended. If you think of leverage as ammunition, your negotiating capital is the number of rounds your gun has. First you are going to target your most dangerous opponents (i.e., the highest-priority points of negotiations); you do not deplete your ammunition on a defenseless one (i.e., a reasonable or insignificant demand).

During the remaining negotiating stages, you must attempt to expend your negotiating capital efficiently and with maximum effect.

Due Diligence

There are many definitions of the term "due diligence." For our purposes, "due diligence" is defined as the thorough investigation/inquisition or audit of your business performed by a prospective investor to confirm all material facts in regard to the potential investment being offered. The prospective investor will examine all material facts of your business pertaining to areas such as finances, legal, tax, labor, intellectual property, debt instrument review, composition and relations with existing stakeholders, vendor relations, insurance, regulatory environment, and current market position to determine whether you are a worthy investment opportunity and, if so, in what price range the prospect should negotiate in. A satisfactory conclusion of due diligence analysis needs to occur before the counterparty is ready and willing to engage in actual negotiations with you. Again, the founders of an entrepreneurial venture also need to perform due diligence to strengthen their negotiating position and judge the suitability of the counterparty as a business partner.

Due Diligence Checklist

The counterparty's delivery of a due diligence checklist usually marks the beginning of this negotiating stage. A due diligence checklist is an exhaustive list of questions that must be answered prudently and accurately. The questions are formally written and typically organized by areas of focus.

Due Diligence Response

The more accurate, clear, and detailed your responses, the greater the amount of trust and certainty you will build up with the counterparty.

Consequently, the smoother, more expeditious, and more favorable the negotiations should be. Your responses will also serve as the basis for the forthcoming negotiation of terms.

You are legally responsible for ensuring that the responses to the due diligence inquiries are truthful and accurate. Should the counterparty discover an inaccurate or less-than-candid response to the due diligence inquiry during the actual negotiations, the entire negotiating process may end, or at the very least it will weaken your negotiating position. An inaccurate or untruthful response discovered after a successful conclusion of negotiations may be grounds for the counterparty nullifying or voiding part of or the entire executed funding agreement. We cannot emphasize strongly enough how important it is to uphold the integrity of your company at all times.

If you have not signed an NDA with the counterparty yet, be sure to complete an NDA that at least ensures confidentiality for the terms of negotiation before fulfilling any counterparty due diligence information requests.

Once a counterparty successfully concludes its due diligence analysis, a basis for negotiations has been established and it is time to negotiate funding terms.

Actual Negotiations

Actual negotiations will commence once the counterparty satisfactorily concludes its due diligence and delivers to you a term sheet. Your management will also need to affirm that the counterparty is a suitable business party before actual negotiations can commence.

Term Sheet

A term sheet is a document prepared by a prospective investor that sets forth the key terms of a proposed investment in outline form. It is a nonbinding agreement expressing the counterparty's intentions and conditions under which an investment will be consummated. Actual negotiations may begin based on the preliminary terms found in the term sheet.

Before we examine the various terms to be negotiated, we discuss appropriate negotiating approaches and best negotiating practices/tactics.

Negotiation Approaches

The negotiating approach you should take is dictated by the type of counterparty you are dealing with. You must recognize differences between the outlook of venture capitalists (VCs) and private equity firms. VCs typically are more preoccupied with risk; thus, they focus on issues of control and their standing upon a possible liquidation. VCs expect a much higher return on investment (ROI) due to the assumption of greater risk. Private equity firms will show the greatest interest in actual performance and when an exit can be achieved. Given their varied focuses, VCs act more like debt holders and downside protection is of utmost importance; private equity firms act more like shareholders trying to secure the best position to profit from an anticipated successful exit.

Negotiating with public funding agencies is an entirely different animal requiring a totally different approach. Such agencies would be very pleased if you made a strong case that their specific mandates regarding employment, economic growth, competitiveness, innovation, and social/cultural objectives can be more readily achieved by funding your venture. The risk they associate with an investment in your business is much different from what private investors think of. Private investors see their risk in financial terms; many public funding agency officers, in contrast, perceive their greatest risk in providing funding to you in terms of career advancement. Public officials view wasting public funds on a venture that fails, changes its objectives away from the mandates of the public agency, or takes the money and runs as detrimental to their career prospects. Demonstrating economic sustainability, a high level of commitment to your business objectives that are aligned with agency KPIs, and easily perceivable interdependence with the specific municipality or jurisdiction of the prospective public funding agency is of primary importance in negotiating for public funding. Trying to impress a public officer with grandiose schemes is apt to scare them off because you diminish the likelihood that you can deliver on what you are promising. Often such officials are preoccupied more with failure than with success.

Best Practices and Tactics

The following are negotiations best practices and tactics to be considered:

- *Speak from a position of strength.* It is important to convey leverage and patience in your conduct, both verbal and nonverbal. This does not mean that you should act brash; however, counterparties should perceive these negotiations as an offer of an attractive investment opportunity for them, not a bailout for you. Counterparties will take advantage of any signs of desperation from you. They may decide to harden their position on many negotiating points or put on the squeeze by employing delaying tactics. Neither is favorable to the successful conclusion of negotiations.
- *Have a tempered passion.* You need to maintain and display balance. Counterparties need to be assured that you have every intention of

battling through any challenge to your baby without thinking that your baby and parenting is perfect. Overselling a business proposition is a big turn-off. As we discuss, counterparties always have some legitimate concerns that must be addressed.

- *Negotiate as a team.* It is beneficial to demonstrate team chemistry, complementary skills and experiences, effective communications, and clear lines of authority (accountability). An experienced investor will closely monitor the interactions and dynamics of your team to judge its future effectiveness to execute business objectives and communicate with stakeholders. Often the personal factor is the most important determinant in the counterparties' investment decision .
- *Exhibit strong corporate governance.* Corporate governance is the set of rules, policies, and procedures through which a company is directed, administered, organized, and controlled. Showing that good corporate governance permeates your venture can serve as a powerful source of leverage as it acts to reduce perceived risk and holds promise for greater performance, thus returns. In Chapter 7, we discuss in greater detail the importance of having strong corporate governance.
- *Take notes (listen!).* There may be some revealing negotiating discoveries that you can use to your advantage later in the negotiations. Information is a source of leverage. Sometimes the other side may accidentally show its cards. If a counterparty inadvertently reveals that a negotiating point is more or less important to them, duly note that information and use it to your advantage later in the negotiations. When counterparties see you keeping notes, they are more likely to be more frank. This will keep them more honest. If they want to do all the talking, let them do so, as long as it is not costing you initiative on any particular negotiating position.
- *Maintain a high level of integrity at all times.* Everything discussed must be candid, sincere, and transparent. Being evasive and downplaying past failures will not help you when dealing with seasoned prospective investors. The faster you can win their trust, the faster you can welcome new business partners.
- *Have a vested mentor.* Although this a mentoring book and I hope the experiences and words of wisdom I impart will be of assistance to you, nothing can replace having a real flesh-and-blood mentor by your side in position to benefit from your success. The best mentors are likely to be people who have had real experience on either side of the aisle—former venture capitalists, institutional investment bankers, or successful entrepreneurs. An effective mentor will be able to place the long and sometimes arduous negotiating process in proper perspective and keep you focused, reassured, and patient while projecting optimism. Remember the auto trip analogy from Chapter 4. Having a passenger who has

traveled the same route before and is just as eager to arrive at your shared destination is a great way to avoid bad traffic jams and find shortcuts. Bouncing ideas, tactics, and strategies off someone who has been there and done that can prove invaluable.

■ *Demonstrate open-mindedness.* Respect all questions that counterparties ask. Counterparties will have legitimate concerns that must be addressed. Maintain a certain level of flexibility in management decision making on both strategic and operational levels to show how receptive you are to advice offered by your business partners to be.

■ *Emphasize your skin in the game.* Prove that if someone invests with you, you are sharing the risks together and you can assure a certain level of dedication. Investors want to know that you are fully committed to the venture and turning their investment funds into huge profits. Part-time efforts and divided loyalties among numerous projects will, at the very least, heighten the sense that your venture is a higher risk, thereby swinging negotiating leverage to counterparties' favor. Do not understate or underestimate all the efforts, achievements, and sacrifices your founding team has made.

■ *Prepare for a game of poker.* Never try to impress prospective investors. They are engaged in a high-risk, high-return game similar to poker. It is to be assumed that they are good poker players who will show you poker faces and try to call your bluffs.

Points of Negotiation (Terms)

Stage of Development

Establish understanding of the stage of development with the counterparty. It is imperative that you initially make a strong supporting case that your venture is at the highest stage of development as can reasonably be expected. Do not be shy in asking for the amount of funding you need because you fear asking for too much may scare away investors. Actually, often the more funding you request, the higher the stage of development your company is perceived to be. Other ways to create the perception that your venture is at a higher stage of development is to showcase those points of your business that would place you by definition clearly in that stage. For example, to establish the perception that you are seeking series A, not seed, funding, earmark the use of funds for executing your go-to-market strategy, not additional research. To secure series B, as opposed to series A, funding, state that the funds will be directed toward activities that will increase your sales volume, market share, or profit margins from already established levels. If counterparties believe you are a lower stage of development, it may be difficult to secure sufficient funds at an acceptable valuation. Remember, the earlier the stage of development, the greater the perceived risk and the greater the expected rate of return. A higher expected rate of return will certainly push down the valuation a counterparty considers acceptable.

Valuation

As discussed in Chapter 1, there are many different valuation models for start-up businesses. A strategic investor will offer the highest valuation, followed in descending order by comparison valuation, pro forma–based valuations, and finally asset-based valuation models. It is in your best interest to convince the counterparty to employ the most favorable valuation model. The importance of your KYI research and inquiries becomes very apparent at this stage.

If you consider your counterparty a strategic investor or have discovered some interests or characteristics that would qualify your venture as a strategic investment for the counterparty, you should present the strongest possible case of your strategic value. To make such a strong case to a strategic investor, you will have to submit a compelling argument that accepting a premium multiple over a credible average price–earnings (P–E) multiple of established comparable businesses. You will have to highlight the superior growth prospects and market player potential of your venture. To establish your venture as a strategic investment you will have to demonstrate that you have far more value than other comparable ventures.

To make the case that a valuation should be based on a comparison-based model, not the default pro forma–based model, you will need to show that the funding you are seeking will catapult you to the stage of development of comparable companies. Persuading the counterparty that the investment will allow you to be at least to be a market participant competing on equal footing, if not establish yourself as a market player, may be sufficient to achieve your objective of being valued on comparable terms.

If the counterparty will not budge and is only willing to negotiate on a pro forma–based model, securing the highest multiple is the objective. During negotiations on valuation, focus on the multiple; do not allow negotiations to make significant alterations to your pro forma financial numbers. Although you should not expect counterparties to fully accept your pro forma numbers, they should accept the numbers for the most part; otherwise likely they would not have entered negotiations in the first place. By scaling down your pro forma numbers, you may harm the credibility of your entire business plan, thereby jeopardizing your already established standing as an attractive investment opportunity. Once you start altering your pro forma numbers, counterparties may try to challenge the underlying assumptions and individual components of your business plan. You do not want to open this potentially nasty can of worms in which your entire business plan is dismantled piece by piece. At the very least, you can expect protracted negotiations if pro forma numbers are revisited. Negotiating an arbitrary number, such as a multiple, is the much more preferred course.

A counterparty will attempt to lower the valuation by using these tactics:

- *Insisting on more conservative valuation models.* As discussed, you must stand your ground and fight for a favorable valuation model. The valuation model chosen will have an order of magnitude effect on the valuation ultimately agreed on.
- *Inserting lower inputs preceding the valuation calculation.* Counter-parties can do this in two ways: by seeking downward adjustments in your pro forma numbers or insisting on a lower P–E multiple. Although you do not want to engage in a series of pro forma number revisions, negotiating a multiple requires prudence as the multiple ultimately agreed on for the valuation calculation likely will have a larger effect on valuation than any individual pro forma number revision.
- *Presenting perceived weaknesses and risks of your business.* You must be intimately aware of your own weaknesses and vulnerabilities so you can deliver counterarguments for each perceived one promptly and decisively. It is always good to counterargue a perceived chink in your armor by referring to specific plans to address such vulnerability and how all that is needed is adequate funding (i.e., the counterparty's money) to execute such plans. If you do not mention the investment as part of the solution, counterparties may ask why you have not addressed the issue before, given you awareness of it. For example, say a perceived weakness of your venture is a weak marketing effort thus far due to insufficient funds. An effective counterargument is to state that the investment funds currently sought would provide the resources to execute your strong marketing plans. A counterargument for a noted risk factor is that such risk has been considered and explained in the risk factors section of prospectus materials, has been accounted for in pro forma numbers, and would be mitigated by specific actions to be taken with sufficient funding.
- *Demonstrating their strong relative leverage.* Counterparties may lower the valuation by making the case that they will contribute much value added as a business partner. If they believe or if you lead them to believe that they are in unique position to offer significant value that no other prospective investor can provide, expect them to wield such leverage on you. A case in point was presented in Chapter 2, where entering a dependent relationship with a strategic investor (partner) placed a founder in a relatively weak negotiating position. Prudent advice would be to dispel any such preconceptions or not provide counterparties with such ammunition to use against you. A counterparty must understand that offering comparatively "better" money gives them an advantage over other prospective suitors but not necessarily entitles them to significantly better terms.

Funding Structure

Successfully securing funds to execute your well-thought-out plans does not ensure operational success for the venture or financial success for the founders. The structure of the funding to be delivered determines the degree of control for the managing founders and the relative returns or asset claims of them and later investors upon a successful exit or liquidation. Agreeing to the wrong type of funding structure can handcuff the management team when making crucial decisions, jeopardizing the venture's business success. It is also the number one way founders lose controlling ownership of their company. If funding disproportionally favors the investor, the founders could find themselves in a situation where they do not earn a satisfactory profit upon a successful exit. There are two ways the founders' ROI is diluted. One is equity dilution as commonly understood as a reduction in the founders' ROI due to the reduction in the founders' percentage equity interest. Funding terms such as antidilution, reverse vesting and performance triggers may permit those "protected" or "entitled" shareholders to gain percentage equity interests at the expense of the founders. However there is a second type of dilution I would like to call structural (or "dirty") Dilution. I define structural dilution as the reduction of Founders' ROI that occurs in addition to the dilution of their equity due to a convertible equity security funding. The amount of dilution is determined by calculating the difference between the amount of return the founders were to receive based on their percentage equity interest at exit or liquidation versus the amount of the exit or liquidation proceeds they are entitled to after the structural dilution terms have been applied. The structural dilution terms include liquidation preference, dividends paid on preferred shares and participation preferred rights. Consequently, the structure of the investment is just as important, if not more important, than the financial terms. The next structural issues require serious deliberation among your management team before negotiations commence.

Preferred Shares   Preferred shares are an equity class that has many features that differentiate it from common shares. These features offer both advantages to each party and potential pitfalls. Preferred shares are senior to common shares, are nonvoting, pay out a dividend that can be cumulative, and have a degree of conversion into common shares if designated as participating. Overall, except for perhaps smaller funding deals, it is better to offer a counterparty preferred shares rather than common shares. However, the founders must negotiate carefully to ensure that issuing this class of equity ultimately is beneficial to them. Next we describe each feature of preferred equity and what should be expected in negotiations.

Preferred shares are senior to common shares in the event of liquidation claims on assets. A counterparty may seek the granting of preferred shares primarily due to their seniority over common shares and the desire to secure a shareholder's higher returns upon a successful exit as opposed to being a debt holder.

For founding partners, preferred shares are attractive because they are nonvoting. This preserves the voting rights and, subsequently, a level of control for the founding management.

A counterparty may demand participating preferred shares. Preferred shares with a participation feature can be converted into common shares upon some future contingency, creating the possibility that the counterparty may have voting rights at a later date. Participating preferred shares and other types of convertible securities, such as warrants can complicate the balance sheet and, in future funding rounds, prospective investors may demand additional consideration to allow such convertible securities to remain in effect. Participating preferred shares already have liquidation preference and have the potential to substantially diminish the returns of common shareholders. The participating feature of preferred shares is certainly a point of negotiation worthy of pitching a battle against. If the counterparty insists on participation rights to mitigate its effects the founders can demand that the contingent requirements for conversion be elevated.

Preferred shares typically pay out a dividend as well. The amount of dividend is usually denoted as a percentage of par value or a stated fixed amount. Avoid paying out dividends if possible, as they are a drain on cash flow, the life blood of a high-growth venture. Dividends also reduce the expected ROI and are counter to the notion of maximizing ROI upon exit. However, you can make an exception by issuing preferred stock, which is more favorable to issue than common stock or assuming debt at earlier fundraising stages. If preferred shares are to be issued, any dividends to be paid out must have minimal impact on your venture's cash flow. The two ways to minimize such impact is to keep the dividend yield low and/or to delay accrual and payout of dividends contingent upon sufficient revenue generation.

A counterparty usually insists on cumulative preferred shares. Any dividend payments missed on cumulative preferred shares will be in arrears and to be paid at some later date. It is, of course, equally important to limit the amount of dividends in arrears as they can have a detrimental effect on future cash flows and reduce your attractiveness as an investment opportunity for future prospective investors who either have to assume such obligations or make additional demands as compensation.

Issuing preferred shares, particularly at an earlier stage of development, offers several advantages over assuming debt as preferred shares will be junior to any future debt raise, preferably at later stages of development, thereby not inhibiting such a future debt raise. Preferred equity looks more attractive than debt on the balance sheet when it is time to secure credit from creditors. You derive no benefit by establishing your company as insolvent from the beginning of its existence. A prospective equity investor examining your balance sheet will not like seeing a load of debt and no equity.

In sum, issuing common shares that do not pay out a dividend or enjoy seniority over shares held by other current shareholders is more favorable than granting preferred shares from a cash flow and asset claim perspective. However, issuing preferred shares with relatively low and/or delayed dividend payouts may be more favorable than piling on debt to your balance sheet that will require periodic interest payments and have senior claims to assets. If your primary concern is the level of control, issuing preferred shares may be more favorable than issuing voting common shares.

Liquidation Preference   A liquidation preference grants the counterparty the opportunity to receive monies before other shareholders in the event of liquidation. Counterparties will define the term "liquidation" broadly during the negotiations to include events involving bankruptcy or sale of much, if not a majority, of a company's equity and/or assets. The liquidation preference is usually depicted as a multiple of the counterparties' proposed investment amount. In other words, if a counterparty insists on a liquidation preference of 1X and is proposing a $2 million investment, it would have first claim on the first $2 million of bankruptcy or purchase proceeds. Counterparties may demand a higher multiple if they perceive an investment in your venture is of sufficiently higher risk. Of course, it is worth your efforts to keep such liquidation preference multiples as low as possible for the benefit of the founders and other shareholders.

When a liquidation preference is being negotiated in tandem with participation rights particular caution is warranted. Participating preferred stock will permit the counterparty to claim a percentage of the remaining liquidation proceeds based on percentage of ownership. For example, if its $2 million investment represented a 50 percent equity purchase of your company and an exit sale was consummated for $5 million, a counterparty will have a claim on half of the $3 million remaining proceeds after the liquidation preference has been awarded to it. Thus the counterparty receives $3.5 million of the $5 million exit purchase. This is a devastating combination and a good example of structural dilution. Either negotiate away the participation feature of the preferred equity or give the counterparty the choice of opting for one or the other.

Receiving participating preferred stock in tandem with liquidation preference terms is a means through which venture capitalists, whether intentionally or unintentionally, can earn a disproportionate share of returns upon a successful exit. I have seen this happen in too many cases. This draconian combination warrants strong resistance. It is best fought simply by making the counterparty aware of such injustice rather than expending valuable negotiating capital.

Voting Rights The issuance of common shares entitles share recipients voting rights that can be wielded to affect decision making at all levels of your venture. The issuance of convertible preferred shares or debt can result in the establishment of voting rights as well. The founders will want to maintain as much control of the venture for as long as possible in order to execute their business plans unencumbered. Typical voting rights afforded to common shareholders include amending corporate by-laws, allowance of agreements affecting the majority interest of the company (i.e., merger or acquisition), and election of board directors. Common shareholders also have the right to exercise their voting rights via proxies. Proxy voting rights occur when a particular shareholder is granted the right by other shareholders to vote on their behalf. The use of proxies allows individual shareholders to vote as a block. The possibility of voting by proxy is very important to be aware of; a management team may believe that the counterparty will be only a minority shareholder and thus does not represent an immediate threat to the effective control currently possessed by the founding management. However, a minority shareholder may be able to accumulate sufficient voting rights via proxy to outvote founding management during a shareholder vote.

Counterparties may negotiate for specific voting rights above what is typically granted to shareholders in order to influence specific areas of decision making as well. Examples of specific voting rights that a counterparty may demand include protective provisions requiring that the authorization from a particular shareholder or shareholding group is necessary to permit indebtedness over certain levels, annual budget approval, or the hiring and firing of key officers. Insistence on such provisions may afford you valuable insight into a counterparty's negotiating priorities and concerns. However, such voting rights can have a significant impact on the future operational and strategic decision making of management and must not be overlooked.

Being responsive to shareholders and being aware of the dynamics that exist within your capital structure and how the counterparty would affect such dynamics is paramount to understanding your control position.

Drag-Along Rights Drag-along rights are another example of a specific voting right. These rights can work in two ways. In the event of liquidation or purchase of the venture below the negotiated liquidation preference, shareholders possessing drag-along rights are granted veto power. This veto power represents a reasonable voting right that can be expected as a demand from a counterparty. It is reasonable because it is usually triggered only when such liquidation or sale event occurs at levels below the negotiated liquidation preference. The counterparty can argue that if you, the founders, did not meet performance expectations, you are not entitled to any kind of return. This may sound harsh, but it is probably not worth expending your negotiating capital to block such a clause. Negotiating capital is better spent warding off less reasonable terms or to secure terms that your team covets.

On the flip side, drag-along rights may also compel shareholders to sell their shares when a specified group (i.e., management) is ready and willing to sell their shares upon the opportunity for a successful exit. This situation can prove favorable to the founders and other shareholders as this prevents one or a few holdouts from blocking a potentially lucrative exit. Unfortunately, there is always the possibility that self-serving shareholders may decide to hold out to extort more favorable terms or demands for themselves. Drag-along rights may prove dangerous to the majority of shareholders if a small group or single individual with absolute authority to negotiate equity sale terms is in the position to accept a sweet personal deal on the side in return for a low price per share sales price.

Board Membership   A more direct means for counterparties to affect the venture's decision-making process is to insist on including a member or members of their investment group on your board of directors. You should reasonably expect such demand for any equity purchase of 20 percent or more of your company. Counterparties likely will insist that the number of board members granted to them is at least proportional to the amount of equity interest they are to purchase. For example, if they are to purchase 40 percent of your company, they may demand two of the five board seats. Having representation on your board of directors permits counterparties not only to vote on major decisions as shareholders but to be intimately involved in the decision-making process. Welcome a new board member from an investment group who can provide nonfinancial assistance; the ideal venue for valuable advice to be shared and applied is during board deliberations.

The issue of board membership can become contentious if the counterparty has either current or potential interests or strategies radically divergent from those of the founders. An example would be having debt holders on the board who, as we mentioned before, are inclined to be more risk averse and prefer strategies and tactics that will not risk their invested principal or disturb future cash flows that would jeopardize your ability to service the periodic interest payable to them. Any decisions in front of the board involving short-term sacrifices for long-term returns may face opposition from debt-holder board members. Often a new board member has invested in your company for one specific reason and may oppose any board decision that does not forward his or her cause. This can happen when you welcome a strategic investor on the board. Decisions to allocate time and resources away from their strategic objective (i.e., crushing a hated competitor, utilizing your innovative technology for a particular application, creating profit opportunities for another of his or her investments) may cause a divide between such a board member and the other members with more varied and broad intentions. Perceived actual or potential contention should not automatically force you to decline a board seat and possibly an investment from a counterparty; however, your team should note such potential board friction prior to negotiations and look for ways to mitigate such future board infighting. In Chapter 8 we discuss in detail ways to manage such potential internal conflicts.

Reverse Vesting   In accordance with a reverse vesting clause, founders are required to set aside their common shares and earn them back over a specified amount of time, usually three to five years. The counterparty negotiates for this structure to ensure that the founders stay around at least through the crucial initial stages of development. Typically entrepreneurs are blindsided by such a demand. However, on the good side, it means that the counterparty values the potential future contributions of the founders. A counterargument is more emphasis on and clarification of your team's skin in the game. In lieu of reverse vesting, the founding members can agree to sign employment agreements for the duration desired by the counterparty. If reverse vesting is still insisted on, negotiate for immediate vesting of a respectable amount of the shares, say 25 percent to 33 percent. The reverse vesting schedule I usually see for early-stage companies is for 25 percent equity upon closing and an additional 25 percent vesting annually for the next three years. The more skin in the game you can demonstrate, the stronger your case for a greater amount of immediate vesting. Your next objective should be to shorten the vesting period so you can earn your shares back sooner; do so by arguing that by the end of the vesting period, the venture would have successfully passed through critical stages of development and reached a point in which the likelihood of flight of the founding management has greatly diminished.

A second dimension of reverse vesting that can lead to contentious negotiations is defining what happens to vesting schedules upon a change of control (i.e., merger or acquisition) during the vesting period. The founders may be justified in claiming they should become fully vested upon such an event because they earned it. Counterparties, as shareholders, will want to minimize the impact of the founders' equity share on their share of the purchase price. Another interest of counterparties and possibly future investors is to maintain sufficient incentive for the management team, which at this point has been successful, to remain. Common language inserted into reverse vesting terms will trigger full vesting of the founders upon the occurrence of a specified single event or two. Such accelerated vesting is referred to as a single-trigger or double-trigger acceleration respectively.

Right of First Refusal   The right of first refusal grants counterparties the ability to maintain their percentage ownership interest in your venture by purchasing a pro rata percentage of shares in a future equity offering of your company. Counterparties will almost always demand this right. They are justified in doing so, as investors do not want their control or potential ROI decimated by poorly managed equity offerings or issuances, which can happen if capital structure is not managed wisely. Granting a right of refusal is more preferable than agreeing to antidilution clauses for similar purposes. However, what may be contended in negotiating this right is the demand for a discount on any future share purchase price. A large discount or, much worse, the ability to purchase shares at their original purchase price would lessen your attractiveness to future prospective equity investors as it increases the amount of immediate dilution that would be incurred on their investment.

Tagalong Rights   Tagalong rights, also referred to as cosale rights, allow passive shareholders to sell their shares when the management team is offering its shares for sale. Often tagalong rights are packaged with the rights of first refusal terms. They are attractive provisions for counterparties that intend to invest as passive investors, who are highly desirable because they do not demand much control, such as a board seat or specific voting rights.

Registration Rights   Registration rights, similar in intentions to rights of first refusal and tagalong rights, compel an issuing company to register the common shares of a shareholder for public sale upon specified occurrences. Registration rights permit shareholders to protect themselves on the upside and possibly the downside by forcing a registration of their unregistered stock, which can now be sold publicly in the event the shareholders do not like the future prospects of the company or desire to have some degree of guarantee to participate in any lucrative exit strategy such as a merger, acquisition, or initial public offering (IPO) that is being offered to current shareholders with registered stock.

There are two types of registration rights:

1. Piggyback registration rights entitle the protected shareholder to participate in any registration initiated by the company or another shareholder. This type of registration right offers upside protection as a noninduced

initiation of stock registration usually precludes an expected desirable public sale.
2. Demand registration rights are considered superior as they allow the protected shareholder to initiate the registration process. In this case the shareholder is afforded both upside and downside protection.

Registration rights are applicable only in jurisdictions with restricted stock, are relevant only upon an IPO, and usually are not a point of contention unless the lawyers wish to make them so. Generally it is not worth expending much time or negotiating capital on negotiating such rights. However, if the counterparty wishes to pitch a fight for such rights, you can certainly entertain them and counter with reducing the potency of comparable, but more relevant, terms, such as rights of first refusal or antidilution provisions.

Antidilution The purpose of antidilution clauses is to protect counterparties from dilution of their convertible securities (i.e., typically preferred stock) in the event of either a future equity issuance through a sale or some form of restructuring (i.e., stock splits, reorganizations, reclassifications, payment of stock dividends, etc.). It is very reasonable to grant such antidilution in the event of a restructuring. Although it is also reasonable for counterparties to seek antidilution protection in the event of a down round, the terms of such an antidilution provision need to be carefully negotiated.

An increase in the total amount of outstanding shares automatically reduces the equity percentage interest held by each current shareholder. However, such dilution is often acceptable to shareholders when future equity sales are executed at higher valuations (i.e., increased price per share). Sophisticated investors commonly insist on such provisions to protect themselves in the event of a down round (which occurs when an equity sale subsequent to their equity purchase is executed at a per share price lower than their prior purchase price). The effect of a down round is a reduction in their percentage equity interest. Similar to rights of first refusal clauses, a mechanism is specified in which the shareholders enjoying antidilution protection will be compensated in some manner, through either an adjustment in share price or number of shares issued.

It is important to understand that any antidilution protection is at the expense of the founders and other shareholders. The two primary problems with granting antidilution protection are that it increases the effective dilution of the equity positions and decreases the relative controlling interest of the founders and other nonprotected shareholders. Consequently this has a third detrimental effect of inhibiting future fundraising efforts as it will have a similar effect for future equity investors.

Trying to entirely block any antidilution protection may be a losing battle. However, the type of antidilution protection will affect the degree to which a trigger of such protection will hurt the equity positions and controlling interest of the founders and other shareholders and the severity of such protective terms is worth contending.

There are two primary types of antidilution: weighted-average adjustments and a full-ratchet adjustment.

A weighted-average antidilution provision limits the amount of dilution suffered by the protected convertible security holder by reducing the conversion price based on the equity percentage interest in the company. In this way no new additional shares need to be issued to enable the protected preferred shareholders to preserve their equity percentage interest. If all equity securities, including convertible securities such as options and warrants, are included, the weighted-average adjustment is considered broad based. If only the existing outstanding securities are calculated in the adjustment, the weighted-average adjustment is called narrow based. By including all outstanding and convertible securities in determining the conversion rate, the broad-based weighted-average adjustment, the most common, is considered less favorable to the founders and other nonprotected shareholders.

A full-ratchet antidilution provision maintains the preferred shareholders' equity percentage interest by adjusting downward the purchase price of their existing shares, thereby increasing the number of shares held by the protected shareholders. This type of antidilution adjustment is much more severe for the nonprotected shareholders as additional outstanding shares come into existence. The increased number of shares created due to the triggering of a full-ratchet antidilution provision results in a more severe immediate dilution of a future equity investor's position, impeding future fundraising efforts as well. This type of provision sets a bad precedent for future funding rounds; future counterparties will feel compelled to demand the same antidilution protections already granted at a drastic additional expense to the founders and other nonprotected shareholders.

My fundraising efforts for a former client were rendered futile by the existence of severe antidilution provisions previously granted to convertible debt holders; fortunately, I was able to renegotiate with the existing convertible note holders to lessen the severity of such provisions. For several months every prospective investor I approached cited the harshness of the current antidilution provisions and justifiably demanded some form of compensation for the considerable immediate dilution of their investment they would be forced to incur. Unfortunately, my client considered the various compensations unacceptable. My time would have been better spent negotiating with new prospective investors, not renegotiating with current stakeholders.

I offer these recommendations when you are negotiating antidilution provisions:

- Attempting to persuade a counterparty to accept rights of first refusal or liquidation preference terms in lieu of antidilution provisions is worth the effort.
- Granting antidilution provisions to protect a counterparty in the event of some form of equity restructuring is fair and just as long as it is proportional to the effects of such restructuring.
- Agreeing on a weighted-average antidilution provision is preferable to a full-ratchet provision, and agreeing on a narrow-based weighted-average adjustment is preferable to a broad-based weighted average adjustment in regard to both dilution and control for all nonprotected parties.
- Agreeing to antidilution provisions at earlier funding rounds when the prospects of requiring a future equity offering is greater is much less favorable. Such provisions can serve as impediments to future fundraising efforts and create the potential for an unacceptable loss of control for founders, nonprotected shareholders, and prospective investors. This is especially true for later-stage investors who typically are investing larger amounts than were invested in earlier funding rounds; thus, later-stage investors are particularly concerned with their relative controlling position. Unfortunately, having to agree to antidilution terms in an early funding round may prove unavoidable as the perceived level of risk at this stage compels prospective investors to demand antidilution protection. If conceding antidilution provisions proves unavoidable, negotiate to mitigate the severity of such provisions.

Use of Proceeds   Counterparties may negotiate for restrictions on the use of their investment proceeds, due either to strategic intentions or uncertainty regarding the financial management of your venture. Regardless, it is important for your management team to know why such restrictions are being insisted on. If you feel the degree or scope of such restrictions will not have a material effect on current planning or substantially reduce flexibility in future decision making, this may not be worth much to fight for. However, if such restrictions are being insisted on due to a fundamental strategic difference or conflict of interest between your management team and the counterparty, you must address such an important division as well as negotiating specifically on the use of proceeds clause. You may not have much negotiating leverage if a weakness of your venture is past financial mismanagement or if your team is simply inexperienced or not sufficiently tested or qualified.

A situation faced by a past client serves as a perfect example of how terms of a use of proceeds clause can result in damaging arguments. My client welcomed onto the board a new equity investor who was interested only in entering a specific geographic market with my client's product. As a condition for his equity investment, my client would need to seek the investor's consent and only under certain financial conditions before any funds could be allocated to introducing the venture's innovative product into a market other than the one preferred by the investor. This proved very contentious when regulatory issues and cutthroat competition in the investor's select market threatened the entire existence of the venture and necessitated pursuing entrance into other more desirable markets. At the very least, what would have served both parties much better was to put in place contingencies that would have permitted the introduction of the product in other markets in lieu of meeting the investor's inflexible financial conditions.

Performance Targets   Performance targets are specified milestones that, when realized, trigger certain actions to occur either in the form of additional funding or the issuance/vesting of additional equity. If structured properly, performance target provisions have strong advantages for both parties. The establishment of stated milestones to be achieved sets a mutual tone of success and mitigates the perceived risk of counterparties in investing by incrementally increasing their investment (i.e., risk) based on agreed-on contingent success markers. This reduced risk perception permits counterparties to be more amendable to commit to larger funding amounts at terms more favorable to you. A benefit to both parties is that funds are committed in a very efficient just-in-time manner. Having a well-conceived financial plan along with your business plan will assist you in successfully negotiating reasonable performance triggers. Set performance targets at milestones that can be reasonably expected to be attained. The amount of funding to be triggered should be consistent with the level of funding you have determined necessary in your financial plan to reach the next performance target (i.e., operational objective). The consequences of failing to reach a performance target in a timely manner should not result in unnecessarily or disproportionally harsh terms.

The type of performance targets depends on the type of counterparty and other negotiated terms. If the counterparty is a debt holder, the terms may oblige the counterparty to lend a specified amount of additional funds at specified amounts and terms. A delay in the release of funds by the debt holder, whether intentional or unintentional, may induce a badly timed cash flow crisis. As a debt holder with liquidation preference over any shareholder, debt holders can apply extortive influence or take ownership of your company. A case in point is what occurred to a former client who had previously agreed to a poorly negotiated senior debt funding. Internal division within the debt-holding group caused a delay in urgently needed funding once a performance target was reached. This cost the former client a golden opportunity to establish a valuable market player position and almost resulted in the seizure by senior debt holders of the controlling interest of the venture, despite the counterparties' responsibility in creating the situation.

If the counterparty is a prospective equity investor, it may be obliged or have the option to purchase a specified number of additional shares on specified terms. Caution is again advised with such stated performance triggers. Poorly set performance target provisions leading to the right to acquire a higher percentage of equity ownership as the company experiences success (reaches milestones) can result in a disproportionately low return for the founders and other shareholders despite the venture's success. Referring to your rating of equity dilution (RED) will help you in determining an acceptable pace and spacing of performance targets.

In the case of reverse vesting, the founders are to earn more shares as the venture achieves certain milestones. The negotiating objective is to set reasonable performance targets to ensure that the founders secure acceptable returns in the event of an exit at any time during the expected time horizon. The use of performance targets to determine when the founders are vested with more shares can create dilemmas as well. Counterparties propose reverse vesting schedules to keep the management team in place during a lengthy period of time. A single-trigger acceleration can be problematic, as when the single-trigger event (i.e., IPO) presents an attractive exit opportunity for key members of management. Such an important event often occurs at a time when retaining the management team is most important. New investors would almost always prefer the existing management team to stay. Indeed, institutional investors often have policies in place that pass on investments where single-trigger accelerations are established.

Employment Agreements Expect counterparties to demand that employment agreements with key members of the founding team be executed as a condition for funding, especially if no reverse vesting clause is part of the negotiations. Counterparties want to commit founders they deem indispensable to the future success of the company to long-term contracts and alleviate their concern that such members will leave the venture too early. This concern is certainly shared with the founders and any future prospective investors as well. Remember, key personnel are the greatest asset of a start-up and often are the primary consideration in the funding decision-making process of counterparties. Sophisticated investors will want to secure your venture's most prized asset. Of all the numerous means through which counterparties attempt to retain key personnel, employment agreements usually are the most favorable way to be locked in if you are a founding member of management.

The important points of negotiation include term, salaries, buy-out options, noncompete clauses, and cause for termination. Equity should be separately negotiated as part of the overall funding agreement; you should not forfeit your equity share forfeited with termination of the employment agreement, nor should be completely dictated by its terms.

The terms (duration) of the employment agreements are typically in the three- to five-year range depending on the expectations of both negotiating parties as to how long it will take for the company to reach a point where key personnel are no longer indispensable. Discussing the point at which you are no longer needed can be a sobering part of the negotiations.

Regarding salary levels, the founders should expect to earn less than what they would receive in a comparable position at another company in which they do not have such a level of vested interest. For founders, the salary's purpose is sustenance and sufficient funds to carry out your expected duties. Securing a salary is a way to mitigate some of your opportunity cost.

Another possible point of negotiation are buy-out clauses that allow the counterparty or other founders a way to release a key team member who has become a liability to the company. This can be regarded as a shared concern as well.

Noncompete clauses should be carefully negotiated. These clauses prevent employees during the term of the employment agreement and for a specified period of time thereafter to work for a competitor. Effective non-compete periods typically are between nine months and three years. The definition of competitors should be prudently deliberated. Employees will not want it to be broadly defined. If you are a software developer, you do not want "competitors" to include anyone who does software development work. Negotiate a more narrow definition that includes only direct competitors of the venture in the particular target market.

In an employment agreement, the most challenging issue to be negotiated often is the cause for termination clause. The definition of cause should be tightly worded so as not to leave much room for interpretation. However, you do not want to include immaterial mishaps or otherwise make it easy to find cause. Note also that the negotiated terms for cause for termination set a precedent for how future employees, including nonfounders, will be expected to perform.

Have a Negotiating Plan

An effective negotiating plan is the key to successful negotiations. A negotiating plan forces the founders to think in a holistic manner. This is important because negotiating is a give-and-take process. It is always wise to enter negotiations knowing what you want to take and what you are willing to give in order to take what you most want. Thinking in a holistic manner will also keep you aware of the interrelationships among the different points of negotiation. Whether intentionally or not, a counterparty may secure from your side terms on a combination of negotiating points that create an untenable position for you in some manner. As mentioned, in some situations, founders of an entrepreneurial venture have unwittingly accepted terms from a counterparty that ensure that no matter how successful the venture is, the founders stand to gain virtually nothing and the counterparty secures a disproportionate share of the returns. Presentation of confusing term sheets intended to conceal such combinations is a tactic of less honorable counterparties. I have seen such term sheets where counterparties inconspicuously increase their equity interest and/or control through some combination of performance targets, rights of first refusal, participating preferred shares, and otherwise innocuous specific voting rights. Once the venture is in position for a successful exit, the counterparty holds nearly all the equity or control. Lethal combinations of negotiated terms can easily be established unintentionally in this way as well.

A winning negotiating plan will recognize the legitimate concerns of each party engaged in negotiations, establish an acceptable range for each point of negotiation, and prioritize them. The execution of the negotiating plan will incorporate the use of leverage and favorable practices outlined earlier and follow a timeline of progressive commitments.

Note Your Concerns and Recognize Legitimate Counterparty Concerns

In doing so, you can avoid potential conflicts of interest, ensure that maximizing the value of all shareholders is the primary objective of all parties, and facilitate the negotiating process as a whole through better appreciation and deeper understanding of the positions of the other side. The following concerns should be deliberated with this in mind. It is derived from the KYI points first discussed in Chapter 2 and referenced in subsequent chapters.

The legitimate concerns of the founders include the dilution of their stock, maintaining sufficient control to successfully pursue an exit, securing sufficient funding to reach the next funding round, and accepting good money associated with valuable nonfinancial benefits and that offers no impediments to future fundraising efforts.

The counterparties have legitimate concerns as well. They include valuation, expected returns, risk mitigation, securing sufficient control to positively influence the decision making, and ensuring both downside and upside protections.

Both parties have a mutual interest in the retention of key employees and the financial positioning of the company after the conclusion of negotiations.

Negotiations ultimately succeed because a mutual respect for the interests of both sides has been reached. This mutual respect also establishes a good basis for continued success as business partners and for the establishment of an effective corporate governance regime.

Composing a negotiating plan is similar to military planning. The first thing that needs to be done is to determine what objectives need to be achieved in a prioritized manner. The second task is to determine how to achieve these objectives by identifying where to attack and defend. The next step is to allocate resources to the execution of these missions based on priority and means. Once a mission has proven successful or required a retreat, what is your relative position on the battlefield and how do you redeploy?

Disclaimer: Again, this is an analogy. You should not treat a funding counterparty and potential future business partner as a mortal enemy. However, the same level of diligent planning will serve your side well. Following the wisdom imparted by Sun Tzu will serve any founders of entrepreneurial ventures well.

Prioritize the Points of Negotiation

Sun Tzu advised leaders to avoid any unnecessary destruction. There is no sense to wage a costly battle with little or nothing to gain. Some negotiating points may be deal breakers for you and the counterparty. In other words, if one of the parties cannot secure certain terms, a deal will not be acceptable. Thus, failure to agree on these points may terminate negotiations. Points that are key to founders may require a show of force (in military parlance) on a certain position. Sun Tzu's advice to avoid a desperate foe by offering an escape may be appropriate when dealing with counterparties' deal breakers. Both parties need to know up front each other's deal-breaking terms to avoid wasting the time of both parties. These deal-breaking terms top your priority list.

The remaining terms are prioritized lower on your list in terms of importance and negotiability. Funding for any product features that differentiates your innovation takes priority over features that are nice to have. Protecting your most critical assets (tangible or nontangible) is of high priority particularly at the earlier stages of development. Funding to enter the most promising target markets or market segments takes priority over secondary markets. Deferring risk associated with negotiating funding structure until liquidation is preferable to assuming risk during your development, go-to-market, and expansion efforts. For example, to appease the dilution concerns of a counterparty, it is better to agree on rights of first refusal or mild liquidation preference terms rather than antidilution clauses, the latter of which can immediately dirty your capital structure and have a greater detrimental effect on fundraising efforts. The importance of negotiating terms is also determined by the type of funding you are soliciting. If you are seeking seed funding, the priority is to preserve control and protect your intellectual property. When negotiating for series A funding, securing sufficient funds to execute your commercial launch is of paramount importance. Funding terms permitting the establishment of sustained exceptional growth via scalability, liberal use of funds, little or no equity dilution, and incremental funding (performance triggers) will be on top of the priority list when negotiating for series B funding. Set lower on the priority list negotiating points that you have ready nonnegotiable solutions for. Negotiating points expected to be more contentious and complicated require a higher priority.

For negotiable terms, it is advantageous to allow the counterparty to perceive that every point of negotiation is of higher priority to you than it actually may be. Utilize the art of deception championed by Sun Tzu to encourage the other side to commit their resources to an unfavorable position on the battlefield. If a counterparty wants to pitch a battle on a point of negotiation not of high importance to you, seize this golden opportunity to put up enough of a defense to position yourself to execute a counterattack and trade for more favorable terms on a point of negotiation of more importance to you. Sun Tzu also advised that that it is advantageous to trigger frustration or overconfidence in the enemy.

You can negotiate away points of negotiation sharing the same position based on overkill as well. Why try to seize or defend every control term negotiated? For example, if you have retained enough board seats to render the granting of a specific voting right moot, why put up stiff resistance to it being negotiated? In military terms, you do not want to fight for the same ground more than once. Sun Tzu preached against any wasted actions.

Establish an Acceptable Range for Each Negotiating Point

Begin negotiating terms at the top of expected range of possibility. The bottom of the range is your minimum acceptable level and the top of the range is the highest you could reasonably expect from a counterpart. Remember that negotiating is a balancing act. If you begin out of this range or set an unreasonable range, negotiations may not last very long. If you start too low, you may have cost you and your shareholders a lot of money and/or control. The bigger the range, the more room (flexibility) you will have in the negotiations, which leaves greater opportunity to resolve sticking points (although negotiations may take longer). The priorities that you set will guide your efforts in establishing these ranges. As we mentioned earlier, you must plan for negotiations done with an understanding of the relationships between the different negotiating positions, thereby allowing you to determine where in the range you intend to start negotiations at or how broad to make the range. If a negotiating stance is a high priority for you, start higher in the range. You may be able to start above what is deemed an acceptable expected range in one area if you are willing to start below an acceptable range on another negotiating point. If you expect negotiations on a particular position to be very contentious, you may opt to broaden the range to negotiate within.

A recommendation from Sun Tzu remains very applicable today: Avoid attacking enemy strong points and attack weaknesses. Expending valuable resources (i.e., negotiating capital) on a strong point to be fought at high cost by the counterparty may not only prove futile but may also weaken your relative strength in future negotiations on other points. The reverse also holds true.

Note When and Where to Expend Negotiating Capital

Deciding when to utilize the leveraging advantages at your disposal is a central objective of any negotiating plan. Once priorities have been set and acceptable expected ranges have been determined, a battlefield has been drawn on which you can maneuver your armies (i.e., leverage).

The founders may be able to preemptively outmaneuver the counterparty by offering a solution to a weakness rather than expending negotiating capital as defense. Reserve your strengths and the associated leverage to be wielded for pressing or high-priority terms. Winning the battle before it is fought would make Sun Tzu very proud.

A famous assertion from Sun Tzu was: "Speed is the essence of war." Engage the counterparty in a decisive manner. If you know what you want and what you are willing to expend to get it, take the initiative. Do not allow the other party to delay the proceedings and reduce the advantage of your clear and concise negotiating plan on a given negotiating point. Additionally, address the highest-priority or expected most contentious points of negotiation first, before you have expended too much of your negotiating capital. Similar to Agile development, in which the highest priority and riskiest features are developed first, you will want to prioritize your negotiating points in the same manner. The objective of Agile development is to ensure that the most desired and needed features are delivered to the client and that complex development efforts are tackled first. The resultant learning curve will serve the development team well during the remaining development efforts. Prioritizing your negotiating efforts is to achieve similar objectives. Whether stated in military or software development terms, your relative position will be more apparent once you have dealt with the most difficult challenges, creating a better opportunity to more effectively redeploy resources (leverage) for the remaining objectives to be achieved.

Sun Tzu emphasized the need to maintain the initiative. Patton's Third Army tactics in relentlessly pursuing the Germans in his march north into Luxembourg and Belgium in World War II is an excellent case in point. Patton never gave the Germans time to mount a defense. He dictated where and when the battles would be fought. If your leverage is a time constraint faced by your counterparty, dictate the pace of negotiations and the order in which negotiating points are to be addressed. Maintaining the initiative would delight Sun Tzu.

When it is time to wield leverage, select the appropriate leverage. If you want to execute an outflanking maneuver, it is best to put into motion your cavalry or armored divisions rather than slow infantry forces. If the biggest concern of the counterparty is uncertainty regarding your product's competitive positioning, the traction you possess would be an appropriate leverage point to champion, as it either directly refutes or mitigates the counterparty's specific concern. If you perceive that securing managerial control is the primary objective of counterparties, compel them to placate your most cherished demand, such as a higher valuation, if they are to be granted such control. If the counterparty is a strategic investor who covets your intellectual property more than anything else, wield your IP in the point of the negotiation you value the most. In this case, the counterparty may want to secure the IP as collateral with a preferred share issuance. Not being able to offer your IP as collateral to future counterparties may require you to employ a counterweight measure and deny them certain levers of control, participation rights, or antidilution provisions that hinder future fundraising efforts.

Secure Progressive Commitments from Counterparties

Sun Tzu was a strong advocate of a divide-and-conquer strategy. Through the use of executing a series of memoranda of understanding, particularly in protracted negotiations, you can commit a counterparty to a position(s) highly favorable to your side and effectively remove what was once a contentious issue from the negotiating table. A demonstration of progress, especially desired in protracted and complicated negotiations, is also a positive result of the utilization of progressive commitments. In military terms, successfully securing the high ground enables you to more favorably redeploy your troops. However, we must offer a word of caution here. Be sure not to lock yourself into a position that you subsequently realize to be unfavorable to your side. In military parlance, by fixing a position, you may become vulnerable to an outflanking maneuver. Again, having a well-conceived negotiating plan in which considerations have been made in a holistic manner mitigates your risk of being outflanked.

For Sun Tzu, obedience was far important than skill. This is important to note because in funding negotiations, you are fighting an opponent that is inherently much more skilled than you in the realm of finance. Having a negotiating plan enforces obedience within your ranks. A disciplined approach will also create an air of confidence in your ranks that will serve you well in the negotiations and make a great and enduring impression on your counterparty, who you hope to be your future business partner.

Concluding Negotiations

Negotiations will finally conclude with either the signing of the funding agreement documents that encompass the terms agreed on or a mutual recognition that continuing negotiations will prove futile.

Successful Conclusion of Negotiations

You know when you negotiated well when the other party grudgingly accepts the terms. Once you have secured acceptable terms, end the deliberations. Do not continue, as you have nothing to gain and only something to lose!

No matter how contentious the negotiations proved to be, the outcome of a successful conclusion to negotiations is a new business partner with mutual interests. It is now time to emulate the strong economic and diplomatic partnership developed between the United States and Japan following their mortal combat in World War II. Working effectively together as business partners is the primary task at hand. The strengths of both sides exhibited during the negotiations can now be wielded in concert to achieve common objectives with the establishment of effective working relationships and strong corporate governance.

Unsuccessful Conclusion to Negotiations

Know when to walk away. It is better to end the negotiations once an untenable pass has been reached. Prolonging futile negotiating efforts will be an unnecessary waste of precious time for both parties and can only lead to a reduction of goodwill.

Do not burn any bridges!

Always respectfully decline terms that are unacceptable and thank the counterparties for their strong interest and willingness to afford you the opportunity to negotiate. In the future, there may come a time that you engage in funding negotiations again with the same counterparty, either one on one or as a participant in an investment syndicate. A future counterparty may approach the current counterparty for a referral. You just never know how the last impressions you make can affect your future fundraising efforts.

Offer the counterparty the opportunity to stay informed of your venture's future developments. A way to do this may be by sending future periodic shareholder reports minus anything considered internal and confidential. Doing this displays sincerity and respect, and counterparties will usually respond favorably. The practical reason for providing information on your continued progress is to give counterparties reason to reconsider their negotiating stances where agreement could not be reached.

Negotiation Postmortem

Whether the negotiations prove successful or not, find out why the outcome was what it was. There are two primary reasons to do so:

1. Often only one or a few issue(s) or point(s) of contention prevented a funding agreement from being executed. There may be a possibility to stay engaged with the counterparty and to reenter negotiations once certain contingencies have been met.
2. This information will prove valuable when dealing with a new counterparty, either now or in the future. The more tense the negotiating process was, the more revealing it may have been in regard to your strengths and weaknesses. Your strengths were challenged, thus measurable, and weaknesses were exposed by the other side. A further refinement of your negotiating plan or a better selection of the type of prospective investor may become apparent. Perhaps from a higher-level perspective, revelations were generated in regard to your overall business or financial plan. The next step is to make the necessary adjustments to improve the prospects of your venture and determine necessary improvements in your corporate governance policies as preparation for welcoming a new business partner. Yes, there are "discoveries" to be identified from a negotiations engagement.

Summary

Entering negotiations to execute a funding agreement is the opportunity you have been preparing for since inception. Your management team is now obligated to negotiate in the best interests of all current shareholders. It is a considerable obligation that must be conducted with the utmost seriousness and skill. The negotiating team must consist of all the key decision makers of the company, and a well-conceived negotiating plan needs to be constructed and pursued. To provide valuable insights and mentoring advice in correct chronological order, the chapter was organized in four major sections: prenegotiations, due diligence, actual negotiations, and concluding negotiations.

Submission of a letter of intent by the counterparty outlining the parameters of the forthcoming negotiations marks the beginning of the prenegotiation stage. The objective of this initial stage is to identify, amass, and organize as many sources of leverage as possible to strengthen your relative negotiating position. Leverage is the ability to exert influence beyond what should be expected, given the amount of financial investment made. Now that you know the identity of the counterparty and have been presented with its outlined negotiation expectations, it is time to conduct more focused KYI research and inquiries to supplement the more general KYI research you have continuously performed.

Due diligence is the next negotiating stage, which begins with the presentation of a due diligence checklist requesting specific information on the material facts of the venture. Your response must be accurate and clear as you are legally bound to represent the facts correctly. The information supplied will serve as the basis for the negotiation of terms. An unsatisfactory response may compel the counterparty to withdraw from negotiations.

The actual negotiations open with the delivery of a term sheet from the counterparty that sets forth the key funding terms that the counterparty wants to negotiate. The appropriate negotiating approach is largely dictated by the type of investor sitting across from you. Several negotiating tactics and practices were discussed, including the benefit of negotiating as a team and demonstrating open-mindedness. A thorough examination of each major point of negotiation was presented, including the various decision-making factors for each negotiating point.

Once all the important points of negotiation have been individually examined and collectively considered, we discussed the preparation of a negotiating plan. Having a negotiating plan is essential to consider the negotiating proceedings in a holistic manner. Thinking in such strategic terms will permit your negotiating team to maximize the value of your leverage, present effective counterarguments, and avoid many of the dangers inherent in negotiating on a large number of terms. The tasks and considerations of formulating a successful negotiating plan include:

- Note your concerns and recognize the legitimate concerns of the counterparty.
- Prioritize the points of negotiation.
- Establish an acceptable range for each negotiating point.
- Note when and where to expend or not expend negotiating capital in the negotiating process.
- Secure progressive commitments from the counterparty.

The chapter concludes with a brief discussion of how to best conclude negotiations. In concluding, unsuccessful negotiations you should assume that you may encounter the counterparty again and/or that the counterparty may have either direct or indirect influence on future dealings you may participate in with third parties. Successful negotiations need to be concluded as soon as the terms have been agreed to, with the recognition that the counterparty is now your new business partner.

With the addition of a new business partner, following good corporate governance practices is even more important. The establishment and pursuance of such good corporate governance policies and practices are topics of discussion in the next chapter.

CHAPTER 7

Establishing an Investment-Grade Organization

A successful conclusion to funding negotiations has been achieved. Now you have the funds to execute at least your immediate operational and strategic objectives. However, the situation is different now. You are spending other people's money. The responsibilities associated with doing so create a new set of obligations that affect the way the business is to be managed and conducted. Professional management, particularly in a number of areas of the business, is now an important requirement in preparation for a successful exit. With a successful exit you will either be acquired or merged into a professionally operated company or become publicly tradable via an initial public offering, assuming the obligations and disclosure requirements commensurate with a publicly traded company.

The particular areas of the business that may require a professional upgrade include the enactment of responsible corporate governance policies and the institution of a program of investor and public relations to execute and convey these policies. You should establish such responsible corporate policies as soon as possible to facilitate implementation and enjoy the benefits, such as giving you the edge in your remaining fundraising efforts, earlier. Sound corporate governance is certainly required before you accept any investment funds from nonfounding sources. The chapter is organized into two sections: corporate governance and corporate governance best practices.

Corporate Governance

In the *Art of War*, Sun Tzu asserts that those skilled in war should cultivate the Tao, or way of humanity and justice. In contemporary terms, the Tao is equivalent to the concept of business culture and the processes that influence the conduct of business. Mastering the Tao requires the cultivation and maintenance of internal rules and institutions. Establishing a strong corporate governance regime accomplishes this.

A corporate governance regime is the set of rules and institutions through which a company is directed, administered, organized, and controlled with the intent to achieve the long-term strategic goals of all the stakeholders. Stakeholders include the board of directors, management, employees, suppliers, strategic partners, and customers/users. A corporate regime consists of the entire collection of rules, processes, policies and institutions through which a company is managed and a corporate culture established. It represents management acceptance that the shareholders are the true owners of the company who possess rights to be honored and interests to be considered above the personal interests of management. The nature of the relationships among the various stakeholders (board, shareholders, executives, customers, vendors, etc.) is dictated by the components and workings of a company's corporate governance regime.

Attributes

A company with good corporate governance exhibits several related and distinguishing attributes. They include:

- *Integrity*. Integrity can be defined as consistent behavior in accordance with good ethical principles such as honesty and fairness. If an individual or institution consistently acts with integrity, its decisions become predictable as its motivations are based on known ethical principles. Integrity can be distinguished by behavior that would be considered acceptable if everyone with the same values acted in a similar manner. Acting in an ethical manner and acting predictably lower the level of perceived risk, thereby facilitating the establishment of trust. When stakeholders invest or participate in the business, they are investing both resources and trust. Trust is one of the biggest assets a company can possess and is the crux of sound corporate governance.
- *Transparency*. Transparency refers to a high degree of openness derived from reporting and disclosing everything of material importance to relevant parties in a clear, factual, readily available, and timely manner. An individual or institution acting with integrity has nothing to hide and thus has no reason not to be transparent. Being transparent is the most

effective way to exhibit integrity and allows for an effective dissemination of information that can serve to enhance performance.

- *Accountability.* This term is synonymous with "responsibility." Every decision must be able to be justified based on sound judgment and ethical principles. Negative consequences must be expected by decision makers whose decisions result in dire outcomes. Transparency, proper accounting practices, and evaluation procedures are prerequisites for effective accountability.
- *Objectivity.* Objectivity refers to the ability to make decisions in an unbiased and measured manner. The existence of actual or potential conflicts of interest creates a situation in which it is difficult to be objective. Decisions that are made in an objective manner respect and consider the rights and interests of all relevant parties. Accountability compels objective decision making.
- *Performance imperative.* Maximizing performance is the highest priority in the decision-making process. Objectivity allows for such prioritization. Every stakeholder stands to benefit from improved performance, thus the interests of every stakeholder are being pursued. This performance imperative represents what should be the ultimate objective of every management team and from which the next benefits of good corporate governance practices are derived.

Benefits of Good Corporate Governance

Most discussions of corporate governance focus on the operations of large corporations. However, good corporate governance practices offer great benefits to start-ups and justify early development.

The benefits for a start-up of exhibiting good corporate governance include:

- Optimizing performance through greater efficiencies and improved decision making.
- Optimal balance between maintaining control of management and receiving favorable advice and assistance from stakeholders. The ultimate success of the business often depends on the ability to fully leverage the expertise, contacts, and other nonfinancial offerings of the various stakeholders without concentrating a controlling interest in any one single stakeholder group. A perception of such concentration of power may dissuade current or prospective stakeholders from further contributions or investment.
- Trust and confidence in management that will serve the company well in any issue resolution, financial challenge, or future crisis.
- Enhancing and cohesively maintaining the image of the corporation.

These benefits assist in generating two additional benefits of particular importance to technology start-ups. The perception of high-quality corporate governance can favorably influence:

- Cost of capital, facilitating fundraising activities
- Share price, permitting the negotiation of higher valuations

Prospective stakeholders will be heartened by evidence that the company follows good corporate governance policies that will ensure that their opinions will receive fair consideration and their interests will be vigilantly pursued with great efficiency. Often prospective investors have to decide between several different investments. A company exhibiting strong corporate governance can possess a decisive advantage.

The ability to showcase a strong corporate governance regime is certainly a powerful source of leverage in negotiations with prospective stakeholders. They will be more amenable to accepting a higher valuation or lower cost of capital offered to your venture for the perceived reduced risk and greater probability of success for their stake in the company. The institutionalization and practice of the following best corporate governance practices allow for such opportunities.

Corporate Governance Best Practices

To achieve all the benefits that can be attained by implementing and following a good corporate governance regime, a number of best practices can be followed. They fall into three broad categories: corporate governance structures, ethical behaviors, and stakeholder relations.

Corporate Governance Structures

A company should be organized with the intention to enable the performance of good corporate governance. Next we discuss organizational best practices to be faithfully practiced and enacted.

No Overdependence on Any One Person or Concentration of Power in a Certain Group

When company decision making is concentrated in a single person, whether formally or de facto, there is very little possibility that the company can be perceived as having solid corporate governance. This issue seldom applies to large, established companies but is a real concern for a start-up dominated by a single founder, particularly as the business grows and management demands become greater and possibly overwhelming. It is much more difficult for a one-person show to raise funds. Prospective investors are looking to invest in a company with either a strong management team or evidence that such a team will be built. Sophisticated investors also understand that businesses benefit from the influence of diverse interests and expertise. As mentioned in Chapter 3, prospective investors place a high premium on a strong management team because they realize that success is all in the execution and that ideas are cheap. Effective execution of any business plan requires effective management of diverse stakeholder interests, which is made possible through sound corporate governance.

An exceptional entrepreneur or visionary does not necessarily make a good executive manager. If a ruling founder is no longer inspired by the monotonous day-to-day activities of a more mature company or prefers innovative work rather than the executive's role, it may be time for that person to consider stepping aside. There have been many sad and ugly examples of founders of successful start-ups failing to recognize when it is time to step down. Such situations may present a challenge in fundraising efforts as well. A former client was dominated by two cofounders who collectively owned a majority interest in the company, called all the shots, and did not have to effectively answer to a governing board. They were very intent on holding their controlling interest. Given their advanced stage of product development, their considerable funding requirements currently being solicited, and their long string of failures in fundraising efforts, many prospective investors questioned why they still maintained such equity interest in the company and how their interests would be considered once they became shareholders. Other prospective investors believed at this business stage, executive decisions needed to be made by seasoned executives, not by the founders, who were critically important to the business and were to be retained in another capacity but had no experience running a company of the size everyone projected this company to quickly become. Almost every prospective investor was sold on the business but not on the current management structure. In this case and others, there may exist a variety of reasons for intransigence regarding the issue of control; however, egos have often been the cause or at least contributed to the demise of many promising start-ups. Remember that it is better to hold a 20 percent interest in a $1 billion company than a 50 percent interest in a $10 million company. When you have vested stakeholders in your business, it is your ethical obligation to pursue the best interests of all stakeholders in accordance with the principles of corporate governance.

It is very common for a founder who considers the venture his or her "baby" to do whatever is necessary to maintain as full control as possible. This can easily result in situations that violate the rules of sound corporate governance to the company's detriment. I witnessed such a situation firsthand. In this case, a single founder attempted to maintain control of virtually all voting rights by making a strong request to a group of investors who had already invested most of the company's early-stage funds to sign proxy rights instruments granting to the founder the voting rights of the shares they were about to be issued. Most of these investors were friends of the founder and were passive investors who were willing to entrust the operations and strategic direction of the company to the capable and very experienced founder. However, by executing the proxy rights instruments, they were creating the possibility of two very real dangers that exist if a single individual or a very small group commands a dominating controlling interest:

- More sophisticated later-stage investors, such as professional institutional investors, may have serious reservations about the integrity of the capital structure and the company's future pursuit of sound corporate governance.
- More opportunistic prospective investors may identify an opportunity to secure a more favorable funding deal simply by offering a package attractive to the individual or small controlling interest to the detriment of the interests of the shareholders as a whole.

Again, any situation where a single founder serves as chief executive and is not checked by an objective board with sufficient supervisory authority should raise a red flag for current or potential shareholders.

Drag-along provisions in the shareholder agreement and a sole founder/ chief executive officer (CEO) not answerable to an objective board with sufficient supervisory authority and who makes all the executive decisions is a dangerous mix. In such cases, opportunistic investors may swoop in. As mentioned in Chapter 6, drag-along provisions are common and are intended to provide protection for the interests of both shareholders and management. However, a management team or single executive not answerable to anyone and shareholders compelled to follow the decisions of the executive nullifies the protective characteristics of such drag-along provisions. Consider the next scenario, which illustrates the dangers of such a mix.

A sole founder/CEO has raised $500,000 in early-stage funds from mostly friends and former business associates. These investors are passive and entrust him to make all the executive decisions and provide the company's strategic direction. Therefore, they do not feel it necessary to elect a supervisory board and are willing to sign over their proxy rights to the founder in the name of decision-making efficiency. For their investment, they have been issued an 80 percent equity interest in aggregate. The founder contributed an additional $50,000 and owns the remaining 20 percent equity interest. In a few years, the company is successful in attracting the interest of prospective buyers and is in position for a lucrative exit. The company is receiving offers to be purchased at a share price based on a valuation of $5 million. At this price, the sole founder/CEO is positioned to make $1 million. The remaining shareholders will share among themselves $4 million. However, a prospective buyer wants to acquire the company cheaply and decides to offer the sole founder/CEO a compensation package of $2 million to retain his services and offers to purchase the company's shares based on a valuation of $1 million. The prospective buyer is getting a good deal as the purchase price is a mere $3 million as opposed to $5 million. The sole founder/CEO is getting a sweet deal, receiving $2 million instead of $1 million. The shareholders are left out to dry. They stand to receive only $800,000, a fraction of the $4 million they would have otherwise been able to receive. Unfortunately, earlier the shareholders did not feel it necessary to elect a supervisory board, and they signed their proxy rights over to the founder, thereby permitting him total freedom to negotiate a sales price and execute a sale. Now the shareholders are forced to sell their shares at this reduced price due to the drag-along provisions in the shareholder's agreement each signed. An executive who lacks integrity is very likely to accept such an opportunity to commit such an act of diminishment and gain another $1 million at the expense of the other shareholders.

Unfortunately, this scenario does occur. Regardless of whether a high level of personal trust exists among founder(s) and initial shareholders, later investors who do not have such a personal acquaintance may see the possibility of such a scenario as a major red flag. This will only hurt the perceived value and safety of the equity you hold. Welcoming as a shareholder a vulture capitalist who is clever about composing funding terms can result in similar situations. The preceding scenario is a glaring example of how a mixture of individually innocuous terms and circumstances can have seriously detrimental consequences, whether unintentional or due to more insidious motivations.

A board consisting of several directors needs to serve as the defender of shareholder interests, no matter the size of the company or the percentage equity interests of individual shareholders. A board consisting of directors of diverse backgrounds is also better able to handle the increasing management demands of a rapidly growing company. The existence of a board also creates a sense of permanence to the business that is assuring to both current and prospective stakeholders.

Establish and Empower a Responsible Board

The primary role of the board of directors is to establish good corporate governance. Thus, this is the body responsible for ensuring that management does not act in its own self-interest but act as long-term investors themselves. As the link between shareholders and management, the board is best positioned to effect good corporate governance and constrain actions of management when appropriate. To fulfill its mission, the board must satisfy these requirements:

- *Composition of the board.* The board must be of sufficient size (at least three to five members) and consist of directors with diverse backgrounds so a broad range of skills and experiences can be brought to bear on the large variety of business issues to be faced. The members must have the ability to analyze and challenge the decisions of management. Board members must be sufficiently committed to uphold their responsibilities and be prepared to constantly review existing corporate governance policies and practices. It is also beneficial to have a mix of both executive (insider) and nonexecutive (independent) members and for the board chair to be an independent director, although this may difficult to arrange in the early stages of a start-up.
- *Supervisory authority of the board.* Board endorsement should be required for all strategic-level decisions and for any actions affecting the capital structure of the company. The composition of a business plan, financial plan, and negotiation plan are all strategic-level activities subject to board review. The latter two will have an effect on the capital structure as well. Protection of the company's assets, including its intellectual property, is a duty of the board requiring supervision of any related management decisions. The board should also craft a policy governing how the company relates to external stakeholders. This is of particular relevance to start-ups when sometimes more than one member of management and/or the board are communicating conflicting information to an external party. The question may arise: Who is in charge at XYZ Company anyway? This is potentially very damaging to the company's credibility and image and is counter to the principles of good corporate governance.
- *Management accountability to the board.* Corporate governance is necessary to resolve the dilemma that occurs when company owners relinquish managerial control. The incentives of management and the interests of shareholders need to be aligned. The board can achieve this alignment by exercising its authority to:
  - Appoint and remove senior members of management.
  - Set appropriate compensation packages that includes performance-oriented incentives.
  - Set directional policies that specify overall corporate objectives.
  - Hold members of management accountable to a published code of conduct.
  - Submit senior management to periodic performance reviews.

If the board is responsible for ensuring that the good corporate governance it formulated prevails throughout the company, who ensures that the board is qualified to construct and uphold those same principles?

Answer: the shareholders.

In a proper corporate governance regime, shareholders have certain authority and duties. Chief among these duties is exercising several checks on the board:

- Ensure that only committed and competent individuals are nominated or appointed to the board.
- Determine the compensation packages of the board to ensure the board directors are sufficiently incentivized to faithfully represent shareholder, rather than personal interests.
- Submit the board to periodic reviews to ensure accountability to the pursuit of good corporate governance. All directors should also be subject to reelection to limited board terms.

Establish Mechanisms to Permit Shareholders to Participate by Voting and Express Their Views in an Informed Manner

Every effort should be made to provide all shareholders sufficient and timely information to make informed decisions and participate in any deliberations, such as at general shareholder meetings. Such information will include the time and place of meeting or voting, the agenda, and accurate background information on each agenda item. Voting shareholders should be permitted to vote in absentia and be allowed to add items to the agenda. For board elections, shareholders should choose from a qualified list of candidates.

Concurrence of Stakeholder Interests into Mutual Objectives

The concurrence of stakeholder interests into mutual objectives requires the establishment of effective mechanisms to include the various stakeholders proportionally in the decision-making process. This task can be the most challenging one for a board, particularly as the complexity of a company's capital structure and the diversity of stakeholders expands, as is often the case for a rapidly growing start-up. Board composition reflective of the diversity of stakeholder interests is a first important step. Two ways to guarantee that mutual objectives are pursued is to ensure that improved performance is one of these mutual objectives and mechanisms are put in place to avoid and treat instances of conflicts of interest. As discussed earlier, the interests of debt holders and shareholders may converge. Multiple share classes both dirty the capital structure and make the convergence of the various stakeholder interests more difficult. Consequently, in order to ensure good corporate governance, it is extremely important to construct a financial plan that takes into account such possibilities. For a higher probability of improved performance, a company's management team should totally be focused on performance. The politics and formulation of strategic objectives for the company should remain the domain of the board.

Ensure that Managers Have Sufficient Authority to Carry Out Their Responsibilities

This is a seldom mentioned feature of corporate governance that is too important to ignore and is consistent with the performance imperative. Occasionally the board may either intentionally or unwittingly place undue constraints on management authority in the name of corporate governance. Both board members and management need to be vigilant against such a situation. If managers are constrained by limited authority they may be impeded or deterred from acting in the best interests of the shareholders. A transparent way to identify any undue constraints on management is to compose a written document listing the duties and authority of management and submit it to periodic board review.

Designate a Corporate Secretary

A corporate secretary is charged with ensuring compliance of the company's corporate governance policies. Although the position of corporate secretary is most likely not a full-time position for most start-ups, it demonstrates an awareness and intention to establish good corporate governance. Furthermore, it sets a good precedent that the company values integrity and accountability and may contribute to the development of a healthy ethical culture within the company as it grows.

Establish Crisis Management Procedures

Crisis management preparation is a critical component of a good corporate governance regime, especially for tech start-ups whose product or service is often dependent on technologies that are complex and advanced, thus possessing a high probability of breakdown. Crisis planning involves the determination of who has the authority to make critical decisions during a crisis and the potential legal issues to be avoided or dealt with. Proper lines of communication both internally and to the public (i.e., external stakeholders) should be dedicated and easily accessible. Contingency plans for any perceptible crisis should be drafted and readied for timely implementation as well. A crisis may hurt not only your business but your brand (i.e., image). Preparing for such an eventuality is essential to having the ability to act with transparency and to display accountability.

Use a Reputable Independent Auditor

An external independent auditor needs to be selected based on competence, relevant experience, and reputation. Financial reporting is an absolute necessity for the effective functioning of any corporate governance regime. To ensure the integrity of financial reporting, an independent auditor should be assigned the task of providing an impartial opinion on the financial performance and condition of the company, including any potential risks and whether the company has the appropriate controls in place. This role of the independent auditor holds true for companies of every size. However, there are additional reasons to have an independent auditor for a start-up. From an internal planning perspective, it is very advantageous for a third party proficient in financial matters to validate your financial assumptions and strategies. Your fundraising efforts certainly stand to benefit from this. Having your actual financial statements and/or your pro forma financials prepared or reviewed by such an independent and reputable auditor will add enormous credibility to the company's financial status and greatly enhance its image by demonstrating adherence to good corporate governance principles. The same applies during negotiations. The company's negotiating positions, particularly deliberations on valuation, are fortified if supported by a qualified and reputable third party. The cost of employing an independent auditor may be easily justified by the increased probability of securing funds at a higher valuation than otherwise may have been possible.

Ethical Behaviors

Ethical behavior can be defined simply as acting with integrity. Whatever the business does will impact its stakeholders. This includes individual actions taken by board directors, management, and employees, not just the actions of the business as a whole. Therefore, it is imperative that individuals are transparent, accountable, objective, and performance oriented.

A business can adhere to good business ethics in several ways. The practices described here represent only a small sample of how a company can comply with good ethical principles.

Encourage Fulfillment of All Attributes Derived from Good Corporate Governance

What distinguishes integrity as a behavior is that it would be considered acceptable if everyone with the same values acted in a similar manner. The development of an ethical corporate culture aims to achieve such a broad acceptance and practice of ethical behaviors.

A business culture of good ethics is cultivated in several ways. Leading by example is one. The development of an ethical business culture begins at the top with moral and committed leadership. Members of executive management attract much attention due to their status. As such, they are susceptible to more scrutiny and are looked on as representatives of the character of the company as a whole. Often board directors are compelled to resign after unethical behavior, whether conducted on the job or in their personal lives, because the behavior of executives is often perceived as reflective of the company's corporate governance practices.

Designing a work environment conducive to ethical behavior is another path to encouraging ethical behavior. An example is the use of certain processes. My friend is a leading evangelist and practitioner of Agile software development. The Agile development process is an excellent vehicle to ensure compliance with the good corporate governance principles of transparency, accountability, and the imperative of performance. Agile software development is different from the traditional models of software development in that costs and duration are fixed (per iteration of typically two weeks) and what remains variable are the features to be developed. Planning is conducted in a very transparent manner because there are no hidden costs, no surprises regarding deliverables that are not revealed only at the very end of the project (working software is delivered at the end of every iteration), as is traditionally the case in software development, and the customer constantly prioritizes features through frequent periodic iterative meetings. Accountability is compelled on two different levels. Daily stand-up meetings during which all team members present brief updates on their work to all the other team members ensures accountability among the development team. The obligation to deliver working and integrated software upon every iteration completion holds the developer effectively accountable to the customer. Performance is optimized by the use of small but dedicated cross-functional teams and the completion of the highest-priority features first. Those who subscribe to the Agile thought process are more likely to extend ethical habits to other areas as well.

It is advantageous to incorporate good corporate governance practices in a small start-up, as such practices and ethical behavior can quickly permeate the entire company. It is also good reason to incorporate a good corporate governance regime as soon as possible.

Whenever I speak on the value of corporate governance to founders of a start-up, the usual response is along the lines of "Dave, there are only three of us."

My response has three parts:

1. Good. Then it should be very easy to establish and implement good corporate governance procedures.
2. You do not need to be a large company to make the impression that your venture is and will continue to be guided by good corporate governance principles.
3. Establishing such an impression will increase your chances of attracting investment funds for the reasons previously stated.

This last point particularly grabs their attention.

I like to tell the story of my first business venture when my business partner and I established what our futures clearing merchant dubbed the smallest registered CTA (Commodity Trading Advisor) in the world. My partner and I took great pride in defying all doubters and actually identifying a way to incorporate a business and use it as a vehicle to sponsor us each to take the required series 3 test. He and I were both broke and young (in our mid-twenties) but somehow we scrounged up enough money for a shared office space with common conference rooms and a receptionist. We did not share responsibilities, however. Rather, we divided responsibilities and accountability between us. My business partner had an academic management background, was much better at computers, and more familiar with the trading platform than I. Thus he was our chief operating officer (COO) and chief technology officer as far as we and the outside world was concerned. I managed the finances and possessed the legal background to handle the compliance issues. Thus I assumed chief financial officer (CFO) and compliance responsibilities. He and I unknowingly practiced good corporate governance procedures in a fun manner. As a newly registered CTA, we attracted the attention of futures exchanges and futures clearing merchants soliciting for our interday currency trading business. Everyone assumed we were a large financial institution like most other CTAs. When exchanges or futures clearers called, they usually asked to speak with a specific executive, such as our COO, trading supervisor, CFO, or compliance manager. When one of us answered this type of call we would pause for a few seconds, determine which one of us was responsible and accountable, given the nature of the inquiry, and introduce either the other or have the other introduce us as the executive the caller would like to speak to. So when XYZ exchange called to speak with our COO or our trading floor manager, I would ask my business partner if either was available. He would say something like "Give me a minute while I wrap up an issue on the trading floor." For another inquiry he would jokingly say, "I suppose you want me to speak with him."

As a small start-up, you can begin good corporate governance practices by clearly defining the responsibilities and accountability of each founding partner, referring all incoming inquiries to one person ultimately responsible, and creating the impression that your company has good corporate governance procedures like those in a big corporation and they will continue to grow with the company. As we mentioned in Chapter 3, one objective in composing the management team section of the business plan is to delineate the division of responsibilities (i.e., accountability) among the executive officers.

Leading by example, establishing a work environment conducive to ethical behavior and clearly delineating lines of responsibility and accountability are ways to foster a strong business culture of good ethics.

Your company is never too small to draft and have all team members sign a written code of conduct. A written code of conduct applicable and distributed to every employee at every level for mandatory signing and return is the most common means of fostering a healthy ethical business culture. A business code of conduct sets forth standards of behavior and responsibilities all employees are to comply with to ensure all legal and ethical obligations can be satisfied and that the company's reputation as an adherent to good corporate governance is preserved. Again, no matter how small the team may be, executing a simple code of conduct can only be beneficial. Future employees who are asked to sign the code of conduct will appreciate knowing that it has already been signed by the entire management team, whose members hold themselves accountable to the same code.

Ethical Behaviors toward External Stakeholders

Acting with transparency toward external stakeholders is one example of exemplifying strong corporate governance. Often start-ups contract with a service vendor or a supplier to support either continued research and development and/or operations. Start-ups typically rely on either erratic revenue streams or investment funding to finance their operations. Relationships with vendors and suppliers, especially strategic ones, are extremely important and should not be jeopardized by a lack of forthrightness. If the management of a start-up foresees a cash flow crisis, they should inform their vendors of such possibility. Withholding such notification and forcing vendors to face a cash flow issue themselves due to your failure to pay in a timely manner can cause irreparable ill will. Remember, you are a high-risk venture that shareholders were willing to invest in because of the prospects of a high return. Do not compel vendors to share such high risk without the prospect of a high return. Reasonable vendors who choose to deal with you after a funding crisis would be totally justified in requesting an equity interest in your venture or another risk-mitigating demand.

Another situation where practicing sound ethical behavior can strengthen relations with external stakeholders is to notify relevant parties of a foreseeable conflict of interest. Often start-ups and a vendor/supplier, particularly a large vertically or horizontally integrated one, may have interests that may conflict under certain future circumstances. Set up contingencies in advance with the vendor to ensure that such conflicting interests are avoided or at least mitigated to mutually acceptable levels. Such candor will certainly be rewarded with stronger working relations.

Your transparency will be of enormous value in developing trusting relationships with your external stakeholders and is just another instance of how practicing good corporate governance will contribute to the success of your venture.

Unethical Behaviors to Be Vigilant Against

After reviewing sample codes of conduct, you will discover a list of common unethical behaviors. However, other unethical behaviors also exist, beyond those mentioned in standard codes of conduct. One client had stakeholders willing to wield their perceived unfettered financial leverage for self-serving interests. It is of critical importance for a business and an ethical responsibility of the board as defender of stakeholder rights to ensure that no stakeholder group obtains a level of financial leverage that is difficult to challenge. Two possible unethical actions mentioned earlier are selective liquidity and Rolodex of proxies. Selective liquidity occurs when an investor with unfettered financial leverage chooses to withhold investment funds to compel a cash flow crisis and demand highly favorable terms at the expense of other shareholders. In extreme cases they may reserve investment funds for an eventual takeover of the company. Such a stakeholder may utilize a Rolodex of proxies as well. This occurs when the stakeholder tries to accumulate greater control by referring new prospective investors who will grant them future proxy voting rights, either formally or de facto. These stakeholders act stealthily and conceal their true intentions. Unfortunately, a previous client faced both tactics from the same stakeholder group. Whenever the client faced a cash flow problem, the stakeholder group simply stated that it was not liquid. However, whenever the stakeholder group's control position was challenged or when it could extort highly favorable terms, all of a sudden it would discover that somehow it did have funds after all or had "friends" who would invest under their guidance. In addition, a member of this stakeholder group who was on the board advised a current shareholder who wanted to invest more funds during a critical juncture for the company to wait until a "better time." What was a "better time"? After this incredible opportunity to gain a valuable strategic partner had passed? When it was time for the stakeholder group to practice selective liquidity and advise another down round? Either way, that board member should have been held accountable for not upholding his ethical responsibilities to the remaining stakeholders whose interests were compromised by this action.

Capital Structure Integrity to Be Preserved

Maintaining a clean and healthy capital structure, as discussed in Chapter 1, allows a company to exhibit the following cherished attributes of strong corporate governance:

> *Integrity.* A capital structure is deemed fair and credible when no shareholders, following successive fundraising rounds, believe they received a bad deal considering relative risk/returns.
>
> *Accountability/Objectivity.* The capital structure is to be managed to ensure no single partial investor group secures a disproportionally

large or dominating position of control in which potential conflicts of
interest may arise and opportunities for extortion are possible.

Transparency. A complicated dirty capital structure heightens the level
of uncertainty by creating confusion and injecting many unknown
variables. Transparency is much more difficult to practice and/or
convey under these circumstances.

Performance imperative. A clean and healthy structure will not impede
fundraising efforts. Efficient management of capital structure will
afford the opportunity to secure the highest valuations throughout
the duration of fundraising efforts, due to less perceived risk, and
ultimately upon a successful exit.

Expected Use of Funds

If investors invest funds based on uses specified in the prospectus materials
delivered to them, you must have every intention of allocating such funds
accordingly. If use of funds is not specified, you should nevertheless try
to honor shareholder expectations as much as possible and be prepared to
justify any decisions as driven by the performance imperative.

Stakeholder Relations

Stakeholder relations are conducted based on the set of rules, processes,
policies, and institutions through which a company strives to communicate
and execute its corporate governance activities. Such activities are to be
accomplished by exhibiting favorable corporate governance attributes and
executing the corporate governance best practices it has decided to
implement.

Stakeholder relations involve communicating the company's financial
strategy and its broader strategic direction to stakeholders. The stakeholder
relations function also includes the dissemination of information to stakeholders relevant to ensuring that effective corporate governance practices can
be pursued. Stakeholder relations best practices are discussed next.

Stakeholder relations best practices include communicating any corporate governance activities and events in a timely, clear and accurate manner,
proper reporting/disclosure, establishing effective public relations and crisis
management procedures and building strong credit.

Communicate Corporate Governance Activities and Events in a Timely, Clear, and Accurate Manner with Proper Disclosure, and Reporting

Reporting to ensure the direction of information flow for optimal decision
making is realized is a worthy best practice: To satisfy the performance
imperative, it is essential to ensure that critical information is disseminated to

the relevant parties in a timely manner so informed decisions can be made by all stakeholders.

Demonstrating that you are aware of and stay abreast of industry best practices by distributing such current event news to the appropriate stakeholders is an indication of your adherence to the performance imperative.

Proper Disclosure/Reporting to Stakeholders

Fulfilling the transparency standards of good corporate governance is your ethical obligation to existing stakeholders. Prospective stakeholders will take note of how you treat existing stakeholders. Ensure that confidential information remains confidential. When you distribute information, make sure the appropriate recipients receive it. Make any required disclosures in a clear and accurate manner. Deliver such disclosures in a regular format and, when possible, periodically to reduce perception of selective timing or doctoring reports.

What needs to be disclosed?

- Disclose the various corporate governance policies that have been enacted and the rights and responsibilities of all the participating stakeholders.
- Disclose terms of use, privacy policies, and other such documents executed with exterior stakeholders. These also reveal your adherence to good corporate governance principles and reduce the impression of risk.
- Disclose anything that has a material effect on the rights and interests of the various stakeholders. These include board membership changes, voting participation, nature and timing of exit, expected return on investment, a planned funding round, a significant change in strategy, and welcoming a new strategic partner.
- Disclose any actual or potential conflicts of interests.
- Disclose anything that alters the capital structure or any efforts to ensure capital structure integrity. Disclose capital structures or any other arrangements that enable certain shareholders to obtain a degree of control disproportionate to their equity ownership.
- Disclose any deviations from shareholder expectations regarding use of funds.

How is such disclosure performed? There are three primary ways to deliver such information: a formal corporate code of governance, distribution of a periodic shareholder letter, and shareholder notices to disseminate more precise and timely information.

Publishing and making easily accessible a corporate code of governance is an excellent way to provide standard disclosure information. A corporate code of governance is the means for a company to codify its corporate governance regime and avoid any misunderstandings that could occur.

As mentioned in Chapter 5, distributing a shareholder letter is another effective way to periodically convey current investor relations activities and external and internal events.

Shareholder notices are issued only to relevant stakeholder interests when necessary to present urgent and important matters that likely require a certain action or response from the recipients.

Effective Public Relations to Convey the Attributes of Good Corporate Governance

Implement a well-conceived and orchestrated public relations campaign to take advantage of third-party credibility, leveraging relationships, and corporate responsibility. Such a campaign would include providing favorable news bulletins to media outlets, such as bloggers and industry periodicals, publicizing association with reputable strategic partners in an appropriate manner, and securing membership in prominent industry organizations. The openness exhibited by an effective public relations campaign is a sign of transparency and accountability.

The importance of third-party credibility when attracting the attention of prospective investors who are bombarded with other investment opportunities and possess very short attention spans cannot be overstated. Human nature dictates that praise from a credible third-party will carry more weight than any self-promotion could. This is just another instance of how strong corporate governance practices can improve the prospects of attracting investment funds.

Effective Crisis Management

A crisis may not only be an operational event but a public relations event as well. It should be seen as an opportunity to increase one of the most valuable assets of a company: trust. Effective public relations practices made possible by crisis management preparation discussed earlier affords this golden opportunity.

Trust is built by acting in a transparent manner (transparency), accepting responsibility (accountability) for the problem, and demonstrating a strong determination to improve (performance imperative).

During the crisis, you must accept responsibility while at the same time providing timely and accurate reporting. Crucial information to be reported are the commencement time of the crisis and an estimate of when the problem is expected to be resolved. By doing so, you show that you are committed to operating in a transparent manner. When you place yourself in the position of a customer/user and do what you would expect to be done as a user, you are acting with integrity. Such reporting allows those who are affected to make their own plans to deal with the crisis and preempts any speculation that may damage - the company's brand or image.

The reporting does not end once the crisis has dissipated. You must publicly distribute a detailed summary report to illustrate the cause(s) and chronological events of the crisis and what lessons have been learned. The various stakeholders will need to know what actions are being taken to prevent a repeat occurrence. This summary report can serve as a valuable internal reference for future crisis prevention and management as well as prompting necessary revisions to operational plans and/or codes of conduct.

To use an analogy when good crisis management procedures are appreciated and valued, I will submit the frequent occurrence of being stuck on the local elevated rail system in the city in which I reside. Given the terrible traffic congestion here, the elevated rail system has been a blessing for local commuters. Unfortunately, it is subject to frequent delays for a variety of reasons. I have grown accustomed to such disruptions in service but would appreciate more information from the authorities when a delay does occur. When the elevated train comes to a halt and we commuters are stranded, the public announcement system on the train is activated and a preprogrammed apology for the inconvenience is announced. No other information is given for us commuters to decide whether to get off at the station we are currently stuck at or disembark at the next station if stuck between stations. Why has the train stopped? Is there a power outage, as is typically the case and according, to local sources, not the fault of the rail authorities? Is there a fire or explosion on the line? How long will the delay last? If indefinite, how frequently will updates be provided? Should we expect that this delay in service is just one of a series of halts in the immediate future, as is sometimes the case? I need the answers to these questions so I can make an informed decision on what I need to do. If there was an explosion or accident at a station up the line, my informed decision would be to get off at the earliest possible opportunity. If it is just a power outage or waiting for another train to clear and I am rushing to a meeting, I want to make an informed decision on whether I should disembark at the earliest opportunity so I can take a taxi if the auto traffic is not too bad. How will this recent disruption affect my long-term view on the use of this elevated train and my opinions of the rail operators? The cause and frequency of such disruptions will certainly be a determinant in my future decisions to commute on the local elevated rail. Should I look for a regular alternative mode of transportation and abandon the use of the elevated train, or do I just need to make contingency plans?

Consumers or users of your product or service will certainly be asking similar questions when a crisis arises. Seize this opportunity to enhance your brand image and generate loyalty among your customers by acting with total transparency and holding yourself accountable.

The discussion in this chapter related to crisis planning and management is based on "The Upside of Downtime: How to Turn a Disaster Into an Opportunity," by Mr. Lenny Rachitsky. This informative and well-conducted presentation can be viewed at http://www.youtube.com/watch? v=6MF2Pu6IW3Q.

Build Strong Credit

A company can take several actions consistent with good corporate governance principles to build strong financial credit. Such actions include:

- Collecting a list of good credit references so you can compose a credit reference sheet
- Requesting credit reference letters from your best creditors.
- Open a credit reporting account with a reputable business credit reporting agency, such as Dun & Bradstreet. A credit reporting account typically works in this way: A company adds vendors/creditors into its account and allows the reporting agency to track payments to its creditors. A third party who subscribes to the reporting agency service may purchase a report on the company's credit history to assess the risk of doing business or extending credit. Opening a credit reporting account is especially favorable to a young start-up with little credit history and little physical assets to offer as collateral as it helps prospective stakeholders to ascertain risk and increases the possibility of securing more favorable credit terms. The cost of opening a credit reporting account is minimal compared to the financial benefits of achieving a lower cost of capital to the benefit of all stakeholders. Taking actions to improve your credit standing is an excellent way to adhere to the performance imperative. Next is an example of a credit reference sheet that should be composed, updated and made available to any prospective creditors.

Credit Reference List Sample

References for Credit

ABC Corp.
2981 Valley Road Suite 334
Chester, New York 29856
Phone: 443–823–7329
Website: www.abccorp.com
Year Started: 2001
Dunn & Bradstreet#: 15–439–22976
Tax ID: 235917385

Bank Information

U.S. Savings Bank
42 Rose Street

Chester, New York 29856
Check Account#: 23494758691
Contact: Mr. Bob Alvarez Tel: 443–328–7554

Credit References

1. ABA Software Solutions   High Balance: $120,000
   2904 33rd Court Street
   Miami, FL 33987   Current Balance: $45,000
   Tel: 943–887–4539
   Attn: Ms. Charlotte Gomez
2. XYZ Manufacturing, Inc.   High Balance: $37,000
   3557 Margaret Road
   Justice, Missouri   Current Balance: $8,000
   Tel: 233–193–6639
   Attn: Mr. Robert Smith

Past Senior Creditors

1. Mr. William Glen   High Balance: $100,000
   392 Fourth Avenue
   Ft. Dodge, New York 34992   Current Balance: $0
   Tel: 433–287–3448
2. HBC Investments   High Balance: $250,000
   9886 Fifteenth Street
   Ayers, New York 35448   Current Balance: $75,000
   Tel: 433–287–4372

Summary

Corporate governance is the set of rules and processes through which a company organizes and directs itself to achieve the long-term mutual objectives of its stakeholders. The establishment and implementation of good corporate governance principles is necessitated by the assumption of trustee responsibilities that occur when company owners relinquish managerial control to a management team that may have personal interests that diverge from those of the owners. The favorable attributes exhibited by a company possessing effective corporate governance include integrity, transparency, accountability, objectivity, and the imperative of performance.

There are several benefits to be obtained through the pursuance of good corporate governance practices. They include improved performance through greater efficiencies, enhanced corporate image through greater trust, optimal leveraging of shareholders' nonfinancial contributions, higher valuations, and lower costs of capital.

To secure these benefits a series of best practices can be implemented. These corporate governance best practices may be placed into three broad categories: structure, ethical behavior, and stakeholder relations.

Organizational best practices entail structuring the company to facilitate the performance of good corporate governance at both the institutional and the individual level. No overdependence on any one person or shareholder group should be permitted. A responsible board with authority to defend shareholder interests must be in place. Shareholders need to have sufficient participation and opportunities to express their views, and managers must be granted sufficient authority to carry out their responsibilities. The interests of all stakeholders need to converge into mutual objectives. Establishing crisis management procedures, designating a corporate secretary to oversee compliance with good corporate governance, and the use of a reputable independent auditor are additional structural measures to ensure that good corporate governance principles will be upheld.

A corporate culture that encourages the fulfillment of all the attributes derived from good corporate governance is the first important step in pursuing the practice of beneficial ethical behavior. There are ethical behaviors to be practiced and unethical behaviors to be vigilant against. Ensuring the integrity of the capital structure and allocating funds based on what is expected are other ethical behavior best practices.

Stakeholder relations involves the communication and execution of corporate governance principles vis-à-vis all stakeholders. Best practices start with communicating any corporate governance activities and events in a timely, clear, and accurate manner. Proper disclosure of all important material information to the various stakeholders is a necessity as well. Taking steps to build strong credit, employing effective public relations, and using crisis management practices are additional ways to pursue strong corporate governance.

To determine whether a particular act or decision diminishes or strengthens the corporate governance of a company, consider the effects of such an act or decision on the ability of the company to fulfill and communicate the five core attributes of sound corporate governance: integrity, transparency, accountability, objectivity, and performance imperative.

Employing strong corporate governance practices is a crucial piece of the puzzle necessary to achieve a successful exit.

CHAPTER 8

Financial Decision Making for Optimal Performance

In Chapter 7, we discussed the numerous benefits associated with establishing a strong corporate governance regime. Two of the benefits included improved performance through greater efficiencies and optimizing the leveraging of nonfinancial contributions offered by the shareholders, some of whom will be new business partners serving decision-making roles. The primary means to secure such benefits is to manage financial decision-making processes and establish financial decision-making structures consistent with the performance imperative.

To achieve a successful exit, you must consistently and decisively make the right financial decisions on all levels. You must allocate judiciously the appropriate decision-making authority and responsibilities to ensure successful execution and sufficient accountability respectfully. Deem processes in any business as natural inefficiencies, and streamlining them should be a goal. Decision-making structures, particularly for an entrepreneurial venture, need to accommodate the periodic addition of new business partners who also serve as decision makers.

To examine the various critical elements related to establishing effective decision-making processes and structures, the chapter begins with a discussion of financial decision-making processes, which include employing sound corporate governance practices, managing financial expectations, and understanding the dynamics of your decision-making regime. The next topic is establishing financial decision-making structures. After articulating the objectives to be pursued, we examine the means to establish the appropriate decision-making bodies and procedures, the proper allocation of decision-making authority and responsibilities, and the placement of individual decision makers in the most appropriate decision-making bodies. The chapter concludes with a thorough investigation of financial decision making in practice. The areas covered include strategic financial planning/fundraising, budgeting, operational (day-to-day) financial decisions, financial dealings with external parties, and exiting.

Financial Decision-Making Process

Managing the financial decision-making process provides an opportunity to preserve a certain level of control, maintain the focus of the company, and ensure efficient decision making. It serves as a base for establishing the most effective decision-making structures.

Practicing Sound Corporate Governance

As we discussed in Chapter 7, instituting a strong corporate governance regime is both an acknowledgment that management (i.e., the decision makers) have been granted decision-making authority by the owners (i.e., shareholders) and that such authority is to be wielded in the interest of the owners. The corporate governance structures and practices you have instituted will have a significant effect on both the decision-making structures you elect to establish and the financial decision-making procedures conducted in all decision areas.

A responsible board serves as a check on the decisions and actions of management, particularly in regard to strategic-level decisions that require some form of board consent. The board sets the strategic objectives of the company, sparing management from involvement in stakeholder politics and permitting apolitical decision making necessary for honoring the performance imperative. The board also is required to grant sufficient authority to each decision-making body to enable decisions to be made and executed effectively.

Aspects of corporate governance particularly relevant to effective ongoing financial decision making are listed next.

- A balance of power among the decision-making bodies needs to be maintained to ensure that no one decision-making authority is overworked, that too much power is not concentrated, and that diversification of stakeholder interests is properly managed.
- Potential conflicts of interest need to be identified early before individual decision makers are delegated to important financial decision-making roles, assigned to specific decision-making bodies, or permitted to participate in financial dealings with outside parties.

- Relevant and actionable information needs to be accurately disseminated to each decision-making body in a timely manner to ensure optimal decision making.
- Any real or potential cash flow crisis or conflicts of interest need to be shared with external stakeholders (i.e., key vendors and strategic partners).
- All levels of management, particularly those directly involved in budgeting and financial planning, should be keenly aware of the expected use of funds and be able to justify any deviation from such expected usage.

Every financial decision made and the actions of every financial decision maker must be firmly based on and consistent with the five core attributes of corporate sound governance: integrity, transparency, accountability, objectivity, and performance imperative. In addition to practicing sound corporate governance, understanding the dynamics of your financial decision-making process and managing financial expectations enables you to pursue these attributes.

Understanding Existing and Potential Decision-Making Dynamics

An intimate understanding of the dynamics of the financial decision-making process within your venture, given the personalities, background, and interests of the various decision makers is essential to optimize effective decision making.

In Chapter 7, we mentioned the concept of Tao as postulated by Sun Tzu. The Tao both impacts and is impacted by decision makers at all levels. Interplay between Tao and decision makers creates a dynamic environment that must be understood in order to cultivate a favorable Tao.

Acquiring a strong understanding of such dynamics is both critical and challenging, particularly for entrepreneurial ventures, which experience both rapid growth and the relatively frequent addition of new decision makers who often represent previously outside interests.

In Chapter 2, we talked about how important it is to know your investors (KYI). We also need to know our management, which is often composed in part of formerly prospective investors. It is useful to answer the following questions.

To what degree are interests aligned?
Are there factions, partial interests or potential alliances?
Are there decision-makers that may be considered centers-of-influence?
Are there actual or potential personality clashes?
To what degree are expectations aligned?

To What Degree Are Interests Aligned?

It is virtually inevitable that decision makers with different stakes in the company will have different interests. This fact will become more evident as the number of stakeholders represented by decision makers increases. Very little can be done to change such interests once decision makers have gained participation in the decision-making process. Again, the importance of KYI #4 related to selecting good business partners and avoiding bad money cannot be overstated. However, you can manage the existing varied interests represented within your decision-making bodies effectively if they are adequately understood. I find it a very helpful exercise for entrepreneurs to draft a document, kept in confidence, listing the different interests of all those participating in the venture's decision making. Identify common interests and interests that may conflict or prove very difficult to achieve simultaneously. Keep this list in mind when articulating the venture's current position/traction, setting forth financial objectives and an exit strategy. Emphasize common interests, and avoid stating a status, objective, or strategy that may reveal a real or potential conflict of interest or have a perceived counterproductive effect. Refer to this list when it is time to assign individual decision makers to decision-making bodies.

Are There Factions, Partial Interests, or Potential Alliances?

The list of interests you create will assist you in identifying potential allies and adversaries in the various decisions to be deliberated and made. Identifying allies may provide an opportunity to establish productive working relationships. For example, if you have a decision-making body primarily responsible for financial negotiations with outside parties establishing a working relationship and including two individuals in that particular decision-making authority with complementary abilities is a good idea. For example, one decision maker has intimate knowledge and strong contacts with a key strategic partner and another has a successful track record negotiating financial agreements in the relevant industry. In decisions in which a strong representation of the diverse interests that exist will stimulate debate and eventually lead to a necessary broad consensus, the participation of individuals with opposing views may prove advantageous. In a situation in which two factions have opposing views, both of which are considered extreme, a heated debate may serve to moderate the views of each side and result in a more moderate decision.

Understanding the relative positions of the various decision makers is a valuable tool that enables you to foresee potential disagreements related to specific decisions and provides you with an opportunity to make the necessary preparations to mediate or mitigate such disputes. For example, say you have identified two potential opposing camps in the budgeting process.

One side is taking a longer strategic view and would like to see more money allocated to research and development to enhance product features that will give a competitive advantage and perhaps secure greater future market share. Another side is more concerned with the more immediate need to improve current cash flow and would like to prioritize funds for a direct marketing campaign that is expected to increase immediate revenues. As a founding chief executive officer, you may want to mediate the expected battle by offering an alternative way to increase current revenues. The importance of securing valuable intelligence, maintaining the initiative, dividing and conquering, and winning battles before they are fought are all tenets advocated by Sun Tzu.

Are There Decision Makers Who May Be Considered Centers of Influence?

People may be considered centers of influence (COIs) if they possess significant influence on other decision makers due to professional status or strong persuasive skills. A COI could be a powerful adversary or advocate, depending on the degree to which his or her interests are aligned to yours. If a COI has interests different from yours, you may need to make contingency plans to counter any influence the COI may attempt to wield on certain future decisions. If COIs generally are in agreement with you, they may prove invaluable advocates in your efforts to manage expectations, serve as an excellent conduit in communicating your objectives, and offer credibility to any decisions you support. Regardless, they are possible candidates to serve presiding roles in decision-making bodies as they have the strong capability to secure consensus. This is especially important in areas where decisions need to be made in a timely manner, heated deliberations are to be expected, and/or a strong consensus is eventually needed.

Are There Actual or Potential Personality Clashes?

It may be beneficial to maintain a safe distance between two individuals with personal issues between them. A "safe distance" may mean keeping them off the same decision-making bodies. However, often this is not possible and the two clashing personalities participate in decision-making proceedings together. The existence of opposing personalities in a decision-making body can be harmful when it disrupts deliberations or clouds the objectivity of the individuals in question or others influenced by the personal clash. In the former scenario, you can only hope for or encourage professional decorum. In the latter scenario, participant awareness of the personality clash is usually sufficient to maintain objectivity. In any credible decision-making deliberation, procedures must be in place to ensure that only objective evidence and analysis receives serious consideration and that personal opinion is deemed as just opinion. Another potential difficulty to be aware of when two rival personalities exist is the possibility of personal competition for greater decision-making authority. Caution is advised when it is time to place such people in decision-making positions to ensure that neither one is in a position to thwart the legitimate concerns or presentations of the other.

To What Degree Are Expectations Aligned?

The difference between interests and expectations is subtle but very important to recognize. The best way to explain the difference regarding a particular decision is if interests are aligned, everyone will say "yes"; if expectations differ, qualifications will be demanded and the extent to which the decision is executed will vary. Unfortunately, most decisions will require more than a simple "yes" or "no." The chemistry among the decision makers may be strong, but if there is a large variation in expectations, the reactions to significant financial events can also vary. Varying expectation levels among decision makers, regardless of the existence of shared interests, can prove to be a challenge when attempting to reach consensus; a shared expected effect of a specific decision may be deemed acceptable by some and not sufficient for others with loftier expectations. This is a matter of the relationship between risk and benefit discussed in Chapter 1. Decision makers with relatively high expectations will demand that riskier decisions be made or that higher risk is assumed to achieve greater results. Consequently a decision made by decision makers with similar interests but different expectations may have radically differing views regarding execution of the decision as well.

Next we discuss how to determine and manage such expectations.

Managing Financial Expectations

Financial expectations should be maintained at the minimal level that keeps people from feeling disenchantment. Expectations that are too low can lead to a defeatist attitude that can prove self-fulfilling. Expectations that are too high will narrow the permissible margin of error afforded to management and possibly apply undue pressure to achieve unreasonable objectives. At the very least, expectations that are too high likely will lead to a higher level of dissatisfaction, regardless of financial status or outcome.

The relative expectations of decision makers is equally important. A greater range of expectations may lead to greater dissention and detrimentally affect the decision-making process. It is not a good situation when a founding chief operating officer (COO) would like to make a high-risk decision to take advantage of a short-lived market opportunity she believes is essential to achieve financial objectives more ambitious than the ones currently stated. However, a new chief financial officer (CFO) appointed by a new shareholder group would like to take a more cautious approach; he recognizes that the high-risk decision is not necessary to achieve the stated objectives and may induce another funding round sooner than planned and before a higher valuation (i.e., higher price per share) can be justified. Consequently, this decision could dilute the recent investment made by the new shareholding group represented by the CFO more quickly than desired.

Financial expectations are expressed in two primary ways: stated Financial objectives and expected exit strategy. Setting and stating reasonable financial objectives easily discernible to all decision makers and having an agreed-on consensus on what would be the most desirable type of exit are two ways to keep expectations among the various decision makers aligned. Just as financial objectives progress on a timeline, so do the expectations of individual decision makers. Remember that an exit strategy is expressed in three ways: type of exit (initial public offering, merger, etc.), return on investment (ROI), and time. As with financial objectives, a consensus on the type of exit and ROI can be more easily tracked and maintained with effective communication. Time is the most likely dimension of an exit strategy where a consensus breaks down and is not readily apparent. It is nice that everyone agrees on the stated progression of financial objectives on the way to being acquired by an agreed upon shortlist of prospective purchasers. It is good that all stakeholders agree that a desirable ROI upon acquisition is 10X. However, if some stakeholders believe such an exit should occur next year and others three to five years from now, the decision makers representing the latter stakeholders will be more conservative in their decision-making positions. Another situation to stay vigilant for is when there exists a consensus on an acceptable ROI. Decision makers representing the interests of different stakeholder groups who invested at different price levels often have different ROI expectations in real terms. The best way to avoid such a situation is to state ROI in terms of the latest investors or the investors who paid the highest purchase price. Hopefully, no down rounds occurred, and the last investors did indeed pay the highest purchase price. The additional challenge of managing expectations effectively after the occurrence of a down round is just one more reason not to have a down round.

How can stakeholder expectations be tracked and managed?

Tracking expectations require expectations to be measured in real terms. The dimension of time is a basis for the subtle difference between interests and expectations. Agreeing to a set of financial objectives and the exit strategy is not merely a matter of "yes" or "no." Measuring expectations in real terms requires the use of a timeline.

The first step in managing expectations is to determine a safe range of manageable expectations. Periodically solicit the expectations of various stakeholders of diverse interests and different perspectives to determine such a range. If you find that the expectations of an individual stakeholder or a particular stakeholder group has moved out of the safe range, some direct consultation may be required. If you discover that the expectations of numerous stakeholder interests have markedly changed, it may be necessary to reassess what should be considered a safe range.

Avoid any excessive reactions to any significant financial event, whether good or bad. Managing expectations is easier when demonstrated progress is steady. Expectations of the various decision makers often start to diverge after a significant financial event occurs; it may be a good time to assess expectation levels.

If financial objectives are too strongly associated with volatile conditions, it is advisable not to define progress in their terms. Reasonably space out stated financial objectives to be attained on a timeline. The more often financial objectives are to be achieved, the greater the frequency of the possibility of expectation changes.

When discussing worst-case, expected-case, and best-case scenarios direct expectations near the bottom of the expected range. The progression of financial objectives should lead to this point in the expected-case scenario. The principle is similar to beginning negotiations on a particular point at the most favorable level within the range of possibility, as discussed in Chapter 6. Provide the decision makers with some reasonable working margin.

Financial Decision-Making Structures

The existing corporate governance regime, the dynamics of your decision-making process, and the financial expectations of your stakeholders and decision makers will determine what decision-making structures are established and their scope of responsibility and authority.

The aim in devising financial decision-making structures for your entrepreneurial venture is to find the optimal balance in which:

- Decision-making structures (individual officers or bodies) responsible for every potential financial decision are vested with sufficient authority to ensure that decisions are decisively made and dutifully executed.
- Decision-making efficiency is achieved by avoiding the possibility of turf battles, delineating clear and simple decision-making procedures, and ensuring that each decision-making body is of suitable size and composition to arrive at a decision (reach a consensus) in a timely manner as determined by the scope and nature of the decision.
- The maximum participation desired by each decision maker can be granted.
- The maximum value to be secured from each decision maker is achieved by persuasively assigning/placing each decision maker in the decision-making bodies most suitable for their experience and interests.
- The decisions made by the various decision-making bodies can be coordinated most effectively and do not conflict.

Successfully striking such a balance will create a lean, mean fighting machine capable of honoring the performance imperative discussed in Chapter 7.

Establishing Appropriate Decision-Making Bodies and Procedures

A decision-making body can be defined simply as an entity that is responsible for making final decisions on a specific issue or multiple related ones. A decision-making body may be an individual (i.e., CFO, project manager) or a committee (i.e., finance committee, negotiating team, etc.). Decision-making procedures include the mechanics and processes associated with deliberating and eventually achieving a consensus on a decision to be accepted, understood, and implemented by all the relevant parties.

Based on what major financial decisions will need to be made, the following considerations will be necessary: the time requirements to make each major decision, the level of consensus desired, the experience and expertise required to be drawn into the deliberations of a particular financial decision, and the degree of interdependence and required coordination with other decision-making bodies.

Time Constraints Associated with Each Decision

Some financial decisions need to be made within a few days once they arise. Certain tactical level or day-to-day decisions, such as deciding what software tool to purchase given the requirements of a particular development project (i.e., made by a project manager) or the decision on how to pay for the purchase of computers (i.e., decision by the CFO), are examples. The procedures required to make such decisions should be very straightforward, and the decision maker or decision-making body responsible for making such decisions should have immediate access to the relevant information and have sufficient authority (greater discretion) to make the decision quickly. Other financial decisions require a longer-term decision-making process. For example, how to finance a go-to-market strategy requires collection and analysis of a relatively large amount of information from multiple sources, and a decision does not need to be made before the actual go-to-market strategy is executed. Any decisions related to finance or fundraising may very well necessitate lengthy research and/or negotiations before a decision can be reached.

Necessary Consensus Required for Each Decision

For some decisions, simply reaching a decision is not sufficient. Securing a broad consensus may be necessary due to the importance of the decision, the number of stakeholders directly impacted, and/or the complexity of both deliberating and executing it. An example of a decision that should be made with a broad consensus is how best to structure the next funding round. Should you offer a debt or equity placement? How much money should you raise, and to what extant would you be willing to pledge valuable intellectual property (IP) as collateral? It is advisable to secure very broad consensus on such important decisions due to their direct impact on all stakeholders and the necessity to include and address the diverse interests in the deliberations. Another decision that requires strong consensus is agreeing on the financial terms to be proposed in negotiations with a comarketing partner, due to the strategic nature of the decision and the complexity of executing it. Typically decisions with more immediacy require less consensus. The processes and procedures associated with making decisions requiring a high level of consensus must be very inclusive, offer sustained forums for deliberation, and set stricter conditions for a decision-making vote.

Necessary Participants for Each Decision-Making Body

Necessary participants can be categorized into three classes: information providers, responsible decision makers, and decision implementers. Information providers are those individuals who possess the relevant and critical information necessary to make an informed decision. For example, a project manager responsible for infrastructure maintenance is probably a good person to participate in the decision-making body responsible for computer hardware purchases, whether this person has voting authority in the decisions of the body or not. Responsible decision makers include all those who will be held accountable for making a particular decision. Naturally, those with voting authority should be held accountable. However, excluding an individual from the deliberations or denying him or her voting authority in the decision-making process of a particular decision he or she ultimately will be held accountable for it is neither fair nor prudent; such a person can become a scapegoat for those who were collectively responsible for making a costly decision. The third class of necessary participants is the decision implementers. They are the managers responsible for successfully carrying out the decisions. There are three reasons not to exclude such participants in the decision-making process of a decision they will be directly responsible for executing, whether they are granted voting authority or not.

1. They may serve as important information providers, advising on what is and is not feasible.
2. They may be more capable of executing the decisions if they have participated in the decision-making process and have a good understanding of how and why the decision was made.
3. Their decisions will command more credibility (authority) among their subordinates who realize their direct superior participated in the higher-level decision making.

Coordination with Other Decision-Making Bodies

Some decisions require either a mechanism for joint deliberations and shared responsibility among multiple decision-making bodies or an actual decision-making body established for a particular decision in which diverse decision-making responsibilities can be channeled effectively. The primary examples of such decisions are related to crisis management. Two elements make a situation a crisis: time and importance. Crisis management decisions are the most difficult to make because they have very short time requirements; however, typically they require a considerable amount of consensus and coordinated execution as well. There are two ways to structure a decision-making process that can accommodate such demands. One is to identify those decision-making bodies responsible and accountable for decisions directly related to the crisis. Draw up contingency plans for each decision-making body specifying urgent emergency deliberations and streamlining internal decision-making procedures to reach a crisis decision in a timely manner. Each decision-making body must delegate one of its own to represent it in a separate decision-making body empowered by the board to make timely crisis-related decisions and be ultimately accountable. Another way is for the board to simply cut out the decision making to be made within each otherwise relevant decision-making body and assign participants selected from decision-making bodies otherwise responsible for the relevant decisional areas to a separate crisis-related decision-making body. This crisis-related body, which may have board representation as well, has overriding authority to demand relevant and critical information from whatever decision-making body and independently deliberate, make, and execute crisis-related decisions. Although the latter option may result in more expeditious decisions, I would recommend former option if possible. Due to the importance of crisis-related decisions, the stronger consensus and more powerful sense of accountability among the decision-making bodies derived from the first option more than justifies its selection.

All other decisions made under noncrisis circumstances also have varying levels of required coordination. The higher the level of coordination required, the greater the level of access to both information providers and decision implementers and the greater the need for a nexus where all information is collected and disseminated. This imperative is true for decisions requiring a high level of consensus as well. For decisions requiring a high level of consensus, the degree to which decision-making authority is concentrated is low; decisions requiring a high level of coordination need one or a few responsible decision makers to enable a more expeditious decision-making process.

A simple way to illustrate decision-making structures for optimal decision-making is to create a chart listing all conceivable potential financial decisions on the vertical axis. They can be classified into five broad categories: financial planning/fundraising, budgeting, day-to-day financial decisions, financial dealings with strategic partners, and exit. On the horizontal axis, list time requirements, level of consensus required, degree of coordination required and necessary decision participants. (See Figure 8.1.)

The chart will serve as a useful tool in determining what decision-making bodies should be established, the composition of each body, and what procedures will be appropriate in each body. The list of decisions on the vertical axis provides a means to allocate individual decisions to appropriate decision-making bodies. The considerations shown on the horizontal axis help you determine the appropriate procedures to be instituted in each decision-making body.

Allocating Decision-Making Authority and Responsibilities

The objective of effectively allocating decision-making authority and responsibility is to ensure that overall effective power is not too centralized or decentralized in particular decision-making bodies. Chapter 6 discussed the necessity to remain vigilant against negotiating a compromising combination of otherwise innocuous individual financing terms; it is equally important to avoid granting an individual decision-making body too much overall decision-making authority. Concentration of too much authority in a single decision-making body may enable it to render decisions of other decision-making bodies moot. This can occur because the decisions made by the other, effectively subordinate, decision-making bodies cannot stand alone and are too dependent on the decisions of the omnipresent decision-making body for execution.

When decision making is too decentralized, the ability to execute decisions effectively will be diminished, a deficiency in the sense of accountability may be created. and the decisions made by the various decision-making bodies are more likely to conflict, possibly resulting in paralyzing turf battles.

To avoid either excessive centralization or decentralization, each decision-making body must possess three As in sufficient quantities:

- *Authority*. The ultimate authority to make each specific decision must reside in a single decision-making body for three reasons. One is to avoid paralyzing turf battles during which two or more decision-making bodies argue over who has the responsibility to make a decision. Clear lines of authority must be established, particularly in crisis situations when rapid decision-making among multiple decision-making bodies needs to coordinated.

  Another aspect of authority to consider is that associated with ensuring the dutiful execution of any decisions rendered. Sometimes decision implementers receive conflicting directives on how to interpret and execute a decision if multiple decision-making bodies are involved.

Financial Decisions	Decisional Considerations			Necessary Decision Participants		
	Time Requirements	Level of Consensus Required	Degree of Coordination Required	Responsible Decision Makers:	Information Providers:	Decision Executioners:
Strategic Financial Planning/ Fundraising:						
Setting progressive financial & operational objectives	Low	High	Moderate	Board & executive mangement	All analysts and management	All levels of management
Decision to commence another funding round	Moderate	Very high	Low	Board & executive management	Financial Analysts	CFO & fundraising team
Selecting type of funding & prospective investors to Solicit	Very low	High	Low	Board & CFO	Financial Analysts	CFO
Budgeting:						
Monthly sales & marketing expenses following commercial launch	Low	Moderate	Moderate	CFO/Controller and CMO	CMO, market researchers, sales managers	Sales managers
% of profit margins allocated to Capex	Low	Low	Very low	CFO	Executive management	COO
What amount of new investment funds allocated for product development?	Low	Low	Low	CFO, & CTO, and COO	Project and R&D managers	Product managers
Operational Financial Decisions:						
How should we finance the purchase of 6 computers for new hires?	High	Low	Very low	CFO/Controller	Procurement officers	Procurement officers
How much should we retain in a cash reserve?	Low	Low	Low	CFO & controller	Financial analysts	Controller
Should we develop our own project management tool or subscribe to one?	High	Low	Moderate	CFO, CTO, and COO	Project managers	CTO

(Continued)

Financial Decisions	Decisional Considerations					
	Time Requirements	Level of Consensus Required	Degree of Coordination Required	Necessary Decision Participants		
Given our current burn rate, can we hire another tester?	Very high	Moderate	Moderate	CFO & COO	Controller	Hiring managers
How are contingency funds allocated and managed in crisis situations?	Very high	Very high	Very high	Board & executive mangement	All analysts	CFO
Financial Dealings with External parties:						
Which strategic partner is offering better comarketing agreement terms?	High	High	Moderate	CFO, COO, and CMO	CMO	COO
What should we demand to offer exclusive terms in licensing agreement?	Moderate	Moderate	Low	Board, CFO, & CTO	CTO	COO
Should we enter a long-term supplier agreement with a key vendor?	Low	Moderate	Moderate	CFO & COO	COO	Procurement officers
Exiting:						
Should we pursue an IPO or look for a strategic acquirer?	Very low	Very high	Very low	Board & executive management	CEO, CFO, & COO	CFO
Under what circumstances do we seek an exit?	Very low	Very high	Very low	Board & executive management	CFO & COO	CEO & CFO
What is the basis of our valuation and the price per share we should demand?	Low	High	Low	Board & executive management	CFO and financial analysts	CFO

FIGURE 8.1 Decisional Chart

This could cause confusion and turf battles among multiple bodies responsible for executing the decisions, resulting in poor execution. Another situation to avoid is when the decision maker lacks the authority to compel people to carry out the decisions. A glaring example of such an occurrence in American history is when President Jackson, who disagreed with a Supreme Court decision led by Chief Justice Marshall regarding the issue of native Indian removal, allegedly declared, "John Marshall has made his decision; now let him try to enforce it." I hope your venture will never face such a conflict, which can occur when the interests of lower management are not aligned with a new executive management group perhaps placed by a new controlling interest of the venture. A situation in which a necessary decision implementer was carelessly denied participation in the decision-making process can result in such a conflict as well.

- *Accountability.* Accountability (i.e., responsibility) and authority are intimately related. As we have mentioned several times, authority must be paired with responsibilities. This was demonstrated in the first situation discussed in which a decision implementer receives conflicting directives. It is also important to certify that the ultimate authority to make each decision resides in a single decision-making body so it is very clear which decision maker or decision-making body is to be held accountable. Accountability may become less clear if a decision is rendered moot by diminished ability to carry out a decision due to confusion about execution. Who should be accountable for an otherwise good decision that failed to meet expectations due to poor execution? In hindsight, it may be easy to determine who is to blame for a failed decision. However, our objective is to create decision-making structures in which the sense of accountability permeates all the relevant parties to induce everyone to faithfully ensure that decisions do not fail due to poor decision-making or implementation. In the second situation discussed allegedly involving President Jackson and the US Supreme Court, a sense of accountability may be eroded to a greater extent if the decision-making body cannot force the execution of a decision in accordance with the decision maker's intentions. Who should be held accountable for the failure to carry out the Supreme Court decision? The Supreme Court or President Jackson?
- *Access.* Sufficient access to both information and relevant management must to guaranteed. This is certainly a rudiment of sound corporate governance with the objective to ensure that the performance imperative can be pursued effectively. Not only does relevant and actionable information need to be disseminated accurately to each decision-making body in a timely manner but also a direct line of communication with both higher and subordinate management needs to exist to certify that

decisions are made consistent with higher-order strategic objectives and can be executed pursuant to their spirit and intentions. Both forms of access are required to ensure optimal decision making.

Placing Individual Decision Makers on Appropriate Decision-Making Bodies

To ensure that each decision-making body can best reach decisions within its areas of responsibility, you must assign individual decision makers to the most appropriate decision-making bodies.

A financial decision maker is defined as any individual having direct influence on a decision financial in nature. Typically the CFO is the only individual decision maker participating in every financial decision. The CFO usually serves as the presiding officer as well. Obviously, the CFO is a financial decision maker. However, a financial decision maker may be a person without a financial background who is granted the right to affect the outcome of a financial decision, whether by having the opportunity to cast a vote, by providing an opinion, or by participating in the deliberations of any decision related to finances (i.e., information providers and decision implementers). For a young start-up, the founders are usually the sole financial decision makers. Regardless, you should construct a decisional chart showing clear lines of decision-making responsibilities and accountability. As the entrepreneurial venture adds investment partners, much of the strategic-level financial decision making will reside with the board of directors, which may include representatives of new business partners. The CFO answers to the board. Individual board members or executives may be charged with specific financial decision-making responsibilities, such as negotiating with outside stakeholders, cash flow management, budgeting, and others. As the venture matures further, a professional experienced CFO and/or accountant (controller) may be hired; lower-level managers may be charged with submitting project-level budgets; and eventually the board may commission and select directors to serve on a finance committee to make political strategic-level decisions and perform well-defined financial oversight responsibilities. As you can see, as the venture grows, more and more financial decisions below the strategic level are delegated to executives and managers. Consequently more decision-making bodies filled with capable individuals are required.

Key considerations in making specific assignments include compliance with sound corporate governance principles, comparable backgrounds of individual decision makers, existing/expected decision-making dynamics, and the level of willingness and capacity of each person to assume decision-making responsibilities.

Compliance with Sound Corporate Governance Principles

Individual decision makers cannot be placed in decision-making positions in which they may have difficulty honoring one or several of the five core attributes of sound corporate governance: integrity, transparency, accountability, objectivity, and the performance imperative.

As we noted, as the venture grows and welcomes new stakeholders who have demanded board seats and/or management positions, potential conflicts of interest may arise. Such conflicting interests need to be identified before individual decision makers are delegated to important financial decision-making roles. For example, a decision maker with a vested interest in an outside stakeholder should not be permitted to participate in the deliberations of the decision-making body responsible for negotiating a comarketing agreement with the same outside stakeholder. A decision maker should not be assigned to a decision-making role in which he or she may be compelled to break an existing legal obligation to which he or she currently is bound. For example, a venture capital firm invests in your venture. The agreed terms call for the firm to select a COO to manage the venture's operations. However, that COO may have previously served in the same position with a comparable business and is bound to confidentiality agreements that restrict the ability to apply and/or share all of his or her expertise and experience. Perhaps the new COO is restricted from dealing with key suppliers or strategic partners as well.

Sometimes situations occur where an unforeseen conflict of interest arises and the decision maker has already assumed and performed in the decision-making position in question. In such cases, the decision making may have to be persuaded or compelled to withdraw from the deliberations of this particular decision.

To honor the corporate governance principle of maintaining a balance of power, you must seriously consider the ramifications of assigning an individual decision maker to more than one decision-making body, particularly several bodies responsible for strategic-level decisions.

Comparable Backgrounds of Individual Decision Makers

Here is your opportunity to finally leverage the expertise, experience, and professional contacts of your new business partners and put their good money to work. First you will have to take an inventory of the backgrounds of each decision maker. Once you have a good understanding of everyone's backgrounds, it is time to match individual decision makers with either a specific decision-making position or appropriate decision-making bodies. Obviously a certified accountant may be useful in the decision-making body responsible for financial planning/budgeting; a former banker may be charged with cash management responsibilities. An objective should also be to establish advantageous working relationships by pairing individuals with complementary skills. For example, a lawyer with negotiating experience and someone with considerable experience and contacts in your space may work well together on a decision-making body authorized to conduct negotiations. Teaming an investment banker with a former marketing executive may be advantageous in decisions related to fundraising.

Existing and Expected Decision-Making Dynamics

Unfortunately, it is not sufficient to man decision-making bodies solely on comparable backgrounds. Here we need to utilize what we learned in our previous discussion on decision-making dynamics.

Alignment of Interests   Based on our earlier discussion concerning the establishment of appropriate decision-making bodies, we know there are strong correlations among the degree to which the interests of the various participants in a decision-making body are aligned, the ease at which they reach consensus, and the necessity of securing a strong consensus. For decisions with short time requirements and a relatively small need for a strong consensus, a closer alignment of interests among the decision makers may be more suitable. For decisions that would benefit from a stimulating debate and/or require a strong consensus that would result in improved execution, a good mix of diverse interests may be preferable. Knowing who will be potential allies and adversaries will help you determine which assignments can be made that would produce advantageous working relationships, moderate the extreme views of two opposing camps, and make prudent preparations in the event of a paralyzing dispute.

Center of Influence   Although COIs have the ability to be effective presiding officers, the founders may not want a COI in such a position if the COI's views radically diverge from their own. If their views and interests are compatible, COIs work well as presiding officers for decision-making bodies in which decisions need to be made quickly and/or require a strong consensus.

Personality Clashes   It may prove very unproductive to place two arch-enemies on the same decision-making body even if they have complementary backgrounds. Such personality clashes may result in the deficiency of all five core corporate governance attributes. Integrity is compromised if their arguments are based on personal differences and unpredictable emotional responses. A lack of transparency may occur if each chooses to work behind the other's back. They may blame each other for failed decisions (not being accountable), injecting personal antagonisms may cloud objective debate, and any form of personal competition may trump the interests of shareholders. This would be a clear violation of the performance imperative.

Alignment of Expectations A misalignment of expectations may challenge attempts to secure a consensus on a decision and how it should be executed. Unlike a mix of diverse interests, which offers decision-making benefits under certain circumstances, mixing diverse expectations is almost invariably bad and difficult to overcome. We hope you have been successful in managing expectations. If not, consider avoiding the pairing of decision makers with diverse expectations.

Willingness and Capacity to Assume Decision-Making Responsibilities

As stated before, an objective for establishing financial decision-making structures is to enable the maximum participation desired by each decision maker. If it is desirable to persuade a new business partner to assume a decision-making role, you must determine whether they are a passive investor not interested in serving any decision-making role or an active investor expecting to be granted one. Ask active investors about the extent to which they would like to be involved in decision-making duties. Ask passive investors how they can contribute in other ways. Perhaps they would be willing to serve on a board of advisors.

Another consideration is to ensure that individual decision makers are not overwhelmed with excessive decision-making responsibilities, whether due to external commitments or assignment to too many decision-making bodies.

As we strongly asserted in Chapters 2 and 3, a strong and complete management team will make your venture much more attractive to prospective investors and provide greater assurance to your stakeholders that the venture ultimately will succeed. Therefore, judicious assignment of decision makers to the various decision-making bodies serves two important purposes: optimal financial decision-making and attracting more investment funds.

Once financial decision processes have been thoroughly examined and understood and the financial decision-making structures have been established, effective financial decision-making may commence.

Financial Decision Making in Practice

There are five primary areas of financial decision-making of importance for an entrepreneurial venture: strategic financial planning/fund-raising, budgeting, operational financial decisions, financial dealings with external parties, and exiting. We discuss the decision-making to be conducted in all five areas based on strategic thinking and established best practices.

Strategic Financial Planning/Fundraising

As mentioned in Chapter 4, there are many benefits associated with sound financial planning. Those that are related directly to financial decision making include assessing what is or is not financially feasible from a business planning/operational perspective, ascertaining the amount of funds that need to be raised, and securing such funds in a timely manner and on the most favorable terms. The objective is to determine a progression of related financial and operational objectives that, if achieved, will result in maximizing ROI upon exit, the ultimate objective.

The decisions are deliberated at the strategic level with input from the board, representing shareholders (i.e., ownership), the CFO (as presiding officer), and select relevant executives. For entrepreneurial ventures, the participants usually include the founding board and executives as such planning should be conducted at the very beginning of the venture.

There are several considerations for decision makers before they make decisions related to strategic financial planning and raising investment funds. To honor corporate governance principles, the strategic direction communicated by the board should be dutifully respected and pursued in both financial planning and negotiating with a prospective investor. In the event investment funds are secured, in the name of transparency, the decision makers will need to communicate the terms to other decision makers, particularly the expected use of funds and other stated interests of the new business partner.

The decision-making body responsible for strategic financial planning has a major influence on managing stakeholder expectations, as the financial plan eventually agreed to will establish the financial objectives and targeted exit strategy that are shared with all other decision makers and stakeholders of the venture. What is conveyed in the financial plan should be realistic and targeted near the bottom of the expected-case scenario. To assist in managing expectations and avoid creating overexpectations that may not materialize, those responsible for deliberating decisions and conducting funding negotiations should not discuss their deliberations with employees and stakeholders outside of the decision-making body. There is enough stress inherent in funding negotiations. Decision makers should not create additional pressure by making premature proclamations.

The practical means for conducting strategic financial planning was broadly discussed in Chapter 4 with the use of the various FREE (fundraising effectiveness and efficiencies) tools. The macro-tier considerations presented are directly correlated with strategic-level financial planning. One of the major purposes for composing a financial plan is to establish a progression of financial objectives. Three of the five primary bases described for establishing financial objectives directly applicable to strategic planning, fundraising, and funding negotiations include optimal selection of financing choices, minimizing equity dilution, and maintaining effective control. Hence the utilization of the FREE tools: ACRE (availability, cost, risk, and effect) charts, rating of equity dilution (RED), and command and control ratings (CCR).

The planning and conduct of fundraising activities was thoroughly covered in Chapter 5. The responsible decision makers for planning fundraising activities will need to answer three initial questions: Who should be approached, when, and how many? The first question is answered based on the venture's current fundraising stage, the stated investment criteria of the various prospective investors, and the use of CCR and ACRE charts to help make good and bad money assessments. Market conditions and the current position on your financial plan time stream will determine your answer to the second question. The answer to the last question is based on time constraints and the ability to manage multiple prospective investors while maintaining optimal leverage.

Funding negotiations were covered comprehensively in Chapter 6. The financial plan and the KYI knowledge acquired serve as valuable guides in devising an effective negotiating plan. Conceiving a negotiating plan in a holistic manner and understanding the interrelatedness of the various points of negotiation also provides a means to ascertain how the results of each point of negotiation will affect the existing or future decision-making structure of the venture. Some propositions worth repeating and directly related to negotiation-related decision making include demonstrating an open mind to convey the impression that the decision makers will be receptive to advice offered by new shareholders. In addition, it is important to remain conscious of possible constraints that agreed-to use of proceeds terms have on future budgeting decisions and any performance targets that may require revision of financial objectives. In the latter case, set such targets reasonably with an amount of funding triggered that is sufficient to enable you to reach the next performance target (i.e., financial objective).

Budgeting

Examining both the macro-tier and micro-tier considerations concurrently along a timeline as set forth in Chapter 4 is of tremendous assistance in making budgeting decisions, as budgeting is the bridge between the higher-level and lower-level financial decision making.

Base budget allocations on the amount of funding available and what is considered sufficient to achieve the agreed-on financial and operational objectives of the venture, as derived from financial planning and consistent with the performance imperative. Thus, the primary bases for establishing financial objectives related to budgeting decisions are revenues and profitability.

Any decision-making body responsible for budgeting should be made up mostly of responsible decision makers and information providers. It is particularly important for a decision-making body responsible for budgeting to continuously stay engaged with decision implementers who are in the best position to share what is and is not financially feasible. However, decision implementers should be used as information providers; they should not have voting authority in the budgeting decisions that will determine how much funds (i.e., power) they are to receive. In more mature ventures, the presiding officer may not be the CFO; instead, a controller may preside over a single budgetary decision-making body. The key information providers typically are project managers; other information providers consist primarily of individuals charged with financial analysis and auditing. Decision makers should be aware of expected use of funds and be prepared to defend any decision that deviates from such expectations.

The central task of budget decision makers is prioritization of spending using both financial and operating objectives as guides. Once spending priorities have been set, the ACRE chart is a valuable tool to allocate funds efficiently. Basically an ACRE chart is a means to making a comparative cost–benefit analysis of available choices to maximize revenues and/or profitability in the short term and the long term.

Operational (Day-to-Day) Financial Decision Making

Now that a financial plan is in place, financial and operational objectives are stated, and budget allocations have been made, we need to discuss how best to arrive at the day-to-day financial decisions that need to be made. The micro-tier considerations set forth in Chapter 4 are correlated with the practical financial decision making at this operational level.

The financial decision makers making these operational or tactical decisions primarily are middle or project-level management responsible for achieving specific financial or operational goals. The decision-making bodies for these particular decisional areas will have the heaviest concentration of decision implementers and information providers. The presiding officer may be an executive other than the CFO, such as the COO or chief technology officer (CTO), depending on the type of decision to be made. In more mature ventures, there may be multiple decision-making bodies responsible for financial decisions at the operational level. Presiding officers likely are financial directors and project managers.

Responsible decision makers should also be held accountable for accomplishing the objectives they are responsible for, given the funds allocated to them.

At the operational level, the financial decisions to be made focus most often on decisions that will expand in scope with business growth. Thus, there is a greater likelihood that decision-making bodies at this level may become overworked, which prevents them from fulfilling their performance imperative. To avoid such a situation, you must monitor workloads and periodically reevaluate the capacity of the existing decision-making structures.

The overall objective of making the various day-to-day financial decisions is for the responsible decision makers to most efficiently manage and expend the funds allocated to them to achieve the objectives of their respective decisional areas.

Day-to-day financial decisions can be divided into three areas: financing, cash management, and procurement (purchasing decisions).

Financing

Securing credit at the most advantageous terms, building strong credit, and progressively reducing the cost of capital are the primary ways to achieve the financing objective of optimizing the selection of financing options. Micro-level financing decisions usually are made by a single individual, such as the CFO for early-stage ventures and a director of finance in later-stage ventures. Again, ACRE charts offer the means to determine the most advantageous financing option, given the amount of financing needed, associated costs, potential risks, and expected effects. The ideas expressed in Chapter 7 on building strong credit will assist in progressively reducing the cost of capital.

Cash Flow Management

Averting a cash flow crisis and maintaining peace of mind are the primary goals of effective cash flow management. The two related primary bases for establishing financial objectives are burn rate coverage and maintaining effective control.

Decision makers responsible for monitoring and managing cash flow need to alert superiors of any pending cash flow crisis so that other decision makers can make appropriate preparations. Doing this is not only consistent with sound corporate governance; it provides critical information that has a profound influence on all other financial and operational decision making. Indeed, managing cash flow properly is usually the deciding factor in the survivability of a start-up. Such decisions should reside with a responsible, trusted, and competent decision maker who has unfettered access to all financial information and the very serious attention of the budgeting decision makers above and the purchasing decision makers below. As asserted in Chapter 4, the first financial objective for any start-up is to be able to internally finance the burn rate. The inability to do so will keep you in a perpetual state of desperation, which will severely limit your flexibility in all other decisional areas.

The first step in effective cash flow management is to create a cash flow statement listing all existing and expected monthly cash inflows and outflows. The second step is to identify which expenses are components of the burn rate. Doing this will allow you to determine the venture's monthly burn rate. Given your monthly burn rate, projected monthly revenues, and cash reserves, you can determine how long your cash reserves will last. That is how long your company can continue minimal operations without any future revenues. Depending on the stage and nature of the start-up, the cash reserve should support a minimum of three to six months If your cash reserve is not that large, you should identify ways to bootstrap—reduce your burn rate.

Rate the remaining nonburn expenses based on the priorities set by the budgeting decision makers. The lowest-rated expenses should be the first ones to be slashed in the event of a pending cash flow crisis. Notify the decision makers responsible for authorizing or incurring such expenses of such contingencies. A high order of transparency is critical in cash flow management as crisis decisions may need to be made.

Procurement

Procurement decisions will be predominated by prioritization and value-added considerations. Spending priorities have been set by the budgeting decision makers and the potential effect of such prioritization has been communicated by the decision maker(s) responsible for cash flow management. It is now the responsibility of decision makers charged with purchasing decisions to make value-added considerations. For each purchasing decision, you must identify the possible purchasing choices. Then conduct a comparative assessment of the direct or indirect impact each purchasing choice would have on the bottom line. The method is similar in principle to utilizing an ACRE chart: The associated costs (price), benefits (increased revenues or cost savings), and risks (durability and reliability) of each purchasing choice are comparatively weighed to determine the purchasing choice offering the highest value-added.

Financial Dealings with External Parties

External parties include key suppliers and the various types of strategic partners. External parties solicited exclusively for investment funds of financing are not included in this discussion.

The objective of negotiating with external parties is to simultaneously maximize revenues/profitability or secure vital inputs, maintain flexibility/control, and secure strategic and competitive advantages. The corresponding gains in traction can be used to attract prospective investors and provide negotiating leverage.

The decision-making body, responsible for negotiating any finance-related deals with external parties usually is a provisional negotiating team composed mainly of executive-level responsible decision makers due to the strategic importance of such dealings. Some form of board consent typically is required for such strategic-level decisions. Either a corporate counsel or a retained lawyer will be needed to ensure that any terms are satisfactory from a legal perspective. Because, in the name of credibility, the venture must express its views in one voice to external parties, typically one individual from the decision-making body is selected to communicate directly with an external party. Both the spokesperson and presiding officer should be an executive of the venture, not a lawyer or other outside representative. The type of deal determines who will likely serve as a presiding officer, decision implementers, and information providers participating in the decision-making deliberations. For example, a comarketing agreement may call for the chief marketing officer/director of sales and marketing to be the presiding officer/chief spokesperson, marketing analysts to be the information providers, and account executives to be decision implementers. The COO may serve as presiding officer over a team charged with negotiating a joint venture. The negotiations for a licensing agreement may be led by the CTO supported mostly by technical staff well versed in the details of the intellectual property being licensed.

Acting with transparency is important in maintaining good relations with external stakeholders. Any real or potential cash flow crisis or conflict of interest needs to be shared, and contingency plans need to be discussed.

The most common agreements entered into with strategic partners are comarketing and licensing agreements. A comarketing agreement is an agreement executed with another company offering a complementary product or service. Both parties agree to assist the other in their marketing efforts via joint advertising, shared use of distribution channels, copackaging, cobranding, and the like. An exclusivity agreement is a type of comarketing agreement that grants one party the opportunity to market the other party's product or service exclusively under specified conditions. Your venture may enter into an exclusivity agreement either as the party granting or the party receiving exclusivity. Note that exclusivity agreements are potent comarketing agreements offering both elevated benefits and elevated risks.

A licensing agreement is an agreement in which the licensee grants the right to use a proprietary product, service, or IP to a licensor. Your venture may enter into a licensing agreement as either the licensor or the licensee. Licensing agreements can include exclusive terms as well. There are inherent risks associated with negotiating any agreements with exclusivity terms. Particularly with exclusive licensing agreements, careless structuring or wording can create or strengthen the counterparty as a future competitor if the exclusive right granted to counterparty to market or utilize your product/service or IP is too unfettered and your right to use your own property is somehow restricted.

When evaluating the attractiveness of proposed terms for agreements with strategic partners, weigh the expected benefits together with the associated costs and risks. To conduct such an evaluation effectively, construct a new version of an ACRE chart.

Alternative options. What options are available other than entering into the agreement under consideration with the counterparty? Are there other potential suitors to negotiate a comparable agreement with? If so, how can their expected terms be compared? An option always available in any decision is maintaining the status quo. In this case, do the additional benefits offered in entering the agreement in question justify the associated additional costs and risks.

Costs associated with executing the agreement. The costs can be both financial and operational. A comarketing agreement often specifies a financial commitment to be made by each party to fund the joint comarketing efforts. Perhaps the financial costs are not stated but assumed. This is the case when expenses are to be incurred related to any integration efforts necessary to fulfill commitments agreed to in accordance with the agreement. From an operational perspective, will you have to redeploy some of your staff, hire new personnel, or change preferred vendors? Will a new decision-making body or coordinating team need to be established?

Risks. There are the risks associated with entering the agreement in terms of the negative consequences of associating with a potentially bad or struggling strategic partner, consequences related to failing to fulfill your commitments pursuant to the agreement, and possible limitations imposed on future decision making. Obviously it is not a good idea to enter a comarketing agreement with a partner that is about to experience a cash flow crisis and will not able to fulfill its end of the deal or a partner about to be experience a public scandal. Other companies may not be so transparent. What happens if, for whatever reason, you cannot uphold your end of the deal? Do you lose market credibility that otherwise would not have been at risk? Certainly you may reduce future opportunities to secure other strategic partnerships. Are there penalties if the product or service you licensed proves faulty? You must assess both the probability that such risks can materialize and the severity of the consequences. Another risk to consider concerns the issue of control. A CCR evaluation should be used to determine the risk of ceding future decision-making control. At the strategic decision-making level four questions should be asked:

- Will you need to choose a new set of financial objectives?
- Will this immediately compel or hasten another funding round?
- Will this inhibit or restrict your ability to engage with other potential strategic partners in the future?

■ Will it limit your exit options by establishing too strong of an interdependent relationship with a counterparty that may offer an exit opportunity: "an offer you cannot refuse"?

At the operational decision-making level, some decisions may be compelled by the terms of the agreement. For example, similar to restrictive use of proceeds terms that may be negotiated in a funding agreement, an agreement with exclusivity clauses may limit your operations, marketing, or choice of vendors in terms of geography, distribution channels and/or selection of product mix. An example of an exclusivity clause with such effect is presented next.

> "Exclusivity: Alpha Corp. agrees to grant to Beta Co. North American exclusivity to market CRM software for Alpha Premium, Alpha SME, and any other products or services created, developed, and/or distributed by Alpha ("Other Alpha Products"). During the Term of this Co-Marketing Agreement, Beta will be authorized to sell Alpha's products on an exclusive basis for the term of this Agreement and sell in the Territory on an exclusive basis. Furthermore, Beta agrees not to joint venture, market, sell, promote, affiliate, or in any way collaborate with competitors of Alpha in the CRM software market.

If your venture represents the grantee (Alpha), you are dependent on the success of Beta to market and sell your products in North America. You are not permitted to compete with Beta to sell your own products either if Beta performs poorly or if you discover a more effective channel of distribution that Beta does not have access to. If your venture represents the grantee (Beta), limitations are imposed in establishing working relationships with other potential strategic partners in the specified geographic territory. Although such restrictions can be mitigated with additional clauses qualifying the exclusivity terms and specifying situations when either party can terminate the agreement, a situation where you have the right to terminate is not very welcoming either.

Effect on finances and competitiveness. What are the financial or strategic benefits to be attained? Will executing this agreement increase revenues and/or increase profit margins? If so, what are the expected increases? Are there substantial cost savings to be realized? If so, how much? Are there certain competitive advantages or a favorable market positioning to be attained? Is a vital input being secured at competitive terms or that otherwise would be unavailable? Will being associated with the prospective strategic partner heighten your credibility in the market? Are risks mitigated with the addition of another revenue stream or the use of an additional marketing channel?

We hope that you have made enough good decisions along the way to be thrust into a new decisional area: *exiting*.

Exiting

The primary objectives of exit decision making are to identify current or potential exit opportunities, determine how well positioned you are to pursue such opportunities, pinpoint the most opportune time to engage, and select the optimal valuation model. The first two objectives have been discussed in Chapters 3 and 6 respectively and the last objective was discussed in Chapter 1.

The participating decision makers likely include the same people involved with strategic financial planning and fundraising. Indeed, exit decision making may be the responsibility of the same decision-making body. However, the primary difference is that decisions associated with exiting occur at a much later stage when the founders may no longer have such dominant influence and the relevant decision-making body has welcomed on board additional members representing the interests of different stakeholders. Again, the CFO likely serves as the presiding officer.

Past efforts to manage the financial expectations of the stakeholders will be crucial in giving the decision makers the flexibility to determine the most lucrative exit.

The decisions related to exiting include identification of ideal exit suitors to engage, selecting the negotiating leverage to be employed, and exit timing.

Identification of Ideal Exit Suitors

A potential exit suitor is any prospective entity that would have either a financial or strategic interest to acquire or merge with you. If the preferred type of exit is an IPO, the potential exit suitors represent the capital markets (i.e., stock exchanges) that you would like to list on and the prospective financial entities that would be willing to underwrite your venture.

The first step is to discover what criteria prospective suitors will use to evaluate your venture. As mentioned in Chapter 3, you should already have considered this issue when you determined how to articulate your corporate objectives. A strategic interest is beneficial. If not, is a potential exit suitor primarily looking for high profit margins, higher revenues, market share/ positioning, number of users, or something else? Keep an open mind when considering ideal suitors. Although you have articulated the type of exit desired in your exit strategy and the venture has achieved all the corporate objectives commensurate with attracting the interest of such suitors and necessary to place you in position to contemplate an exit, often ideal suitors appear from unexpected corners. As stressed throughout this book, the ideal exit suitor is a strategic investor. These are the most elusive types of investors to identify as they may not necessarily be directly related to your space, especially if your innovative product or service has a high level of adaptability and/or applicability.

Selecting the Negotiating Leverage to Be Employed

Once you have identified the potential exit suitors, you can select negotiating leverage to apply. The possible sources of negotiating leverage and the methods to wield them have been broadly discussed in Chapter 6. As with a counterparty in funding negotiations, you may be able to fulfill both financial and strategic interests for a counterparty representing a potential strategic partner. The difference is that the interests of a strategic partner are more likely to be more specific and pronounced, and the corporate governance issues to be deliberated are far less intricate and contentious compared to a non-strategic prospective acquirer. However, you are more likely to identify real or potential conflicts of interests with a strategic partner who probably already operates in your space. Thus, what may be an ideal source of leverage to be wielded with a strategic partner may not be as potent leverage with a prospective non-strategic investor.

Exit Timing

Once you have identified ideal exit suitors and determined what they are interested in and what you have to offer them, you can determine whether an attractive exit opportunity exists now or if it may be preferable to wait.

When is the best time to exit? This is one of the most vexing questions an entrepreneurial venture will need to answer. If you exit prematurely, you may be forfeiting a much more lucrative future exit opportunity. A current exit opportunity may represent a once-in-a-lifetime opportunity.

Not only do you need to consider the interests of your prospective suitors, you also need to consider the expectations of your existing stakeholders. You must consider this decision on a timeline. The longer the shareholders have had to endure, the greater their expected return. Accepting an offer for $5 million may be acceptable now, but in two years it may not be.

There are many possible approaches to determining the best time to exit. One common approach is for the decision makers to not waste any time. They pursue the first and any exit opportunity that presents itself that offers to satisfy the terms of the stated exit. The pro is securing a successful exit in accordance with your stated exit strategy early, forgoing the possibility of a future occurrence that could derail hopes for such an acceptable exit. The con is you may sell yourself short. For example you have received an offer now that presents a ROI of 10X. However, you have not achieved your stated market share goals, which you feel confident you can achieve within the next year. By achieving such market share goals, you will have assumed a market player position and likely will attract strategic investors offering a much higher ROI than what is currently being offered.

Another approach is to pursue an exit opportunity once contingent milestones have been accomplished. When all the stated objectives progressing to the planned exit have been achieved, it is a reasonable assumption that the venture is ready for an exit. This approach can prove to be very inflexible (i.e., you may have to forgo an earlier advantageous exit opportunity). Often such contingencies are not the best determinants of an optimal exit, particularly when you are seeking a strategic buyer whose interests do not depend on any of the milestones the decision makers responsible for exiting chose. Contingent milestones should be used as helpful guides, but it is best not to write such contingencies in stone.

In my opinion, the factors that determine the best time to exit are contingent on whether the ideal suitors you have identified have either a financial or strategic interest and when your negotiating leverage may peak vis-à-vis those ideal suitors.

It is reasonable to assume that from a financial perspective, a successful company will enjoy increased revenues and profits with the progression of time. Consequently, the venture's valuation should grow as well, and the ideal time to exit is later than sooner. Conversely, the highest valuations from a strategic investor may be expected to be higher sooner rather than later because a strategic advantage may have a short window of opportunity.

Additionally, an advantage sought by a strategic investor may have value to him or her that far exceeds what would be reasonably expected if any other potential exit suitor were merely evaluating your financials as a basis for a valuation. For example, if a strategic investor estimates that the strategic value for it to acquire your venture is $10 million, it is in a much better position to offer a higher price than any current nonstrategic investor who, based on your financials, can justify a much lower valuation of $4 million. This perceived difference in valuation may continue to be the case into the future as well. For example, if your planned exit strategy has a time horizon of two more years and an expected exit of $8 million given the successful attainment of all your financial projections, the current offer of $10 million from the strategic investor may remain the more lucrative exit opportunity.

Pinpointing when your negotiating leverage has peaked from a strategic perspective represents another advisable determining factor in when to pursue an exit. You may attain the most advantageous leveraging position when there are multiple offers, when a certain strategic partner has expressed strong interest, when favorable market news is just announced, when a favorable event in your space has occurred, and/or when you have secured a patent or public concession with strategic value. Sometimes such situations occur so fortuitously that you cannot conceive of a better opportunity to exit in the future. In such scenarios, it may behoove you to cash in while you are hot.

What if you cannot identify strategic investors and the ideal suitors consist exclusively of those possessing purely financial interests? For an entrepreneurial venture that has developed and commercially launched a truly innovative product or service, revenues should experience exponential growth for some time immediately after commercial launch. Such growth can be attributed to the high growth in demand and the willingness of the marketplace to pay premium pricing. However, over time, the innovativeness of the product/service fades and the marketplace becomes more competitive, resulting in an eventual flattening of the income curve. Your pro forma financials should depict exponential growth to reasonably demonstrate exceptional ROI to prospective investors and will serve as a means to draw your growth (income) curve. This curve will serve as a valuable reference.

The ideal time to exit is upon reaching the most ideal point on your venture's growth curve. This point occurs just before apogee when you have reached the highest point in the venture's growth curve (i.e., a higher current valuation than earlier points), where you can still show continued exponential growth (i.e., justification for higher price–earnings [P–E] multiples) and before a flattening of growth (i.e., reason for lower P–E multiples) occurs, which happens at some point for most maturing ventures.

The most common way to calculate a valuation of a venture from a financial perspective is to multiply the earnings before interest, taxes, depreciation, and amortization (EBITDA; a measurement of income) by some multiple (given the industry and expected future growth). Thus, the optimal valuation will be at the point on the growth curve where the product of these two factors is at its highest. As a hypothetical example, the ideal time to seek an exit may be when your EBITDA is at $1 million and your multiple remains relatively high at 20. At this point, your valuation is $20 million. If you wait until your EBITDA reaches $1.5 million, your multiple may have leveled off near the industry norm of 10, netting a valuation of only $15 million. If you seek an exit sooner when your multiple is much higher (40) but your EBITDA is also lower ($400,000), your valuation of $16 million remains below the ideal point.

Selecting the Optimal Valuation Model

There is no standard model to valuate a company based on strategic interests. The way to approach valuating your venture when the likely prospective suitors have primarily strategic interest in your venture is how much you would be worth to them once they acquire you and fulfill their strategic interests. A pre-requisite to determining such a valuation, and indeed which prospective suitor may offer the biggest exit, is knowing what strategic interest the prospective acquirer(s) have in your venture. What are you worth to them if they are propelled to a dominant market player position, knock-out a strong competitor, increase sales or profit margins by leveraging your IP, and so forth?

In situations where the prospective suitors may not have exceptional strategic intentions, however, see acquisition of your venture as an opportunity to enter the "space" or complement their existing product/service mix a comparable-based valuation model may be the optimal model to choose if it offers a higher price multiple to calculate your valuation as opposed to a purely pro-forma based valuation model, particularly if your growth rate projections are not sufficient to justify a comparatively high price multiple.

So which valuation model should we use to calculate the valuation in a situation where non-strategic investors represent the likely prospective suitors? Obviously the higher valuations that can be hoped for from a strategic acquirer cannot be expected and it may also be a stretch to insist on a comparable based model unless such prospective acquirer is already intimate with operating in the "space." Asset-based models are never a viable option for a tech start-up, particularly for an exit, and only appropriate for a liquidation sale. Therefore it is reasonable to assume that a pro-forma based valuation model will need to be used. There are many pro-forma based valuation models as we mentioned in Chapter 1. Choose the model that calculates the highest valuation for your venture.

Summary

This chapter explored how managing financial decision-making processes and establishing financial decision-making structures consistent with the performance imperative result in greater decision-making efficiencies. Additionally we demonstrated how this optimizes leveraging the nonfinancial contributions offered by the shareholders, particularly when new business partners are integrated into the decision-making process.

To cover financial decision making, the chapter moved from the financial decision-making process through structures and practice.

Effective management of the financial decision-making processes will result in more efficient decision making and provide a basis for determining how to organize your decision-making structure effectively. The issues covered include employing sound corporate governance practices, managing financial expectations, and understanding the dynamics of your decision-making regime. The decisions and actions of every decision-making body and individual decision maker must be consistent with the five core attributes of sound corporate governance. An intimate knowledge of decision-making processes in your venture and an effective organization of decision-making structures will help you honor the core corporate governance attributes. The diverse personalities, backgrounds, and interests of the decision makers create a dynamic that must be thoroughly understood to ensure that decision making is performed in an optimal manner. The questions to be answered include:

To what degree are interests aligned?
Are there centers of influence among the decision makers?
Are there personality clashes to be aware of?
How aligned are expectations?

The goal of managing expectations is to strike a balance between having unreasonably high expectations that place unwelcome pressure on the decision makers and detrimentally affect objectivity and having low self-fulfilling expectations.

A firm understanding of processes serves as preparation for the topic of establishing financial decision-making structures. The objective in creating decision-making structures is to identify the optimal balance among several related factors, such as ensuring that each potential financial decision is matched with a decision-making body with final authority and responsibility; lines of authority among decision-making bodies are clear; coordinating mechanisms exist for decisions crossing multiple decisional areas; and the maximum participation desired and maximum value to be drawn from each decision maker can be realized. To achieve these worthy objectives, we examined the means to establish the appropriate decision-making bodies and procedures, the proper allocation of decision-making authority and responsibilities, and the placement of individual decision makers in the most appropriate decision-making bodies. Considerations in establishing appropriate decision-making bodies and procedures included what decisions will need to be made, the time requirements associated with each decision, the level of consensus desired, the required experience and expertise necessary to be drawn into the deliberations of each decision, and the degree of interdependence and coordination vis-à-vis other decision-making bodies. A decisional chart was introduced to assist in determining what decision-making bodies need to be established and what procedures would be suitable for each body. In allocating decision-making authority and responsibilities, the goal is to prevent overall effective power to be too centralized or decentralized. To accomplish this goal, each decision-making body should be granted sufficient authority, accountability, and access. To ensure that each decision-making body has the capacity to make effective decisions within its decisional areas, several considerations were investigated, including compliance with sound corporate governance principles, comparable backgrounds of individual decision makers, existing/expected decision-making dynamics, and each decision maker's willingness and capacity to assume decision-making responsibilities.

A comprehensive review of financial decision making in practice concludes the chapter. The areas covered included strategic financial planning/fundraising, budgeting, operational (day-to-day) financial decisions, financial dealings with external parties, and decisions related to exiting. The discussion for each decision area covered the decisions each decision-making body is responsible for, decision-making process and structural considerations, and the practical means to formulate, deliberate, and execute decisions. Many of the practical methods to be utilized and the factors to be considered were covered extensively in Chapters 2, 4, 5, and 6.

I hope this chapter has served as a valuable guide for you in your efforts to integrate new business partners into the decision-making process and establish proper decision-making structures and procedures through your venture's growth stages. The benefit of such is enabling the decision-making bodies to produce well-informed decisions consistent with the core corporate governance attributes, ultimately resulting in optimal performance for the venture on its path to a successful exit.

Afterword

I wrote virtually the entire book based on personal experience as an investment banker, entrepreneur, and mentor. I have written the book in layman's terms simply because I am a layman on the subject matters discussed. Consequently, none of the content of this book should be construed as established academic theory, irrefutable fact, or legal advice.

I am indebted to all my past clients and mentees, without whom this book would not have been possible. All of the ventures I have been involved with, whether successful or not have been sources of inspiration, best practices, and fodder.

I sincerely hope the insights, shared personal experiences, analogies, and illustrations found in the book have been a source of enlightenment and practical benefit to readers.

It is not easy being a technopreneur. If you are a technopreneur living on Ramen noodles and facing the enormous challenges of operating a cash-starved start-up while vulture venture capitalists circle above your head, I feel your pain and hope to provide some relief.

Good luck on all your current and future ventures. Change the world, and make some money in the process!

Sample Financial Plan

Seed Stage
Total Required Funding: $100,000
Beginning RED/CCR: 100/100
Ending RED/CCR: 90/90
Funding Needs: R&D; Construct a Prototype; Patent filing

Tier	Available Funding Sources	Amount	Cost	Risk	Effect on Cash Flow	Effect on Balance Sheet	Command and Control Effect
Macro Tier	Angel: Common equity investment	25,000	10% equity dilution	Dilution of founders' voting rights	None	Additional paid-in capital/shareholders' equity	Neutral: Angel that knows the space. CCR reduction matches reduction in RED.
	Founders' contribution	5,000	None	None	None	Founders' paid-in capital/Skin in the game	Positive control kept in house. CCR addition
Micro Tier	Incubator program	25,000	None	None	Positive: Covers much of burn rate	None	None

Series A Stage
Total Required Funding: $750,000
Beginning RED/CCR: 90/90
Ending RED/CCR: 52.5/57.5
Funding Needs:

Tier	Available Funding Sources	Amount	Cost	Risk	Effect on Cash Flow	Effect on Balance Sheet	Command and Control Effect
Macro Tier	Preferred equity placement	500,000	25% equity dilution	Liquidation preference over founders' equity	None: Dividend payments deferred	Additional paid-in capital/shareholders' equity	Demand a board presence and some restrictions on use of funds (CCR reduced by an additional 5 beyond the correlated reduction in RED)

| Micro Tier | Public funding equity match (2:1) | 250,000 | 12.5% Equity dilution | Dilution of founders' voting rights | None | Additional paid-in capital/shareholders' equity | Positive: Passive investor (+10 on CCR, almost negating correlated reduction in RED) |

Series B Stage

Total Required Funding: **$1,500,000**
Beginning RED/CCR: 52.5/57.5
Ending RED/CCR: 52.5/50
Funding Needs: Scalability development; expansion into new geographic markets; Increase product/service offerings

Tier	Available Funding Sources	Amount	Cost	Risk	Effect on Cash Flow	Effect on Balance Sheet	Command and Control Effect
Macro Tier	Senior term loan	1,000,000	9% annual interest rate	Assets pledged; impediment to future fundraising	Negative: Debt to be serviced	Additional long-term debt	Have senior claim on valuable IP (−10 on CCR)
	Licensing fees	150,000	None	Potentially supporting a future competitor	Positive: Additional revenue stream	Positive: Revenue-generating asset established	Neutral
Micro Tier	Factor financing	250,000	4% Interest and fees	A/R pledged as collateral	Neutral: Collection of A/R directly assumed by factoring entity	Neutral: A/R secured by a third party	Claim on a valuable accounts receivable (−2.5 to CCR)
	Equipment financing	100,000	6% Interest rate	Equipment secured by financing	Negative: Monthly service payments payable	Negative: Additional short-term debt	Neutral: Secured debt
	250k bank revolving line of credit	No draw	10% interest on drawn funds	None: Unsecured line	Positive: Enhance cash management	Any draw considered short-term debt	Positive: Enhanced control of cash management (CCR bonus of 5)

Sample Funding Proposal

Sigma C, Inc. Funding Proposal

This Funding Proposal is dated as of June 17, 2012, and offered by and among Sigma C, Inc., a Delaware Corporation (the "Borrower"), and Prospective Investors (the "Lender").

WHEREAS, the Borrower has requested that the Lender extend credit to the Borrower consisting of a Revolving Credit Facility in an aggregate amount of $2,000,000 (the "Indebtedness"). This proposed funding represents the third funding round of Borrower. The proceeds from the first round of funding totaling $250,000 allowed Company to complete the Research & Development of its innovative subscription service, patent its core technologies, and successfully conclude Beta testing. The proceeds from the second round of funding totaling $500,000 permitted Borrower to finance the successful commercial launch of its subscription service, ongoing customer support, Website maintenance, and initial marketing efforts.

The drawn proceeds of the Credit Facility shall be used to fund the execution of the Borrower's growth and expansion plans into new geographic markets requiring further software development for enhanced scalability and localization of service offering, hiring additional sales and marketing personnel, and paying for fees and expenses related to this Credit Facility. The Lender is requested to extend such credit to the Borrower subject to the terms and conditions hereinafter set forth.

Proposed Funding Terms

Revolving Credit Facility Amount: $2,000,000.00

Term: 48 Months

Interest Rate: Annual Interest paid on drawn funds is 9%.

Credit Funding Schedule: Lender shall extend credit in the following aggregate amounts and on or before the following dates:

Tranche	Aggregate Credit Amount	Credit Availability
1st	$1,000,000.00	Upon Execution Date of a Credit Agreement
2nd	$2,000,000.00	At 6 months following Execution Date

Issuance of Common Shares: Upon each credit extension in the amounts specified in the Credit Funding Schedule above, Borrower shall grant Lender 30,000 shares of Sigma C, Inc. Common Equity.

In order to induce the Lender to extend the Revolving Credit Facility, Borrower hereby represents and covenants the following:

Sigma, Inc. Capital Structure

Total Common Shares Outstanding: 750,000

Total Equity Warrants Outstanding: 100,000

Total Equity Securities: 850,000

All Outstanding Equity Warrants grant holders the right to purchase one share of Sigma C, Inc. Common Equity at an exercise price of $5.00.

Valuation Calculation

Projected EBITDA through end of first year following funding: $2,465,870.00

P−E Multiple: 5

Total Valuation: $12,329,350

Per Share Valuation = Total Valuation/Total Equity Securities

12,329,350.00/850,000 = $14.51/Share

Immediate Dilution

Assuming full Credit Extension as proposed in the Credit Funding Schedule and the exercise of all outstanding Equity Warrants, we would have outstanding 910,000 of Total Equity Securities. The full issuance of 60,000 additional Common Shares to Lender as proposed represented a preoffering equity interest of 7.06% in Sigma C, Inc. The same 60,000 issued Common Shares represented an immediate postoffering equity interest of 6.59% in Sigma C, Inc. Thereby a dilution of .47% of Equity Interest has occurred upon the issuance of the proposed 60,000 Common Shares as a result of a full credit extension.

The following represent additional attributes of our capital structure and financial model favorable to prospective Investor(s):

1. Use of fairly modest assumptions inserted into the financial model.

2. Use of a P−E Multiple substantially below the current average multiple in the industry.

3. Potential extra cash flow generated from proceeds of exercised warrants.

IN WITNESS WHEREOF, the Borrower has caused this Funding Proposal to be duly presented and delivered all as of the day and year first above written.

BORROWER _____

APPENDIX C

Dictums of Entrepreneurial Finance

On Knowing Your Investor

- The primary objective of a prospective investor is to make money, not fund a hobby, not support a cause, or win first prize in a science fair.
- More often than not, the primary determinant of the failure or success of a technopreneurial venture is whether it receives good money or bad money.
- Good investors mitigate their investment risk by helping you mitigate risks associated with your business. Bad investors mitigate their investment risk by trying to establish a comparatively favorable position for them vis-à-vis other stakeholders without much regard for the risks these terms may impose to the business.
- Pay a premium for good money and turn down bad money offered at better financial terms.
- Do not succumb to the mad scientist syndrome. No matter how spectacular and intriguing your innovation, investors are more interested in profits.
- Vulture capitalists focus on desperate people. If you send out the vibe that you are seeking funds to avert the end of your venture, you are lining yourself up to be a hot dinner for a vulture capitalist.
- A strategic investor is the most prized prospective investor offering the greatest perceived valuations for your venture. Your primary objective and challenge is to identify and position your business to attract such investors.
- Investors do not invest in products; they invest in people.

- The way to grab prospective investors is not to impress but to hit their sweet spots and demonstrate command of both your venture and the market.
- In any business enterprise, you do not want to take on a partner who has very little to lose while you are risking and sacrificing everything.
- Debt holders and shareholders have different risk tolerance levels. Debt holders are more concerned with short-term cash flows to service their debt and avoid any moves that may risk the value of assets they have secured from you as collateral. Shareholders are more likely to exhibit patience and be willing to make short-term sacrifices to effectuate a higher ROI upon exit.
- Have passion for your innovation at work, and show passion for your business outside of work.

On Early-Stage Funding

- Treat investors as founding partners in determining the percentage equity interest to be issued based on their offer until you reach a funding round whereby sufficient operational and financial objectives have been achieved to serve as a basis for a valuation.

On Public Funding

- Of primary importance in negotiations for public funding are demonstrating economic sustainability, clear alignment of your business objectives to the agency's KPIs, and clear interdependence with the specific municipality or jurisdiction of the prospective public funding agency.
- If a technopreneurial venture abandons its original vision and objectives to fit public agency funding criteria, it may be seeking bad money.
- Trying to impress a public funding agency official may be counterproductive. Doing so only magnifies the significance of your venture and consequently the risk associated with failure in terms of his or her career prospects. Typically public funding agency officials are more risk adverse than high-risk equity investors, as they do not expect much credit for assisting a successful venture but are likely to be criticized or demoted for assisting a failed one.

On Business Planning

- Your business plan should reflect the progression in your planning. You must specify a problem before you present a solution, and only then can you offer a value proposition. You must define the product and a market before you can formulate a marketing plan and identify competitors. Everything has to be comprehensively described and costs estimated before the business plan ends with the financials and a specification of an exit strategy. Your business venture becomes an investment opportunity only once you have formulated and determined the financials and exit strategy.

- Ideas are cheap. The value of any business is not the idea or product on which the business is built but in the formulation and successful execution of a business plan associated with the idea or product that generates exceptional returns for all its stakeholders.
- A primary objective of any technopreneurial venture is to protect and maintain control of its suite of intellectual property for as long as possible.
- The bigger and more challenging a problem is, the greater the perceived value of any solution.
- A "bigger and better" product does not necessarily secure "bigger and better" profits.
- Do not assume that demand for an innovative product exists merely because it makes complete logical sense that it should. Consumer behavior does not exist in a world of logic. Emotions and other illogical determinants have powerful effects on consumer behavior that can be revealed only by grassroots research, such as customer feasibility surveys.
- If you make a compelling case of why a strategic partner would want to work with you, most likely you have just made a compelling case for why a strategic investor should invest in you.
- What you state may be used against you. Remember that prospective investors may base performance triggers on your operational objectives.
- Do not be too conservative in your financials. Prospective investors will be conservative enough for both of you.
- The strength and credibility of the financial model you use as a basis for your pro forma financial statements are far more important than the actual numbers you employ.

On Pricing

- Your pricing policy can make or break your entire business. If you price too high, you compromise the revenues required for securing initial traction and/or your ability to secure valuable market share. If you price too low, you may make your exterior stakeholders (customers, suppliers) happy, but that is at the expense and scorn of shareholders who expect exceptional returns.

- The objective of your pricing strategy is not to be the price leader (i.e., lowest price); it is to be the price setter.
- If your product is truly innovative, you should be able to charge a premium.
- If you cannot charge a premium for your product or service, you are not demonstrating sufficient differentiation from the competition.

On Financial Planning

- The essence of effective financial planning is considering each individual financial decision in the context of an overall financial strategy.
- If you devise and execute an effective financial plan, the consequent improvement in business planning, the periodic securing of funds on the most favorable terms at the optimal minimum amounts and timing will serve to maximize ROI upon exit.
- Efficient fundraising is a balancing act between minimizing equity dilution while obtaining enough funds to reach the next required funding round.
- Securing the maximum amount of investment funding offered in a given funding round can prove to be a costly mistake.
- Before a technopreneurial venture successfully secures series A funding and commences to generate revenues, the loss of the founders' control more often than not signals pending failure because before that point no one can manage the venture better than the founders.
- Keep your exit options open. Do not try to make yourself particularly attached -to a single exit option by tying yourself too tightly to it. When the time for exit arrives, you will lose negotiating leverage if one prospective purchaser knows it represents the only viable or worthwhile exit option available or that it can take actions that could ward off other prospective acquirers, who may be their competitors.

On Negotiations

- A winning negotiating plan recognizes the legitimate concerns of each party, establishes an acceptable range for each point of negotiation, and prioritizes them.
- When considering relative negotiating leverage, the more attractive a counterparty is as a business partner, the greater that counterparty's relative leverage when negotiating with you.
- The earlier the stage of development, the greater the perceived risk and the greater the expected rate of return. A higher expected rate of return pushes down the valuation a counterparty considers acceptable.

- During negotiations on valuation, focus on the multiple. Do not allow negotiations to make significant alterations to your pro forma financial model. Once you start altering your pro forma numbers, potential investors may challenge the underlying assumptions and individual components of your business plan.
- Negotiations ultimately succeed because both sides gain mutual respect for the interests of the other. This mutual respect is a good basis for continued success as business partners and for the establishment of an effective corporate governance regime.
- In funding negotiations, discipline is far more important than skill. During funding negotiations, you are most likely sitting across from a counterparty inherently much more skilled in the realm of finance than you. Having a negotiating plan forces discipline on your team.

On Corporate Governance

- Trust is one of the most valuable assets a company can possess and is the crux of sound corporate governance.
- Effective execution of any business plan requires effective management of diverse stakeholder interests, which is made possible through sound corporate governance.

Glossary

A

Accountability   Synonymous with responsibility. Every decision must be able to be justified based on sound judgment and ethical principles. Negative consequences must be expected by decision makers whose decisions result in dire outcomes.

ACRE Chart   An effective way to determine how to secure funds on the most favorable terms given stated company and operational objectives. The letters A-C-R-E stand for availability, cost, risk, and effect. They represent the criteria to be assessed to determine the most efficient finance option. The different funding options are listed on the vertical axis. The various criteria to be assessed are listed on the horizontal axis.

Adjusted RED   The raw rating of equity dilution (RED) score adjusted to account for established future uncertainties in the capital structure of a business. An established capital structure uncertainty exists when there is a possibility that further equity dilution can occur without the necessity of executing a funding round. Such an occurrence is primarily possible due to the existence of convertible securities.

Angel Investor   An individual willing to make high-risk investments in early-stage ventures. Typically these individuals have had successful entrepreneurial experience in the areas of investment they consider.

Antidilution   The purpose of an antidilution clause is to protect counter-parties from dilution of their equity in the event of future equity issuance. An increase in the total amount of outstanding shares automatically reduces the equity percentage interest held by each current shareholder. However, such dilution is often acceptable to shareholders when future equity sales are executed at higher valuations (i.e., increased price per share). Sophisticated investors commonly insist on such provisions to protect themselves in the event of a down round.

B

Bad Money The associated risks, impediments, and considerable efforts in securing bad money are too great to assume. Investors offering bad money are impatient, frequently challenge management decisions in a non-constructive manner, have few nonfinancial contributions to offer, impose funding terms that increase risk associated with the venture, and may have self-interests not aligned with the venture's founders or shareholders.

Bootstrapping The practice of sustaining operations and development without raising external capital.

Burn Rate The sum of all the minimum fixed costs of the business. It is a measure of efficiency. Minimum fixed costs include only those costs that would have to continue to maintain the company's existence. The higher the company's burn rate, the higher the perceived investment risk because the burn rate represents a minimal level of commitment to keep the business afloat.

C

Capital Structure The composition of a company's liabilities used to finance (acquire) its assets. It is basically a summary of all your company's executed fund raises. The positions of the stakeholders, narrowly defined as both shareholders and debt holders, will be represented in your capital structure.

Captive Target Market Occurs when potential competition is limited by design for a number of reasons, including the execution of an exclusivity agreement, lack of comparable competition, or when an arrangement exists in which many of your current or potential clientele are existing clients of a comarketing partner. Basically, your target market has very few, if any, alternatives available to meet their demands or expectations.

Centers of Influences (COIs) Generally highly visible individuals who serve as movers and shakers in their respected professions or industries. Their high status and prestige places them in excellent positions to draw on personal contacts to actuate valuable introductions and preferential treatment.

Clean Capital Structure One that is not complicated by numerous funding types and convertible instruments that can be a source of confusion for prospective investors.

Command and Control Rating (CCR)   Calculation of a CCR is an effective way to measure the preservation or loss of financial decision-making abilities of the founders'. You need a clear understanding of the nonfinancial pros and cons of each planned financing on both macro and micro levels to assess their effect on issues of control. CCR permits a comparison of such effects to assist in the selection of the most favorable financing options. It represents a relative estimate of what degree of financial decision-making discretion is expected to be forfeited or gained since the last funding round. A CCR evaluation helps in discerning good money from bad money.

Commercial Launch   Represents the initial offering of your product or service for public purchase through the execution of your marketing plan with the intention to commence generating revenues.

Conference Room Pitch   The audio-visual version of your business plan. It is a formal presentation that usually lasts 20 to 30 minutes. Such presentations should be customized. The audience has had the opportunity to review some or all of your prospectus documents. The typical audience is a group of angel investors or a committee of an institutional investor. The primary challenge in this type of presentation is to demonstrate the efficient organization and smooth functioning of the business in a comprehensive and compelling manner while offering sufficient detail to answer specific questions, whether previously revealed or perceived, and to generate inquiries associated with making an investment decision. The key to crafting a successful conference room pitch is to present your business opportunity in a holistic manner, including every material facet of your venture, and to tie them altogether.

Control   The ability to directly or indirectly influence management decision making. Decisions that may be influenced include business planning, finance strategy, fundraising efforts, operations, research and development, marketing and exit strategy. Control can be intended or unintended. External control is the ability of nonfounding stakeholders to apply such influence. Maintaining effective control of your business is critical to ensure consistent planning, flexibility, a clear path in front of you, maintaining the founders' vision, and a continued focus on a single set of derived objectives throughout the successive stages of development.

Convertible Debt   A hybrid of both private equity and debt in which a debt note is executed and there are conversion terms. The investor usually is permitted to convert the remaining principal and possibly accrued interest balance into equity either at any time during the note term or only at the end of term.

Corporate Governance The means (rules, policies, and procedures) through which a company organizes and directs itself to achieve the long-term mutual objectives of its stakeholders. The favorable attributes exhibited by a company possessing effective corporate governance include integrity, transparency, accountability, objectivity, and the imperative of performance. Demonstration of good corporate governance can serve as a powerful source of leverage as it acts to reduce perceived risk and holds promise for greater performance, thus returns.

Cost of Capital The cost for debt or credit funding. It is the interest rate a lender would charge you under your venture's current financial condition. As your business grows and becomes more successful, your cost of capital will decrease. Achieving progressively lower costs of capital is an important objective for any business.

D
Defined Target Market A target market defined by the technopreneur with two objectives in mind: (1) Define a small niche market in which you can establish a noticeable presence (i.e., become a player) and that is most suitable for your particular competitive advantages and (2) define a market big enough to attract prospective investor interest. Doing this requires an astute balancing act.

Dilution The decrease in the percentage equity interest of each shareholder upon an increase in the number of outstanding shares of the company.

Dirty Capital Structure The opposite of a clean capital structure; a dirty capital structure creates uncertainty due to its complications and numerous contingencies.

Discovery A realization during a planning process that leads to a revision that represents an improvement. A discovery is any important actionable notion that comes to your attention as you are composing your business plan or any other planning document. It is actionable in that it prompts a revision, addition, deletion, or reformulation of a goal, priority, or strategy. Such revelations are key to effective business planning.

Disruptive Innovation One that will significantly alter the dynamics of the marketplace into which it will be introduced; consequently, it possesses the greatest potential value.

Down Round Occurs when an equity sale subsequent to other equity purchases is executed at a per share price lower than the prior purchase prices. The effect of a down round is a reduction in the percentage equity interest of current shareholders. Down rounds are basically death wishes for your venture, as they destroy the integrity of your capital structure, and the prospects of raising future funds will be very bleak.

Downside Protection Any means of protection limiting the amount of financial loss that can be suffered from an investment.

Drag-Along Rights Specific voting rights that may work in two ways. In the event of liquidation or purchase of the venture below the negotiated liquidation preference, veto power is granted to shareholders possessing such rights. Drag-along rights may also compel shareholders to sell their shares in instances when specified group (i.e., management) is ready and willing to sell their shares upon the opportunity for a successful exit. This right can prove favorable to founders and other shareholders as it prevents one or a few holdouts from blocking a potentially lucrative exit.

Due Diligence The reasonable care undertaken by a party before entering into a legal agreement or transaction with another party. It is the thorough investigation/inquisition or audit of your business performed by a prospective investor before they make a decision to enter into actual negotiations. Due diligence is conducted by both parties to fortify their negotiating positions and judge the suitability of the other party as a business partner.

E

EBITDA Earnings before interest, taxes, depreciation, and amortization. To calculate a pro forma–based valuation, this figure denoting a company's income is commonly multiplied by an acceptable multiple to derive a valuation.

Elevator Pitch The shortest of the three types of funding presentations. It is so named because it is used in situations in which you have no more than 30 seconds to speak, such as a chance encounter at a conference. The focus of the presentation should be on the problem/solution dynamic, value proposition, and how you and all the shareholders (i.e., possibly the person to whom you are speaking) will become a market player. In an elevator pitch, you want to establish brand recognition whereby your venture is associated with a valuable service or role.

Equity Warrant Grants the holder the right to purchase a specified number of shares at a specified exercise price. It may or may not specify a term. These warrants share all the characteristics of equity with one important exception. A warrant holder does not have shareholder rights, particularly controlling voting rights, until such warrants are exercised.

Executive Summary The short and sweet version of your business plan and usually the initial prospectus document presented to prospective investors separately. The purpose of the executive summary is to generate enough interest to secure a presentation or request for additional information from a prospective investor.

Exercise Price The price at which a share of convertible stock can be purchased.

Exit Strategy The end game of your venture, denoting how investors get their investment and profits, when, and how much. The components of a stated exit strategy include type of exit, time horizon, and return on investment. The exit strategy you choose will determine what prospective investors to target, how to present to them, and how to prepare both your business and your financial plans.

Expected Range of Possibility A range that you establish on specific terms before entering negotiations on those terms. The bottom of the range is your minimum acceptable level; the top of the range is the highest you could possible reasonably expect. Begin negotiating terms at the top of the expected range of possibility. If you begin out of this range or set an unreasonable range, the negotiations may not last very long. If you start too low, you have potentially cost you and your shareholders a lot of money and/or control. The bigger the range, the more room (flexibility) you will have in the negotiations, leaving greater opportunity to resolve sticking points. However, with larger ranges, the longer negotiations may take.

F

Factoring A form of bank financing that accepts an account payable as collateral rather than the tangible assets usually required as collateral for traditional bank loans. To secure factoring credit, you will need to have an account payable or executed contract with either a client with a strong credit rating or a government agency and typically at least a 6- to 12-month clean payment history with the client or agency. The lender offering the factoring credit will provide funds to you up front based on a percentage of the total account payable or contract amount. The lender will collect the account payable or contract payment(s) directly. In determining whether to award factoring credit, the lender considers the creditworthiness of your client more heavily than the creditworthiness of your company. The beauty of factoring is that you are effectively leveraging the strong credit of your client to secure an otherwise unattainable bank loan at very attractive terms without providing your core assets as security.

Founding Partners   The initial shareholders of a company who, due to the long time horizon to exit and assumption of the greatest risk should have the highest proportional returns upon a successful exit.

Founding Capital   The amount of monetary investment contributed by the founding partners, both initially and continuing through exit. It serves as proof of "skin-in-the-game."

Fundraising Stage   The period during which the cost of funds is comparable throughout the period, whether in terms of equity dilution or rate of borrowing interest. Reaching the next fundraising stage requires progression to the next stage of business development and/or attainment of the necessary financial objectives. This permits solicitation of additional capital at more favorable terms vis-à-vis a higher valuation or a lower interest rate. A financial plan is required to determine the "necessary" amount of funds and to identify the sources of funding currently offering the lowest costs of capital in each fundraising stage.

G
Geek Speak   Enthusiastically talking in highly technical terms at hyper speed. Geek speak is the opposite of speaking in layman's terms. Most non-technical individuals will have a difficult time comprehending geek speak.

Good Money   Money received from an investor who will prove to be a strong business partner as they fully understand your business and market, share your objectives, offer many types of nonfinancial support, and will not impede the execution of your plans.

Go-to-Market Strategy   Your plan to execute a commercial launch of your product or service and all the efforts associated with doing so, including hiring sales and marketing personnel, advertising, required software development or hardware purchases to enable the execution of the commercial launch, and so on.

H
Healthy Capital Structure   One that does not impede the future fundraising efforts of the company.

I
Immediate Dilution   The equity dilution to occur to current shareholders immediately upon a proposed or future equity purchase. Purchased shares will cause immediate dilution by increasing the number of shares outstanding. The financials funding requirements section of a business plan should include an

immediate dilution clause describing the dilution to occur upon an equity purchase.

Incubator Programs   Provide the use of facilities, promotional assistance, business advisement, exposure to prospective investors, and occasionally seed funds for start-up companies. Sharing space, ideas and mutual support with other start-ups can be of enormous benefit to a start-up's development efforts as well.

Initial Public Offering (IPO)   Offering equity for purchase to the general public for the first time. An underwriter is usually secured to execute the public offering. The benefits of going public include the greater ease of raising investment funds, a higher valuation, greater liquidity and credibility, and enhanced exposure. A company that undergoes an IPO will have to make public disclosures thereafter.

Innovation   A new idea that represents a fundamental change in a thought process that presents a value-added result. An innovation can be a technology, process, or proprietary business model. To be innovative requires more than just being new. It has to exhibit a substantial difference that displays a high level of vision. Value and differentiation are the two main characteristics of an innovation.

Institutional Investors   All nonindividual investing entities specifically created to make investments. They primarily include venture capital firms, private equity firms, and banks. As the funding needs of a start-up business outgrow the amount of funding available from individual angel investors and family/friends, the business will need to solicit funding from these larger institutional investors.

Integrity   Consistent behavior in accordance with good ethical principles, such as honesty and fairness. If individuals or institutions consistently act with integrity, their decisions become predictable as their motivations are based on known ethical principles. Acting in an ethical manner and acting predictably lower the level of perceived risk, thereby facilitating the establishment of trust.

Intellectual Property (IP)   Any innovation created through one's own original thinking and experimentation that may offer the possibility of securing legal property rights for the inventor.

Internal Rate of Return (IRR)   The interest rate at which the net present value of costs equals the net present value of the benefits of the investment.

Investment Criteria   Stated requirements necessary to be eligible for funding consideration from a particular prospective investor. The criteria indicate whether funding may be available to a funding prospect, given its needs and stage of development. They also may reveal how suitable the investor may be as a business partner. Types of investment criteria include industry preference, preferred stage of development, funding range, favored funding structure, and choice exit strategy.

K

Kano Analysis   Effectively measures customer responses utilizing a practical and actionable customer preference classification system.

Key Performance Indicators (KPIs)   KPIs are objectives to be accomplished to fulfill the public mandates of a public funding agency. They help public agencies define and measure progress to fulfilling their mandated objectives. Public agencies invest in a venture because they believe that supporting such a venture will assist in fulfilling their mandates. Public agencies are more concerned with fulfilling their mandates than with whether your venture will be profitable or not. Thus a funding presentation to a public agency must focus on how an investment in your venture will help them fulfill their KPIs.

Know the Space   The "space" is the type of business model for your technopreneurial venture, the industry it is or will be operating in, and the market you will be targeting. A prospective business partner that knows your space will be able to understand your business, is intimately aware of the dynamics of your industry and target market, appreciates your efforts and displays greater patience, can make excellent introductions, and can offer valuable advice and other support that goes well beyond the investment funds committed. Consequently such a partner is an excellent stakeholder to have on your team in some capacity and represents "good money."

Know Your Investors (KYIs)   Understanding the expectations and characteristics of the various prospective investors. The greater the understanding, the higher the probability of securing investment funds from the most advantageous funding sources and ensuring that effective working relationships are fostered.

L

Layman's Terms   Terms that individuals not familiar with or expert on the subject can comprehend. A good way to practice delivering your presentation in layman's terms is to test with someone nontechnical and solicit feedback.

This feedback will help you in making the necessary revisions. "Geek speak" is the opposite of speaking in layman's terms.

Letter of Intent (LOI) A signed and affirming acknowledgment by the counterparty of its willingness to enter negotiations in good faith to accomplish specified objectives. Common additional components of an LOI include the parameters of such negotiations, clarification of key points, and safeguards in the event negotiations collapse. LOIs typically are nonbinding. However, they may include nondisclosure and act-in-good-faith clauses that are usually deemed binding.

Leverage Ability to exert influence beyond what should be expected given the amount of financial investment made. Leverage increases the perceived value of your business, which is what you want to impress on the counterparty before and during negotiations. Sources of leverage you may possess include traction, a successful track record, and possession of risk mitigation factors. Additional leverage may exist vis-à-vis the counterparty if you possess the ability to fulfill a prized objective, if you reveal a relative weakness of other party, and if competing prospective investor groups exist.

Licensing Agreement Grants the investing entity some right to utilize one or more of your intellectual property assets in exchange for either an up-front or recurring licensing fee.

Liquidation Preference Grants the counterparty the opportunity to receive monies first before other shareholders in the event of liquidation. Liquidation is broadly defined by the counterparty during negotiations to include events involving bankruptcy or sale of much, if not a majority, of a company's equity and/or assets. The liquidation preference is usually depicted as a multiple of the counterparties' proposed investment amount.

M
Mad Scientist Syndrome The belief that a brilliant innovation is sufficient to impress investors, attract investment capital, and crush any and all competition. Technopreneurs who enjoy the development aspects of their business so much that they forget they are managing a business and fail to seize opportunities to go-to-market. Affected technopreneurs may be strongly inclined to expend a disproportionate share of new investment funds on the most enjoyable part of the venture: research and development. Another symptom of the mad scientist bug is providing a comprehensive and intricately detailed synopsis of the technological marvels associated with your inventions in the product section of your business plan rather than just explaining how the product works.

Market Player   A market participant that warrants the serious attention of every other market participant due to its ability to affect prices, set market standards, service key major customers that influence market demand and tastes, exert control or influence on distribution channels, and/or be in command of disruptive technologies. Basically a market player cannot be ignored because of its noteworthy strength in one or more areas of marketing execution known as the Four Ps: product, price, placement, and promotion. Establishing your venture as a market player is the most effective way to attract strategic investors.

Mentor   Someone who helps people discover how to think and what to think about. The ideal mentor is someone who can do this by imparting personal experiences of both success and failure.

N

Negotiation Brinkmanship   A common tactic for prospective investors is to slow down the negotiating process if they perceive a sense of desperation from you. The objective is to compel the other party to accept the highly unfavorable terms they offer or face consequences far worse if negotiations are not concluded in a timely manner. This is why the best time to secure investment funds is when you do not have a desperate need for them and why you must secure sufficient funds for the next stage of development needs before that stage begins.

Negotiating Capital   The perceived relative strength of the negotiating parties that dictate how strong each counterparty believes it can be during negotiations. Recognize that as such strength is wielded, it is also expended. If you think of leverage as ammunition, your negotiating capital is the number of rounds your gun has.

Nondisclosure Agreement (NDA)   Or confidentiality agreement. A legal contract between two parties specifying what information is considered confidential and not to be shared with third parties. It may also be more detailed, outlining permitted use of such confidential knowledge.

Nontangible Asset   An asset that neither is a physical object or something that can be quantitatively valued due to its original nature. Intellectual property such as a patent or goodwill as a consequence of high brand recognition is an example of intangible assets.

O

Objectivity   The ability to make decisions in an unbiased and measured manner. Decisions that are made in an objective manner permit the rights and interests of all relevant parties to be mutually respected and considered.

Opportunity Cost   The cost of forgoing any other alternative choice. It is assessed not only in monetary terms but also in terms of anything that is of value. A primary opportunity cost of a founder in a start-up venture is the lost opportunity to be gainfully employed in a salaried position. Other opportunity costs include the extra stress and reduced personal time associated with managing a high-risk start-up venture.

P

Passive Investor   An investor who does not want much direct involvement in the affairs of the business and is primarily interested in receiving a high return on investment. Although passive investors are rare, they are ideal in respect to the issue of control.

Performance Imperative   Maximizing performance receives the highest priority in the decision-making process. Every stakeholder stands to benefit from improved performance; thus the interests of every stakeholder are being pursued. This imperative represents what should be the ultimate objective of every management team.

Performance Targets/Triggers   Specified milestones that, when realized, trigger certain actions to occur (either additional funding or the issuance/vesting of additional equity). A lender may not be willing to lend you the total funding amount up front. Instead it will progressively provide funds as your company successfully achieves specified performance objectives. If structured properly, performance target provisions have strong advantages for both technopreneurial ventures and investor/lenders. The establishment of stated milestones to be achieved sets a mutual tone of success and mitigates the counterparty's perceived risk in investing by incrementally increasing its investment (i.e., risk) based on agreed-on contingent success markers. This reduced risk perception makes counterparties more amendable to commit to larger funding amounts at more favorable terms to you. A benefit to both parties is that funds are committed in a very efficient, just-in-time manner. A performance trigger is a powerful control mechanism; failing to meet a performance trigger will cause a direct and immediate reduction in your funding. Thus, management takes every action necessary to achieve these short-term performance objectives, possibly at the expense of long-term objectives and other desirable short-term objectives (i.e., higher profit margins, research and development, etc.).

Postmoney Valuation   Valuation of a business after solicited funds have been secured.

PowerPoint Pitch   The audio-visual version of your executive summary. It typically lasts five to ten minutes and is used when you have the attention of a prospective investor for about that length of time. Common scenarios for use include spontaneous meetings in an airport or a hotel lobby and at events where each participant is allocated only five or six minutes to present. However, the pitch must provide comprehensive coverage of your business. The primary objective and challenge in this type of presentation is to demonstrate the strength of your planning and convince the audience that you know what is required and have the ability to effectively execute it.

Preferred Shares An equity class different from common shares. Preferred shares are senior to common shares, are nonvoting, pay out a dividend that can be cumulative, and have a degree of conversion into common shares.

Premium Pricing Setting the price deliberately high to enhance the perception of prospective consumers/users that your product/service enjoys superior quality and reputation.

Private Debt Placement A nonpublic offering of a debt security, such as a bond or loan, to a select group of prospective creditors.

Private Equity Firms Specifically established to invest in relatively mature businesses possessing at least a modest financial or operational track record that still offer relatively attractive terms in an intermediate time frame (one to five years). Ventures searching for series B funding for their later-stage operations should approach private equity firms rather than venture capital firms.

Private Equity Placement A nonpublic offering of equity securities, such as stock and warrants, to a select group of investors.

Private Placement Memorandum (PPM) A formal comprehensive document offering the equity shares of a private company to a select group of prospective investors. Included in the PPM are details of all the terms of the investment, requirements of the investor, and proper disclaimers and disclosures related to the business and the equity.

Pro Forma Financials Statements prepared in advance of the time periods they cover; thus, they are forecasts. They represent financial projections based on certain assumptions and should extend out at three to five years. The three primary pro forma financial statements to be created and presented are the income statement, cash flow statement, and balance sheet. For technopreneurial ventures, this is the section of the business plan that shows prospective investors how the income is being derived.

Proof of Concept The ability to actually show a product or service to be useful to someone other than yourself and that there is a potential market for it. There are several ways to demonstrate proof of concept. The most common and effective proof of concept techniques include alpha/beta user testing and Kano analysis.

Prospectus Materials   Any documents distributed to prospective investors for marketing or informational purposes. There exist several types of prospectus documents that illustrate different aspects or functions of the business at various levels of detail. They include the executive summary, business plan, funding proposal, shareholder letter, technology brief, demonstration videos, and market research reports. Prospectus materials have two objectives: to entice a prospective investor to request further information or a presentation and to provide more detailed answers to specific questions posed.

Proxy Voting Rights   Occur when a particular shareholder(s) is granted by another shareholder(s) the right to vote on their behalf. The use of proxies allows the possibility of voting as a block, which permits individual shareholders with common positions to vote more effectively. The possibility of voting by proxy is very important to take note of. A management team may have a false sense of security that a counterparty will be only a minority shareholder and thus does not represent an immediate threat to the effective control currently possessed by founding management.

Public Funding   Funding offered by government agencies with mandates to achieve certain business development objectives for their particular municipality. The four most common types of public funding are matching equity, loan guarantees, grants, and incubator programs. The advantages of public funding are that it usually is nondilutive and enhances the credibility of your venture by denoting a certain level of government support.

R

Rating of Equity Dilution (RED)   The percentage equity interest of a company held by the founding shareholders.

Rate of Equity Dilution   The percentage equity interest decrease realized by founding shareholders following each successive funding round. It is a measure of a company's fundraising efficiency.

Registration Rights   Rights that compel an issuing company to register the common shares of a shareholder for public sale upon specified occurrences. Registration rights permit shareholders to protect themselves on the upside and possibly the downside by forcing a registration of their unregistered stock that can now be sold publicly in the event the shareholder does not like the company's prospects or wants to have some guarantee of participating in any lucrative exit strategy.

Return on Investment (ROI)   The ratio of money gained or lost on an investment relative to the amount of money invested. The primary objective of any equity investor is to secure the highest possible ROI on the investments. Typically investors in a high-risk venture, such as a technopreneurial venture, will expect a minimum ROI of at least 8 to 10.

Revenue-Sharing Agreement   The investing party to this agreement provides up-front funds in exchange for a percentage of a current or future revenue stream of the counterparty. Revenue-sharing is nondilutive and does not carry the risk that misuse can lead to a strategic disadvantage, as licensing agreements do. However, a revenue share will consume some of your future operating cash flow.

Reverse Vesting   Requires the founders to set aside their common shares and earn them back over a specified amount of time, usually three to five years. The counterparty negotiates for this structure to ensure that the founders stay around at least through the crucial initial stages of development.

Right of First Refusal   Grants counterparties the ability to maintain their percentage ownership interest in your venture by offering them the right to purchase a pro rata percentage of shares in a future equity offering of your company.

Risk/Return   The greater the perceived risk, the greater the expected return.

Risk Mitigation Factor (RMF)   Any specific characteristic or feature of your business that would reduce a specific perceived risk. By reducing a prospective investor's perceived risk, you increase the likelihood of securing investment funds and at better terms. Common RMFs include multiple revenue streams, high degree of applicability, captive target markets, and barriers to entry.

Rolodex of Proxies   This practice occurs when a current stakeholder tries to accumulate greater control by referring new prospective investors that will grant the current stakeholder future proxy voting rights either formally or de facto. Stealth is employed as the stakeholder conceals his or her true intentions. It is also a favorite tactic of vulture capitalists, who introduce new investors who will serve as proxies for them when it is time to take over the venture.

S

Seed Funding   Usually represents the first funding round for a company. The primary use of seed funds is to develop a prototype, demonstrate proof of concept, and protect any intellectual property.

Selective Liquidity   Occurs when a current shareholder with unfettered financial leverage chooses to withhold investment funds to compel a cash flow crisis and demand highly favorable terms at the expense of other share-holders or, in extreme cases, delay an investment for an eventual takeover of the company. This is a common tactic of vulture capitalists, whereby they provide only enough funding for you to survive until it is time for them to push the founders aside.

Series A Funding   Funding to fuel all the work required to go from prototype to revenue generation. Typically series A funding is called go-to-market funding as these monies are used to finance the commercial launch of a product or service.

Series B Funding   Funding to finance the growth stage at which your company progresses from revenue to profitability.

Skin in the Game   A demonstration of personal and financial sacrifices personally incurred. Sacrifices include such things as opportunity costs, actual financial investment, placing at risk personal relationships and professional reputations, assumption of stress, time away from family, and the like. A value needs to be placed on such sacrifices when determining an appropriate share of potential financial returns.

Soft Launch   Occurs when you commercially launch your product without the capability to fully execute the marketing plan. This typically occurs when it is deemed necessary to not delay the commercial launch for strategic or other reasons. Reasons may include securing "first-to-market" advantages, avoiding prohibitive delay costs, seizing a short-term market opportunity, or not having sufficient funding or not completed preparations with comarketing partners to fully implement their marketing plans. In a soft launch, you may forfeit the opportunity to compare different placements, different promotions, and effectively analyze your pricing.

Stakeholder Relations   Communicating the company's financial strategy and its broader strategic direction to its stakeholders and disseminating other information relevant to ensuring that effective corporate governance practices can be pursued.

Strategic Investor Perceives an attractive investment opportunity as offering a way to enter a market more easily, leverage existing operations and investments, gain a competitive advantage, or simply dominate a given market or industry. Attracting the attention of a strategic investor should be the objective of any ambitious technopreneurial venture. No other investor type will be willing to offer a higher valuation for you company.

Strategic Partner A company that has a strategic reason to establish a working relationship with you. Vendors that provide a product or service to you for the sole purpose of profit are not considered strategic partners. However, vendors with additional nonfinancial intentions may be considered strategic partners. Examples of potential strategic partners include comarketing partners, joint developers, licensees, and distributors. Prospective investors view strategic partner(s) as reducing risks and increasing returns.

Structural ("Dirty") Dilution The reduction of founders' ROI that occurs in addition to the dilution of their equity due to a convertible equity security funding. The amount of dilution is determined by calculating the difference between the amount of return the founders were to receive based on their percentage equity interest at exit or liquidation versus the amount of the exit or liquidation proceeds they are entitled to after the structural dilution terms have been applied. The structural dilution terms include liquidation preference, dividends paid on preferred shares, and participation preferred rights.

T
Tagalong Rights Also referred to as cosale rights. Allow passive shareholders to sell their shares when the management team is offering their shares for sale.

Tangible Asset A physical asset or an asset that has an easily quantifiable value.

Target Market The market(s) into which you intend to introduce your innovative product or service. Target markets must be delineated and described in any prospectus documents. Prospective investors want to know the size of the market (potential revenues) and any niche market opportunities (profit margins, market player positioning).

Term Sheet A document prepared by a prospective investor prior to negotiations that outlines the key terms of a proposed investment. It is a nonbinding agreement expressing the intentions of counterparty and conditions under which an investment will be consummated. Actual negotiations may commence based on the preliminary terms found in the term sheet.

Traction   Current impact on target market. Traction includes such measurements as market share, number of users, and revenues. Other factors include level of innovation, brand/product recognition, and strategic partners. Traction is also defined as recognized instruments of leverage that can readily be employed.

Transparency   A high degree of openness derived from reporting and disclosing everything of material importance to relevant parties in a clear, factual, readily available, and timely manner. Being transparent is the most effective way to exhibit integrity and allows for an effective dissemination of information that can serve to enhance performance.

U

Upside Protection   Holder of such protection is able to profit from the successful exit of a venture at the comparable level of returns enjoyed by the highest risk-taking stakeholders.

Use of Funds   An itemized statement of how you intend to allocate the funds secured in a particular funding round or placement. A use of funds statement is a component of the financials section of your business plan. Prospective investors want to see what their investment funds will be spent on. They strongly prefer that funds are allocated to value-added activities.

V

Valuation   What a company is worth. A company is worth how much a prospective buyer is willing to pay to purchase it. Ultimately the valuation of a company is determined by negotiations between company and investors.

Value-Based Pricing   Utilizes the measured perceived value of your product/service among target consumers/users to determine a price level.

Value Proposition   Securing recognition that your innovation is a solution to a significant and challenging problem that will hold value for someone. To support a value proposition, these questions must be definitively answered: How do potential users or consumers benefit? Would someone be willing to pay a premium for its use? How does your innovative product or service compare with more expensive and less expensive alternatives?

Value Added   The effect on one's bottom line by either reducing costs or increasing revenues and/or profit margins. Features that are value added enable, facilitate, clarify and enhance the consumer or user experience. Value-added activities have a positive effect on your income statement whereby the associated costs of the activity is less than the profits derived.

Venture Capital   Investment funds allocated to high-risk ventures.

Venture Capital Firms   Firms specifically established to invest in high-risk ventures that offer potentially high returns. Such firms raise funds to capitalize investment funds of which they manage. Their investors entrust them to identify investment opportunities matching their specified and shared set of criteria and expectations, which govern the investment decisions of the fund managers. The series A fundraising stage is the domain of venture capital firms.

Vulture Capitalists   An opportunistic subspecies of mainstream venture capitalists who prey on vulnerable ventures. Their objective is to take advantage of a venture's precarious position and offer terms very unfavorable to the venture regarding both equity percentage holding and control. They structure their funding proposals to create almost no-lose situations for themselves by assuming small amounts of risk in a highly disproportionate manner.

About the Author

David Shelters currently resides in Bangkok, Thailand, where he provides investment banking, business brokerage, and financial advisement services through his company Karon Business Consulting. He is also an active participant in the local tech entrepreneurial scene presenting at numerous Bar Camps and other tech conferences. He currently mentors several local software start-ups and has served a leading role in efforts to strengthen the Thai start-up community and foster ties with start-up communities in neighboring countries. Recently, David launched his blog "Finance for Geeks." His blog represents a continuation of his efforts to impart mentoring advice to tech start-ups and can be found at www.financeforgeeks.com. David possesses over 15 years of entrepreneurial experience as a founder, cofounder, and financial advisor to numerous tech start-ups in both America and Asia. He holds a B.A. in history and political science from the State University of New York at Albany, an M.S. in international affairs from Florida State University, and has completed coursework for the master's in international business studies degree at Georgia State University. He was formerly Series 3 and Series 7 licensed in the United States, which permitted him to trade on both the stock market and the futures markets. During his free time, he likes to travel, play basketball, and read history.

About the Website

Please visit this book's companion Website at www.wiley.com/go/financial fraudfortechnopreneur, password shelters123. The Website includes these documents to supplement the information in the book:

- Sample executive summary
- Sample business plan
- Sample pro forma financials
- Sample letter of intent
- Sample nondisclosure agreement
- Sample term sheet
- Sample due diligence checklist
- Sample code of business conduct

Please also visit the author's Website at www.financeforgeeks.com to view other related materials. In addition to the supplementary materials, the Website also provides further valuable information and resources for technopreneurs.

Index